# GILDED YOUTH

# GILDED YOUTH

*Privilege, Rebellion and the British Public School*

James Brooke-Smith

REAKTION BOOKS

*For Leo and Freya*

Published by Reaktion Books Ltd
Unit 32, Waterside
44–48 Wharf Road
London N1 7UX, UK

www.reaktionbooks.co.uk

First published 2019
Copyright © James Brooke-Smith 2019

Printed and bound in India by Replika Press Prt. Ltd.

A catalogue record for this book is available from the British Library

ISBN 978 1 78914 066 8

# Contents

Harrow School Bill, 2001.

# Introduction:
# Permanent Adolescence

'Neither the British jury, nor the House of Lords, nor the Church of England, nay, scarcely the monarchy itself,' opined Leslie Stephen in 1873, 'seems to be so deeply enshrined in the bosoms of our countrymen as our public schools.'[1] Today few would echo Stephen's belief in the mass popularity of public school education. Exclusive private schools are more often the subjects of heated debates about elitism and stalled social mobility than of misty-eyed veneration. But his comments nevertheless capture a perennial feature of the public school mystique, a set of associations that have clung to these institutions for most of their history, and continue to do so today. More than just an educational institution, the public school is a symbol of privilege and a shorthand for a particular vision of British national identity. With its elegant architecture and evergreen playing fields, it encodes a powerful myth of organic tradition and national heritage. As Stephen suggests, it is part of a network of ancient institutions that have proved remarkably skilful at adapting to historical change in order to maintain their position at the centre of national life.

The very first public schools were religious communities that contained grammar schools in order to instruct aspiring clerics in the Latin tongue and liturgy. Winchester College, founded in 1382, was housed in the diocesan grounds of Winchester Cathedral. Its original architecture was monastic: cloisters, chapel, chantry, vestry, warden's lodgings, brewhouse, gardens and a small schoolroom. Eton, the most elite of English schools, was founded in 1440 by King Henry

VI concurrently with King's College at Cambridge University. This act of institutional largesse was part of the King's duties as *Fidei Defensor*, defender of the faith and steward of the Church in England.

Almost all of the early foundations, including those of the nine 'great' schools – Eton, Harrow, Winchester, Westminster, Charterhouse, Rugby, Shrewsbury, Merchant Taylors' and St Paul's – made provisions for the education of the poor. William of Wykeham, founder of Winchester, stipulated that the school should provide board and tuition for seventy 'pauperes et indigentes' as well as fee-paying pupils. Eton's founding charter set aside funds – and still does to this day – for seventy 'collegers', who would be educated for free alongside the wealthier 'oppidans'. In reality, this meant that the schools catered principally for the sons of tradesmen, merchants, professionals and the rural gentry. Classical education was of little practical use to the labouring poor, and many of the sons of the aristocracy continued to be educated by private tutors in the great houses until well into the eighteenth century. In the early 1700s the register of pupils at Eton included the sons of a baker, bookseller, brick maker, cheesemonger, grocer, innkeeper, tobacconist, mercer and coach maker.[2]

But the schools' original charters were gradually circumvented through long years of corruption, inertia and the influence of prosperous families who sought the benefits of public schooling without the coarsening presence of scholarship boys from the lower classes. Throughout the seventeenth and eighteenth centuries, the schools were transformed into the elite establishments that they remain to this day. On the recommendation of the Clarendon Report of 1864, the first serious attempt by government to regulate the public schools, many of the original charters were amended to offer up scholarships to general competition, rather than leaving them in the gift of individual administrators or boards of governors. But this merely served to consolidate the grip of the already wealthy, as it ensured that only the sons of families who could afford expensive tuition had any chance of winning prizes. The process of class cleansing had reached its apogee by the 1920s, when George Orwell, who famously classified himself as 'lower upper middle-class', described his time at Eton as 'five years in a lukewarm bath of snobbery'.[3]

This tangled history is why the modern 'independent sector', as politicians and publicists like to call it, is still known to most people as the 'public schools'. In reality, this term encompasses a huge variety of institutions that exist outside the state system, from the nine 'great' schools, to former 'direct grant' grammar schools, private schools owned by individuals or corporations, and a host of institutions that cater to particular constituencies and needs. It was not until the nineteenth century that the state considered mass education to be part of its remit at all. The first government-run schools were known as 'board schools', due to the fact that they were administered by local education boards, and are now part of the 'state sector'. The schools founded in the fifteenth, sixteenth and seventeenth centuries were entitled to be called 'public' in that they were charitable trusts, administered by boards of governors for the education of those who might not otherwise be able to afford private tutors. In the 1960s, under pressure from a Labour Party whose official policy was to nationalize all schools, the PR consultants hired by the Headmasters' and Headmistresses' Conference, the national organizing body for the public schools, successfully introduced the new term 'independent schools'. This was a calculated makeover designed to deflect attention from the glaring contradiction between the way in which these institutions functioned to entrench the privilege of the wealthy few and their original purposes as charitable trusts for the deserving poor.

And function they still do. In September 2014 the Social Mobility and Child Poverty Commission, an advisory body to the Department of Education, found that 71 per cent of senior judges, 62 per cent of senior officers in the armed forces, 55 per cent of parliamentary secretaries in Whitehall and 53 per cent of senior diplomats were educated at private schools. Similar figures applied throughout the upper echelons of British society: 44 per cent of people on the *Sunday Times* Rich List, 43 per cent of newspaper columnists, 36 per cent of cabinet ministers, 26 per cent of BBC executives and 22 per cent of shadow cabinet ministers. All of this in a country where a mere 7 per cent of children enjoy a private education. The standout phrase from what was otherwise a bland and bureaucratic report was the assertion that Britain suffers from 'a closed shop at the top', an unrepresentative elite that is disproportionately composed of the privately educated, the Oxbridge educated, the wealthy, the white and the upper-middle class.[4]

THIS BOOK TELLS the story of how a small group of elite schools has come to occupy such a dominant position within British society; how they have shaped the experience of adolescence for successive generations of upper-class youth; and why they continue to hold such a powerful grip on our social institutions and cultural imagination. My aim is not to mount an overtly political argument for or against private education.[5] In my view, the findings of the Social Mobility and Child Poverty Commission make it abundantly clear that if we are to be serious about meritocracy, fairness, equality of opportunity or even – heaven forbid! – greater equality of outcomes, then the independent sector must either be radically reformed or incorporated within the state sector. This is the only way to break the connection between family background and social advantage that is so strongly cemented by private education.

Rather than a political polemic, this is a historical study that traces the myriad ways in which the public school has exerted – and continues to exert – an outsized influence not only on the privileged few who can afford to pay for an elite education, but on the wider reaches of British culture and society. One thing that the Social Mobility Report failed to capture was the deep sense of historical inertia that many people in modern Britain feel when confronted by the persistent inequities of private education. In spite of the enormous gains of post-war social democracy, which have extended access to education, healthcare, pensions and National Insurance to the whole population, our elite institutions suffer the lingering after-effects of an education system that never fully threw off the hierarchical assumptions of the Victorian era. While the arguments for and against public school education – often in their most simplistic, emotive forms – have been rehearsed in the media ad nauseam, in their haste to take up stances commentators have largely ignored the fundamental question of *how* these institutions have managed to exert such influence. This is the question that I set out to answer in this book.

One of the reasons for public schools' startling ability to evade reform over the years is the imaginative hold that they exercise over their former pupils. In 1938 the literary critic Cyril Connolly formulated his theory of 'permanent adolescence':

> the experiences undergone by boys at the great public schools, their glories and disappointments, are so intense as to dominate their lives and to arrest their development. From these it results that the greater part of the ruling class remains adolescent, school-minded, self-conscious, cowardly, sentimental and in the last analysis homosexual.[6]

Private education has always been, and continues to be to this day, as much a matter of culture and identity as of academic excellence. For hundreds of years, the great majority of Britain's most powerful men (and later women) went through the same adolescent rite of passage. Having been separated from their homes, governed by arcane customs, ruled by the prefect elite, dedicated to the study of two ancient languages, subjected to corporal punishment and wrapped in an atmosphere of clannish solidarity, many ex-public schoolboys bore the mental and emotional imprint of their schooldays for the rest of their lives. This was true not only for the nation's leading politicians and civil servants, but for its writers, artists and intellectuals. And it was true not only for the well-behaved boys who conformed to school discipline, but for the rebels and refuseniks who kicked against the pricks. We get a sense of the enormous power of nostalgia for the old school both in the case of the Victorian prime minister Lord Roseberry, who had the 'Eton Boating Song' sung to him on his deathbed, and the Communist double agent Kim Philby, who insisted on wearing his old Westminster scarf while in exile in Moscow.

The sense of national significance has also been reinforced by representations of public schools within popular culture. In spite of its elite demographics, the public school is an iconic space of Englishness that has informed the attitudes and ideals of countless generations of young people, both within and beyond its imposing stone walls. It was Great Britain, after all, that gave the world the genre of the boarding school novel. Thomas Hughes's *Tom Brown's Schooldays* (1857), Rudyard Kipling's *Stalky and Co.* (1899) and Frank Richards's Billy Bunter stories (1908–61) are still widely read and much beloved. Indeed, just as *Downton Abbey* has recently reinforced the status of the aristocratic country house as a symbol of national identity, so too has J. K. Rowling's *Harry Potter* series revived the boarding school as an icon of deep, mythic England.

In these fictionalized forms, the public school has also been the source of some of the modern world's most influential narratives about youth, gender and identity. The masculine heroes of classic British adventure fiction, including John Buchan's Richard Hannay, Sapper's Bulldog Drummond and Ian Fleming's James Bond, are all embodiments of the cultural archetype of the 'public school man', who combines in varying degrees the qualities of charm, guile, physical strength and a bluff confidence in his own fitness to rule half the globe. When the first girls' public schools were founded in the Victorian era, they quickly produced their own female archetypes, from the Angela Brazil-style tomboy to the finishing school debutante. By the end of the nineteenth century, the public school ethos of self-discipline, loyalty and 'fair play' had been converted into an instantly recognizable educational template that could be exported around the globe. Public school values were adopted by the Boy Scouts, the Boys' Brigades, the first organized sports leagues, the early Olympics movement, the borstal system for housing young offenders and elite schools in India, the Caribbean, Canada, Australasia and South Africa.

But the influence of the public school does not begin and end with popular novels and Muscular Christianity. There is a tendency within academic studies, such as Isabel Quigly's *The Heirs of Tom Brown* (1982) and Jeffrey Richards's *Happiest Days* (1988), to focus only on the most familiar or canonical forms of public school culture, such as boarding school fiction in the mode of Hughes and Kipling.[7] Dominic Sandbrook takes the same approach in his recent study of British popular culture, *The Great British Dream Factory* (2015), in which he discusses modern reboots of the public school novel in the form of George MacDonald Fraser's *Flashman* series and Rowling's blockbusting *Harry Potter* books.[8] But while boarding school fiction is an undeniably distinctive and influential feature of British popular culture, its prominence can deflect attention from the myriad ways in which the public school has wormed its way into the popular imagination. Over the years, public school life has been represented in an enormous variety of genres and forms, including scurrilous eighteenth-century political pamphlets, Victorian nonsense verse, flagellation pornography, avant-garde magazines, Cold War spy novels, Ealing film comedies, pop songs, Monty Python skits and newspaper gossip columns.

This vast cultural hinterland has often been a site of resistance and refusal, rather than loyalty and acceptance. Just as important as the mainstream culture of the public school – the classical pedagogy, organized sports and gentlemanly character-building that are so prominent within existing historical accounts – are the subcultures that flourished in the corners of institutional life. Today we tend to think of youth culture as classless and democratic, the product of the city streets rather than the cloistered retreats of Eton and Harrow. But some of the very first 'moral panics' about feral youth originated in the public schools.[9] When eighteenth-century schoolboys took up arms against their masters in support of the principles of the French Revolution, the popular press was filled with alarmed commentary about the decline of moral standards and the waning of adult authority. Medical experts in the Victorian period wrung their hands over the vice of masturbation that seemed to be sweeping boys' dormitories like a biblical plague. The schoolboy aesthetes and dandies of the 1910s and '20s were cast by teachers, parents and journalists as avatars of an insidious decadence that threatened to undermine the moral fibre of the Empire. The tabloid press of the 1930s fumed about the 'red menace' that was brewing among the nation's disaffected public schoolboys, some of whom were thought to be in the pay of the Soviets. In the 1960s, real-life scenes of teenage revolt similar to those depicted in Lindsay Anderson's film *if . . .* (1968) unfolded at private schools around the country, as pupils refused to join in the rituals of school life, rejected the values of their teachers and parents and immersed themselves in the arcana of the hippy subculture.

Against the backdrop of the symbolic space of the public school, these episodes were more than just outbreaks of adolescent bolshiness:

they were struggles to define the values and identity of the future leaders of the nation. Throughout modern British history, the public schoolboy has been a symbolically overloaded figure. On the one hand, he is the embodiment of the nation's future. At more or less any point between 1750 and 1950 one could safely assume that sitting at the desks of the nation's public schools were the next generation of statesmen, civil servants, clerics and generals. The identities and ideals of those leaders were shaped under the influence of school discipline. In the figure of the public school man, upper-class society could comfortably envision its own continuity between generations. And yet, on the other hand, the public schoolboy has also been a register of deep-seated anxieties about youth and change. Consistently throughout the history of the institution there have been public outcries about riotous behaviour, homosexual scandals, cultural decline and radical politics. In the figure of the mercurial adolescent, as yet uncommitted to the values of the older generation and dangerously susceptible to external influences, upper-class society has envisioned its own instability, the unknowability of its offspring and their potential for revolt.

On the face of things, a history of Britain's elite private schools might not seem like a particularly edifying prospect. Who really wants to read about crusty old teachers and their hyper-privileged pupils? But one of the most appealing aspects of studying the enclosed world of the boarding school is that it enables the reader to enjoy the aesthetic pleasures of miniaturization. Like a cutaway of a model ship, it enables us to view in minute detail the inner workings of one of the central mechanisms through which upper-class society seeks to reproduce itself. At this scale, we are able to pick out not only the broad outlines of the process, but its quirks and ambiguities, its comic misfirings and simmering tensions. From a distance, everything seems to function smoothly, but up close we can see the strains in the system and its potential for collapse.

IN SPITE OF the radical changes in ethos and curriculum over the years, the most important aspect of public school education remains the same as it was during the system's Victorian heyday: an almost subliminal confidence in one's own capacity to succeed. Thomas Hughes captured this attitude back in 1857 in *Tom Brown's Schooldays*. Hughes describes East, Tom Brown's mentor on his first day at Rugby, as being 'gifted with the most transcendent coolness and assurance', a self-satisfaction that Tom finds 'aggravating and hard to bear, but couldn't for the life of him help admiring and envying'.[10] This is the secret ingredient of private education, the 'X factor' that exceeds mere pedagogy. East's 'coolness and assurance' is 'transcendent' because it seems to come from his innate charisma rather than his enormous social privilege. Over the years this obscure property has gone by many different names, from the Renaissance Italian *sprezzatura*, to Victorian gentlemanly 'reserve', to the 'effortless sense of superiority' that today's public school graduates are often said to possess. The technical term used by sociologists is 'habitus', which refers to the way in which social class is registered not only in terms of the contents of your bank account, but in the subtle markers of judgement, taste and behaviour that are first acquired at school but later come to seem like inherent properties of the self.[11] Call it what you will, the shifting terminology points to an abiding feature of elite education: the way in which it confers upon its pupils an almost magical belief in their own worth and abilities that is the very essence of class privilege.

Until very recently, however, the privilege of a public school education was often accompanied by astonishing forms of institutional violence. In some cases, schools provided cover for criminal acts of sexual and physical abuse. Evelyn Waugh famously quipped of English schoolmasters that, 'some liked little boys too little and some too much'.[12] Waugh's bone-dry joke deflects attention from the hidden history of abuse that has unfolded within the hallowed space of the boarding school. The flip side of Leslie Stephen's idealized image of the public school as a symbol of national heritage is that of the gothic institution, cut off from society at large, stifled by repressive authority, wreathed in silence and suffering. The legacy of this dark tradition can still be felt today. The journalist Alex Renton has calculated that teachers from 62 different private schools have been convicted of sex crimes against children in the last twenty years, and 130 other schools have been subject to similar allegations.[13]

But in most cases, psychological damage was simply an offshoot of the institution's official system of discipline and training. It is a singular fact of modern British history that the great majority of its ruling class were sent away from home at the age of seven or eight to live in the self-enclosed, all-male world of the boarding school. The domestic affections of fathers, mothers, siblings and nannies were replaced by the rigid discipline of the school. Discipline was enforced both through overt forms of corporal punishment and the unwritten code of emotional suppression that determined how young men should interact with their fellow pupils and masters.

For much of the nineteenth and twentieth centuries the ill effects of the system were invisible to most people because they were regarded as 'normal', part of the unquestioned furniture of upper-class existence. Today, however, psychologists refer to the damaging effects that can arise from being sent away to school as 'attachment fracture' and 'privileged abandonment'.[14] Sufferers from 'boarding school syndrome' display symptoms of emotional coldness, an inability to empathize with others, detachment from family and friends, fragile ego formation and anger management issues.[15] What now looks like a form of psychological abuse was for a long time an integral part of the training for membership of the ruling class. The psychotherapist Nick Duffell has described the recipients of this peculiar form of mental conditioning as the 'wounded elite'.[16] While we tend to think of educational privilege in terms of what it enables its lucky recipients to achieve – better qualifications, better jobs, a wider range of experience, a more assured sense of one's place within the national culture – it can also be a profoundly disabling force.

And yet there are many different ways of wearing one's privilege, many different strategies for embracing or rejecting the advantages that are the result of one's position near the top of a hierarchal society. Where one schoolboy becomes a prefect, another becomes a rebel. Where one adopts the values of the institution as his own, another chafes against the phoney *esprit de corps* and meaningless discipline. Where one assumes that his successful career and comfortable life are purely the products of his own hard work, another may feel a nagging sense of unease at the sheer luck of having gone to the 'right' kind of school. Where one wears his old school tie with pride, another seeks to erase all traces of his class background by adopting the speech and uniform of an alternative subcultural tribe. The variety of possible responses to the sheer arbitrariness of privilege can range from arrogance and entitlement to shame and disavowal, and all the various shades of feeling in between.

One of the central arguments of this book is that public school education has not only influenced the mentalities of the ruling elite, but given shape to an alternative tradition of dissent, a kind of upper-class counterculture (from Percy Shelley to George Orwell, and from Peter Gabriel to Richard Branson) that was forged in opposition to, but obliquely mirrored, the values of the school. One of the questions that I wish to explore, however, is whether privileged radicals can ever really renounce the values of the old school, or whether their gestures of dissent are always doomed to be co-opted by an institution that has proved uniquely capable of adapting to critique in order to maintain its position at the very pinnacle of British society. Throughout modern British history, privilege and rebellion have often gone hand in hand. Yet the consequences of adolescent misbehaviour are unevenly distributed throughout society. If you possess the right connections and pedigree, youthful riotousness is part of the rite of passage that marks the boundary between juvenility and maturity. If you don't, then it's more likely to lead to the prison or the gutter. Many of the figures that appear in this book rebelled against what they took to be the 'establishment' of their day. They defined their youthful identities in opposition to the dominant ideals of their schools and class. And yet, over time, they found themselves in positions of authority and power within the self-same establishment they once denounced. For a certain kind of public schoolboy, anti-establishment rebellion is an alternative means of becoming a member of the club.

It should be abundantly clear by now that this book is mainly about overprivileged white men. For most of their history, the nation's most prestigious schools were exclusively masculine zones. It was not until the Victorian era that a parallel school system emerged in order to furnish middle- and upper-class girls with a similar kind of academic training to the one their brothers enjoyed. This training was adapted to the supposedly different needs of young girls: in place of leadership, girls were instilled with the values of 'service'; rather than physical bravery, they learned elegance and grace. Eventually, however, girls' schools would become academic powerhouses in their own right, regularly topping league tables and filling Oxbridge scholarship lists. In the 1970s this prompted the first of the traditionally male public schools to introduce co-education at the sixth-form level. But prior to this, gender segregation was integral to their role as training grounds for the ruling elite. To exercise political power was to be male; and a public school education was a training in both leadership and masculinity. This form of masculinity was defined by the violence of the institution, both the official forms of corporal punishment and physical conditioning and the unofficial forms of bullying and repression.

But this is not just the story of individual lives and identities. It is also the story of an institution, a supra-individual structure that is made up of rules and regulations, traditions and customs, norms and ideals, architecture and topography. In many tales of public school life the collective identity of the institution appears as a kind of disembodied *genius loci*, a ghostly presence that clings to but exists somewhere beyond the physical reality of the place. In *Goodbye to All That*, his bitterly critical 1929 memoir of Charterhouse, Oxford, the Great War and his eventual exile from Britain and 'all that', Robert Graves recounts his conversation with a friend on their final day at school. The two boys discuss how they would like to remake the school, starting from scratch with new staff, new pupils, new rules and a new curriculum better suited to their own ideals. Eventually, however, they decide that even this radical process of reform would not be enough: 'the school buildings being so impregnated with what passed as the school spirit, but what we felt as fundamentally evil, that they would have to be demolished and the school rebuilt elsewhere under a different name'.[17] Graves uses the metaphor of the school 'spirit' to convey his sense of the power of the institution above and beyond the lives of its particular members and its physical existence. The institution seems to have a spectral life of its own, a metaphysical force that haunts the minds and shapes the identities of successive generations of masters and pupils. It is this ghostly institutional life that I trace in this book.

BEFORE I BEGIN, however, I feel that I should come clean: I too am a former public schoolboy. In 1992, at the age of thirteen, I entered the enchanted landscape of Shrewsbury School. Nestled in its eyrie above the River Severn, the school stretches out over almost a square kilometre of playing fields, dotted with boarding houses, classroom blocks, a cricket pavilion, concert hall, theatre, chapel, swimming pool, shooting range and clusters of elegantly spaced oaks and elms. At the main gates stands a bronze statue of Sir Philip Sidney, old boy, courtier and poet, whose heroism at the battle of Zutphen in 1586 set the archetype for the public school warrior-gentleman. Protected by the natural fortification of the riverbank and wrapped in the gossamer-fine webs of class and privilege, the school seems to occupy a fissure in the fabric of time and space.

Rather than making the most of the incredible riches that the school had to offer, my response was to rebel. I smoked, drank, took drugs and offered surly opposition to the school's authority. I wish I could say that my hatred of the school was based on rational argument and egalitarian principles, but it was not. My revolt was instinctive, driven by a creeping sense of unease in the school's stifling micro-climate rather than a reasoned analysis of its structural conditions. I just felt a dumb rage at the myriad ways in which the institution set itself apart from the rest of the world. I hated the elegant grounds and lavish facilities. I hated the ridiculous school slang. I hated the oversized rugby shirts and scuffed boating shoes that students wore during leisure hours. I hated the floppy hairstyles. I hated rowing. And most of all I hated the constant, chivvying familiarity, the assumption that we were all on the same team, pulling in the same direction.

It should come as little surprise, then, that before I finished my third year at Shrewsbury I was 'asked to leave'. It is only in the most extreme cases of bullying or drug use that pupils are 'expelled' from independent schools, but they are often politely told that they should look elsewhere for their education. Operating in a highly competitive industry, and free from the legal frameworks that govern 'exclusion' in the state sector, headmasters often find it easier to remove mildly troublesome pupils than address the causes of their behaviour. Thus, halfway through my GCSE year, it was decided that I would complete my academic work at home, return to school to sit my exams and then move across town to a state sixth-form college. This was a move for which I had longed. I saw it as an escape from the enclosure of the school into the great outdoors of the real world. There would be no more self-satisfaction, no more arcane tradition, no more school spirit and no more oppressive seclusion from what I took to be the bright reality of everyday life.

But the real world turned out to be a profound disappointment. The two main features of life at a public school were the constant struggle to evade the authorities and the intense camaraderie that this struggle forged among my small band of friends. It was only after being kicked out that I realized what a great luxury it is to have a clearly defined enemy, a provocation for righteous anger and antagonistic self-definition. At sixth-form college the tension between authority and rebellion evaporated. Outside the classroom, my life was my own. My teachers didn't care a great deal whether I smoked, took drugs, stuck pins through my eyebrows, developed a rounded moral character or fulfilled the highest ideals of the institution. All of a sudden, without any authority to challenge, I lacked a project. What was once a high-stakes game became simply a daily round of listening to music, getting high and mooching about a small provincial town on the Welsh borders.

I do not kid myself that I have somehow escaped from the privileges of my class and education. Even though I hated my school and did everything I could to express my displeasure, the training that I received there has smoothed my path through life in ways that I can barely fathom. This book is a product of my own public school education in more ways than one. Any confidence in its voice or panache in its style are products, at least in part, of the excellent education I received as a teenager. And yet the very best feelings that I can drum up for my old school are ambivalent ones. I cannot help but acknowledge the quality of the education I received, but any gratitude I feel is curdled by the knowledge that this sort of education was inaccessible to most of my peers. Its value is diminished in direct proportion to its inaccessibility. And yet, in spite of my better judgement, to this day I remain 'school-minded' in the sense that Connolly described in the 1930s with his theory of 'permanent adolescence'. I still think that my years as a schoolboy rebel were the best I've had. I like to tell myself that this is not simply a case of thirty-something nostalgia, a craving for lost youth born of the frustrations of adulthood, but rather a residue of the clarifying freedom of hatred. Everything that I cared about in those days – the music, the books, the drugs, the friendships – were intensified by their implicit challenge to the culture and traditions of the school. These things were good in and of themselves, but they were even better as tokens of resistance in a battle against repression and bad faith. The wish to have that intensity of feeling again is a profoundly juvenile desire. Far better to grow up, move on, look forward and enjoy the milder but more enduring pleasures of maturity. But the hex of the school is strong.

'Barring Out; or Party Spirit', from Maria Edgeworth,
*The Parent's Assistant; or, Stories for Children* (1856 edn).

# ONE

# *Floreat Seditio*

Winchester College, 1793. Sometime in early spring. More than forty senior boys have gathered in Commoners' Hall after evening prayers. This boxy, brick-built edifice stands just outside the main College buildings, in the lea of the chantry and its gloomy medieval cloisters. The masters are all at home in their private dwellings. The Warden is in his lodgings on the other side of Chamber Court. The Ushers are off-site until early morning call-over. This is safe ground, ruled by the boys themselves.

Everyone is angry at the Warden. He forbade the boys from attending last week's performance by the visiting Buckinghamshire militia band in Cathedral Close. That was shabby dealing in itself. What could be wrong with an afternoon's musical entertainment? Pretty harmless stuff, and certainly less offensive to the school authorities than some of the boys' more rumbustious pursuits: a spot of poaching here and there, the occasional evening at the White Hart, or maybe a rendezvous with some of the town girls. But tonight their blood is up. Gathered in the gloom of Commoners' Hall, their shadows cast upon the chipped wainscoting by the light of the fire and a few guttering candles, the young Wykehamists work themselves into a heady steam of indignation. The Warden has acted as only a tyrant would. He has insulted their dignity. They have a right, as honourable gentlemen, to plain dealing and respect.

When he swore the boys off the concert, the Warden promised that anyone found to be in breach of the law would be punished individually. Only if the school sinned en masse would it be sanctioned collectively. But when he discovered a single boy – a college prefect, no less – among the crowd listening to the jaunty melodies of the military band, the Warden denied all senior boys leave to dine out with friends on the coming Easter holiday.

Petty regulations are to be expected from this punctilious little man. Evading his strictures is part of the game of school life. The Warden presides over the many rules and regulations that govern the institution: the timings of call-over and lock-up, the organization of half and full holidays, the bounds set around College, the order of service in the dining hall, access to the town and the playing fields where pupils go for their afternoon exercise. Every boy has at some time broken the strict letter of these laws. That is how life in an ancient public school works. Authority and transgression must find a workable median, a tacit yet stable order in which some minor infractions go unnoticed so long as the foundations of school authority remain unshaken. But this time the Warden has gone too far.

After the boys have poured their collective scorn on the pettifogging official, forty members of the Upper School pledge an oath of fellowship and swear vengeance for the insult to their honour. They then draft a letter in Latin stating their grievance and demanding an apology. Privately they agree that if the Warden does not comply, revoke the sanction and issue a full apology, they are prepared for outright rebellion. There is ample precedent for this: school lore tells of previous uprisings at Winchester and other public schools. And word travels fast: legendary tales of mutiny and riot are part of the schoolboys' oral tradition, passed around at dormitory feasts and holiday visits.

The Warden does not deign to answer that first letter, but on receipt of a second, he pens a desultory response accusing the rebels of arrogance and impertinence. Enraged, the boys write to the masters declaring that they will not attend school.

The uprising begins when a group of students, armed with clubs, attack an Usher, Mr Goddard, and throw marbles at him. The Usher later reports that, on entering the school, he found the once-tractable schoolboys 'metamorphosed into serpents'. He retreats to safer ground and the serpent-children proceed to smash windows throughout the school and drag desks, chairs and wainscoting into the courtyard to burn. On hearing the news of the uprising, the Warden sends a note to the boys asking to negotiate a truce. Giddy with the delight of fire and destruction, the boys refuse. Later in the day, they manage to steal a set of keys from one of the porters and occupy the Second Master's house, which is also located within the maze of poorly lit corridors and passageways that snake through the school's ancient site. Having established their redoubt, the rioters blockade the passage to the Warden's lodgings with chairs and desks. When the Warden and Usher return, the rebels ambush the two men and hold them hostage overnight. The following morning, a chanting horde of boys escorts the prisoners from the school grounds. They lock the gates and return to their positions.

Eventually the High Sheriff of Hampshire arrives with a 'loyal address to the crown' – a document that proclaims the Riot Act and calls the militia into action against the treasonous mob. He finds the school gates blockaded and the paving of Chamber Court torn up for use as ammunition. The boys are gathered throughout the school buildings, armed with swords, bludgeons, sticks and stones, ready to defend their territory. Four boys have loaded pistols, stolen from the Second Master's house on the first day of the rebellion. Some are strategically situated on the roof of the main school building, whose Gothic parapet they have loosened in readiness to tip down on to the onrushing forces. Also on the roof of the school a red cap of liberty flutters in the breeze atop the flagpole. The 'Phrygian' cap is rich with revolutionary symbolism. Originally worn by freed slaves in ancient Greece, adopted by Brutus as the symbol of Rome liberated from the tyrant Caesar and recently sported as an item of revolutionary dress on the streets of Paris, the cap semaphores the Winchester boys' demand for freedom. But exactly what kind of freedom remains unclear on this bright spring morning.

Returning the following day, the High Sheriff musters three companies of the North Hants militia in College Street, which runs along the front of the school. He now reads the Riot Act, which grants the members of the crowd an hour to disperse, after which time they are officially deemed to be treasonous and hence subject to the full force of the law. When the Warden arrives to negotiate, he agrees to a general amnesty and states that in future he will not punish the whole school for the sins of individual pupils. Running low on supplies and ill prepared for a prolonged siege, the boys grudgingly leave their positions. Now, the life of the institution resumes, but only for a brief morning. Prayers are read in chapel; lessons are delivered; boys present hastily cadged translations of Thucydides and Virgil to their somnolent masters.

But then trouble flares again. When the Warden demands the return of the Second Master's stolen pistols, the enraged ringleaders demand to see the line in the school statutes that requires this course of action. The boys also discover that, even after siege negotiations had begun, the school authorities contacted their parents to urge the rebels to surrender. This further instance of deceit sparks more mutinous fervour. In a pact of solidarity, 35 senior boys resign their places in the school. The rebellion ends with almost all of the oldest boys walking out in protest, with many of their juniors joining them in solidarity. Over the next few weeks, the pressure on Dr Thomas Warton, the headmaster, mounts to an insupportable pitch and he resigns.[1]

WINCHESTER'S 'GREAT REBELLION' of 1793 was not an isolated occurrence. There had been riotous uprisings at the school in 1770, 1774 and 1778 and subsequently in 1818 and 1828. Nor were events of this sort confined to one school. Between 1768 and 1851 there were armed rebellions in almost all of the nation's oldest and most prestigious schools. There were riots at Eton in 1768 and 1818. Westminster was up in arms in 1793, Rugby in 1797, Harrow in 1805 and 1808, Charterhouse in 1808 and Shrewsbury in 1818. The last of the great boarding school rebellions took place at Marlborough on Guy Fawkes Night, 1851, when a group of boys lit gunpowder charges, set off more than a thousand petards, built enormous bonfires and instigated over 24 hours of pitched battles and rioting. But the Marlborough rebellion signalled the end of an era, one last hurrah for a soon-to-be-lost world. When the uprising was put down, the new headmaster enacted a series of reforms that were to be repeated throughout the nation's booming public school system: organized sports, compulsory chapel attendance, narrow bounds, strict surveillance by the prefects, and an unstinting focus on the moral 'character' of students. This was a new system of managed adolescence, designed to put an end to the previous era of schoolboy rebellion.

But what exactly was at stake in the boarding school rebellions of the late eighteenth and early nineteenth centuries? What wrongs did the sons of the ruling class seek to put right by occupying their schools and battling their teachers? What rights did they claim? What freedoms did they seek? Contrary to my ex-public school-boy's desire to discover a prior generation of student radicals battling for freedom and equality for all, the rebellions of the late eighteenth and early nineteenth century were not progressive critiques of the system. Rather than asserting the rights of junior boys to be free of indentured servitude, or pressing for reform of the antiquated classical curriculum, or even demanding improvements in domestic conditions, the rebels sought to protect the traditional rights of schoolboys to self-governance.

Life in an eighteenth-century public school was a curious mixture of extreme liberty and severe discipline. There was very little in the way of organized sports and extracurricular activities, and certainly none of the Victorian mania for surveillance and control. While the classroom and chapel were legitimate zones of teacherly authority, the dormitories, cloisters, courtyards and surrounding countryside were relatively free spaces in which students governed themselves through the prefect-fagging system. This rigidly hierarchical and often astonishingly brutal system produced a kind of self-governing polity, in which juniors submitted to a year of grinding servitude in the hope that they themselves would in due course rule over their own band of snivelling fags. Headmasters, Assistant Masters, Wardens and Ushers would intervene only in matters that impacted on the broader life of the school or which were in particularly flagrant breach of the rules.

Public school rebellions were often deeply conservative affairs in which the boys fought to preserve old rights and freedoms rather than to win new ones. The great majority of school rebellions were sparked when pupils' liberties were infringed upon by overzealous masters who were keen to assert their authority and enact reform. Uprisings grew out of local disputes over the mundane details of institutional life – the setting of bounds, the quality of the food, the scheduling of holidays and so on – but these elements of school routine were embodiments of a wider culture that granted schoolboys an enormous degree of autonomy as a self-governing tribe. Many of the rituals of institutional life stretched back to the public schools' medieval origins and were seen by pupils and masters alike as expressions of ancient ideals of chivalry and sodality. This tangled web of customs was guarded with a fierce, almost mystical devotion.

And yet the rebels were not *just* fighting to defend entrenched privileges. There was also something new here, something more familiar to modern eyes. In the sixteenth and seventeenth centuries pretty much all of the recorded instances of schoolboy rebellion were carried out by individuals or very small groups. Histories of the public schools relate numerous tales of drunkenness, whoring, buggery, fighting, bribery, extortion and even one or two murders. Another regular feature was the schoolboy runaway, who stole out at night and made for the nearest highway or forest. But the mass uprisings of the late eighteenth and early nineteenth centuries were a more modern phenomenon. What we see in this later period is a readiness to identify – and to fight – as a group. Public school rebellions gave voice to a new, as yet dimly perceived, group identity, one that would be of profound significance in the centuries to follow: youth. All of the rebellions pitted young against old. They may have been triggered by local disputes over institutional procedure, but they blossomed into battles to assert the rights and defend the honour of boys against masters.

This was precisely the kind of generational struggle that inspired the Winchester rebellion of 1793. The rebels were standing up for a particular sense of honour and fair dealing. They decided to mutiny when the Warden preached one doctrine but practised another. And they framed their objection in the official – indeed, highly *officious* – form of a letter written in Latin, which invoked the moral authority of that ancient language. This was a calculated piece of rhetoric that not only highlighted the Warden's wrongdoing but asserted, indirectly, the nobility of the boys themselves. When the Warden's response eventually arrived, it could not have been better calculated to enrage the boys' sense of wounded honour: 'If the Scholars are so forgetful of their rank and good manners as to insult their Warden by letters of consummate arrogance and extreme petulance, the Warden can give no other answer than that he shall continue to refuse all indulgence till the Scholars behave better.'[2] This is the language of juvenile chastisement. The Warden addresses the students as boys who have got above their station, rather than as young men deserving of equality and respect.

Today these boys would be called 'adolescents'. They would be granted a greater degree of autonomy than children, but still less than fully grown adults. They would be assumed to have needs – moral, social, psychological – that pertain to their specific stage in life. Historians often point to the turn of the twentieth century as the moment when adolescence emerged as both a widespread cultural formation and a topic of intellectual inquiry.[3] Although the word 'adolescence' dates back to the classical world, it was not until 1904 that it was fully codified as a social scientific concept, in G. Stanley Hall's treatise *Adolescence: Its Psychology and its Relations to Physiology, Anthropology, Sociology, Sex, Crime and Religion.* Hall cast this tempestuous phase of life as a 'recapitulation' of humankind's progress from barbarism to civilization.[4] Hall's treatise helped to found a whole new scientific field that sought not only to understand the psychosocial processes of adolescence but to manage those processes (usually within institutions such as schools, hospitals, youth clubs and detention centres) in order to alleviate the social problems they were thought to cause, from juvenile delinquency to cultural decline.

But there were earlier formations of adolescence that preceded the social scientific treatments of the early twentieth century. Philippe Ariès, the pioneering historian of childhood, observes that 'until the eighteenth century, adolescence was confused with childhood'.[5] Prior to this, childhood was a largely undifferentiated time that stretched from the end of infancy right through to marriage, when the period of juvenile dependency upon the family or some other sheltering institution – such as a guild, army or seminary – came to an end. It was over the course of the eighteenth century that adolescence came to assume many of the social and cultural meanings that it has today, especially for those sectors of society that could afford to furnish their male offspring with an extended period of leisure before entering the worlds of work and adult responsibility.[6] In his educational treatise *Emile* (1762), Jean-Jacques Rousseau defined adolescence as a distinct phase of his young charge's education. According to Rousseau, this period was akin to a 'second birth', which consisted of 'a change of temper, frequent outbursts of anger, a perpetual stirring of the mind'.[7] Johann Wolfgang von Goethe ascribed similar qualities to the suicidal hero of his novel *The Sorrows of Young Werther* (1774). *Werther* became a sensation of European literature, spawning a spate of copycat suicides and its own trend in fashion. The Werther 'costume' – blue tailcoat, yellow waistcoat, yellow trousers – became a sartorial shorthand for disaffected youth, an early forebear of the subcultural styles of the late twentieth century. In these two hugely influential works, youth was cast as changeful, tempestuous and unstable, while at the same time retaining a purity of sentiment that was uncorrupted by society at large.

These were the ingredients for a whole new conception of what it meant to be young: change and purity; instability and honesty; a skittish state of becoming coupled with a naive moral authenticity. And as this list of qualities suggests, youth quickly took on a new political significance. As adolescence became recognized as a time of profound personal change, it was but a short step to detecting these same qualities in the great social and political upheavals of the age. Looking back on the French Revolution, William Wordsworth uttered the now canonical statement of political youthfulness: 'Bliss was it in that dawn to be alive, / But to be young was very heaven!'[8] Wordsworth's lines invoke a triple dawning: of a new day, a new self and a new society. Written from the distance of maturity, they memorialize the deliciously incomplete promise of youth and revolution.

Of course, eighteenth-century public schoolboys were not fully fledged teenage rebels as we would recognize them today. These schoolboy mutineers would have dressed much like their teachers and fathers, in breeches, frock coats and cravats. They shared the same pastimes, attended the same events, spoke the same sociolect. They were, in almost all respects, miniature versions of their elders, sent away to school in preparation for the same life of authority and privilege. Among the Winchester rebels of 1793 were young men who would go on to assume positions of high authority within Britain's ruling elite: John Colborne, 1st Baron Seaton; Sir Lionel Smith, much-decorated Admiral in the British Navy and Governor of Jamaica; Sir James Charles Dalbiac, hero of the Peninsular campaign; Thomas Silver, Professor of Anglo-Saxon and Fellow of St John's College, Cambridge; Richard Mart, Bishop of Down. For the rowdy school-boys of the late eighteenth century, a chequered report card proved no barrier to membership of the ruling elite. Boarding school mutinies were vehemently prohibited and strenuously punished, but they were also seen by some as expressions of the same instincts for valour and self-reliance that were the most highly prized attributes of the ruling class. Sir Francis Burdett, the great parliamentarian and opponent of William Pitt the Younger, honed his leadership skills as a boy when he led his Westminster schoolfellows in an armed revolt in 1786.

And yet in their readiness to take up arms against their masters, public school rebels also embodied a new spirit of youthful activism. Riot is always a semiotic act. The choice of where to gather, when to assemble, what to smash, what to wear, who to include, who to exclude, what to sing, chant or cry: these are all choices, conscious or other-wise, which convey meanings beyond the bare act of destruction. As with any language, rioting was governed by rules and conventions. In his history of mob violence in eighteenth-century London, Robert Shoemaker points out that 'riotous protests were regulated by shared cultural understandings of honour and fairness which severely limited the amount of interpersonal violence actually committed.'[9] We see a similar set of 'shared cultural understandings' at work in the board-ing school rebellions of the era. In some cases, before they mutinied, boys would draw up official letters that set out their grievances to the school authorities. Frequently, rioters entered into negotiations with school authorities after the first flush of rebellion subsided. These negotiations were not always productive, but the willingness to parley indicates a respect for the right of the opposing side to fairness and plain dealing. Rioting schoolboys often selected highly symbolic items for destruction, further confirming the semiotic rigour with which they rebelled. At Harrow the rioters smashed the headmaster's desk. At Marlborough they burned the headmaster's manuscript on

Sophocles, which was ready to be sent to his publishers in London. At Eton a group of boys stole the 'flogging block' and broke it into pieces to keep as souvenirs. These are calculated decisions, which levy eloquent violence against the emblems of headmasterly authority: the pen, the book and the rod.

Many public school rebellions drew explicitly on the language and symbols of the French Revolution. In the midst of the rebellion at Rugby in 1797 a group of boys nailed the Declaration of the Rights of Man to the central noticeboard. At Harrow in 1808 pupils rioted in protest when the headmaster banned them from parading at the Guy Fawkes celebrations a banner that read 'Liberty and Freedom'. And at Eton in 1818 rebellion broke out when the headmaster, 'Flogger' Keate, punished a popular senior boy for missing lock-up. The boys smuggled a sledgehammer into the main school and smashed Keate's desk to smithereens, before daubing revolutionary slogans on the walls, including 'Down with Keate' and '*Floreat Seditio*'. The latter slogan subverts the school motto, *Floreat Etona* or 'May Eton Flourish', with an injunction to let sedition bloom in its place. The word 'sedition' alludes to the repressive laws – the Seditious Meetings Act of 1795 – introduced by parliament to suppress radical political groups in the wake of the French Revolution.

The sheer physical presence of a 'mob of boys' declaiming revolutionary slogans in the symbolic space of the public school gave spectacular expression to deep-seated fears about the maintenance of social order, especially among the moralistic middle classes who did not share the schools' aristocratic values. The connection between public school rebellions and radical youth politics was exploited for maximum effect in a satirical pamphlet published in London in 1792: *A Sketch of the Rights of Boys and Girls, by Launcelot Light of Westminster School, and Laetitia Lookabout of Queen's Square, Bloomsbury*. Masquerading as a radical tract penned by two enlightened schoolteachers, *A Sketch of the Rights of Boys and Girls* makes the case for the complete freedom of children from adult authority.

Among the list of rights that the pamphlet claims for schoolboys are the right 'to learn what they think proper'; 'the right to choose one's profession and situation in life'; the right to be free from 'tasks'; and the right not to attend public worship.[10] But Launcelot adds to this list a further right that plays directly upon adult fears about the public school system of pupil self-governance. This is the fundamental right

> that we choose our own masters. That we cashier them for misconduct. That we form a government of ourselves. These . . . are the fundamental rights of the people of England, of which people, Westminster men, Eton men, Harrow men, Winchester men, not to omit Hackney men, form no unimportant portion.[11]

The anonymous author draws an implicit connection between the revolutionary language of natural rights and the traditional system of pupil self-governance that was practised within England's public schools. He or she also voices the fear that the freedoms enjoyed by upper-class boys while at school contain the seeds of revolution. The last sentence imagines the nightmare scenario in which the public schoolboys' 'fundamental right' to self-government is extended to lower-class 'Hackney men', a prospect that would have appalled many readers.

Launcelot also declares that the appropriate way for schoolboys to cashier their masters for misconduct 'must be a kind of public act, and what in great public schools is usually, though absurdly, denominated rebellion'.[12] Having made this reference to the recent history of school uprisings, Launcelot quickly corrects himself and rejects 'rebellion' in favour of what he thinks is the more appropriate term, 'revolution'. This again plays upon the fear of contamination beyond the confines of the school, scaling up from the microcosmic language of 'rebellion', which refers to a limited uprising within a specific institution, to the macrocosmic language of 'revolution', which indicates a general uprising within the wider space of the nation itself. The pamphlet gives voice to the fear that the public school system of pupil self-governance and the recent outbreaks of student unrest cannot be dismissed as localized affairs. Instead they threaten to spill over into society at large, cascading from the little world of the school to the wider world of the nation.

*A Sketch of the Rights of Boys and Girls* is a piece of knockabout satire, a cheap pamphlet designed to sell quickly and make hay with the flimsy progressive notions of the day. But the very topicality and populism of the pamphlet also make it a powerful register of the wider cultural meanings attached to public school rebellion. The public school has often been described as a microcosm of the British state, a little world that prepares its charges for a life of authority and rule. The public schoolboy thus becomes both an emblem of futurity – the guarantor of the establishment's continuity between generations – and an object of intense social anxiety. By this logic, student rebellions spell national disorder. The seeds of rebellion sown in the school will bloom into a cankerous growth in the body politic. Many commentators were appalled at the prospect of the nation's elite schools run to riot, as this presented in microcosm the exact fears they held for the nation at large: a generational struggle between the young and the old, a questioning of ancient right and long-held tradition, violence, lewdness, anarchy.

IN THE LATE eighteenth century the school day at Eton included four timetabled hours of lessons, at 8 a.m., 11 a.m., 3 p.m. and 5 p.m., except on Fridays when the first afternoon lesson ran from 2 to 3.30. Each night, 'absence' was called at six o'clock, by which time all Collegers – that is, the boys who received scholarships – had to be inside the school buildings. At 7 p.m. they had to sit and read under the supervision of a prefect for an hour, then at 8 they attended prayers in the Long Chamber, the vast, draughty hall in which the hundred and more Collegers slept. By this time of day, the Oppidans, or fee-paying students, were off-site in their lodgings with masters or private families. All members of the school attended chapel at 10 o'clock on Sunday mornings. There were numerous holidays, including Founder's Day, Royal birthdays and the major holidays of the Church calendar. On whole holidays, boys were free to entertain themselves, but there were still two chapel services to attend, one at 11 a.m. and the other at 3 p.m.

The curriculum was devoted almost exclusively to the study of classical texts, although sometimes, for a little light relief, students translated essays from back issues of *The Spectator* from English into

Latin and Greek. Pupils of the fifth and sixth forms had to 'construe' ten times each week – that is, they had to prepare in advance, then orally translate, an assigned passage from a classical text. They also had to recite from memory passages of between 35 and sixty lines apiece seven times a week. There was a thriving black market for 'cribs', or English translations of assigned texts, and where this market failed the more capable juniors were often pressed into service as translators. The earlier forms worked on writing, arithmetic, geography and algebra, as well as Greek and Latin.[13]

For all of the detailed scheduling, this is not an overly crowded timetable. Four hours of classroom time each day is pretty minimal, especially considering that as soon as pupils had delivered their own construes, they were free to leave the class. Other schools at the time had similar workloads. During Lord Byron's time at Harrow in the first decade of the nineteenth century, he was obliged to attend a mere 21 hours of lessons each week.[14] Byron quickly discovered that, as academic standards were generally low, he could get away with minimal preparation and spend his spare time pursuing his own interests. Indeed, many intellectually curious boys gained a sound education while at public school simply by reading under their own steam. Byron claimed to have read over 4,000 novels while at school, as well as vast swathes of more learned material. But he also made sure that he was 'never *seen* reading, but always idle and in mischief or at play'.[15] Ever the easeful aristocrat, Byron acknowledges the role of the public school culture of *sprezzatura*, or the assumption that the learned gentleman should wear his erudition with a seemingly careless grace.

More significant than the structure of the curriculum, though, were the institutional expectations of how students should behave outside of class hours. The key here was that there were very few expectations, beyond the basic requirement of following school rules. Officially, the eighteenth-century public school sought to produce 'compleat scholars', but this was a matter for the classroom rather than the boarding house or the sports field.[16] Outside the official domains of classroom and chapel, boys were largely left to entertain and police themselves. Order was maintained through the prefectfagging system, in which junior boys acted as servants for seniors. On entering the school, each new boy, or fag, was assigned to a fag-master – a senior boy in the fifth or sixth form for whom he would polish shoes, wash and brush clothing or prepare food. At Shrewsbury fags were known as 'douls', which derives from the Greek word for slave, *doulos*, a piece of school jargon that suggests the entire subordination of the fag to his master. In the pages of the *Edinburgh Review*, the writer George Lewis characterized fagging as 'the only regular institution of slave labour enforced by force which exists in these islands'.[17] Defenders of the system, however, cast it as the ideal preparation for a future life of leadership: by learning the positions of both subjugation and authority at school, boys were better prepared for wielding true power in the wider world.

Before the Victorian period, fagging was an unofficial feature of school life, a kind of shadow system formed through long custom among the boys themselves and tolerated as a matter of convenience by the often harried and overworked masters. In the second half of the eighteenth century staff numbers failed to match the growth in school rolls. This growth was as yet a minute fraction of the middle-class boom of the Victorian period, but it had significant implications for school discipline. Masters were often heavily outnumbered by their charges, both in the dormitories and in the classrooms, where a single teacher might find himself in charge of a room of more than a hundred boys. When John Keate was appointed headmaster of Eton in 1809, he had seven assistant masters to help him run a school of 515 boys. The prefect-fagging system was thus a matter of convenience as much as it was an expression of principle. It was only with the reforms of Thomas Arnold, the famous headmaster of Rugby between 1828 and 1842, and his many Victorian imitators that prefect-fagging became an official part of school routine, an instrument of surrogate discipline controlled from above by an all-powerful headmaster.

The ratio of masters to pupils, and the tenuous grip on authority that this entailed, meant that beatings were a regular feature of the school day. One account of life at Winchester in the first decade of the nineteenth century estimates that there were roughly twenty beatings each day in a school of only 150 pupils.[18] At Eton in 1810, 'Flogger' Keate caned a hundred senior boys in a single session. Rebellious behaviour seems to have been tolerated as an unavoidable by-product of the system. For this earlier generation of pedagogues, before the evangelism of the Victorians and the depth psychology of the Freudians, forbidden acts were to be met with physical sanctions. The deeper motives and moral qualities that underpinned transgressions were of little concern. Rebellion was part of the 'game' of school life, in which the self-governing commonwealth of the boarding house would attempt to win as many liberties from the authorities as possible. Arnold Whitridge, in his biography of Thomas Arnold, referred to 'the atmosphere of guerrilla warfare' that prevailed in the unreformed schools. Under these conditions, rebellions were accepted 'like outbreaks of cholera, as being unfortunate but inevitable'.[19]

Insofar as there was any pedagogical theory attached to eighteenth-century public schooling, it was one of aristocratic libertarianism. Not all of the boys who were sent to public schools at this time were descended from noble families, but a large proportion were. This meant that most pupils were the social superiors of their masters, who tended to be drawn from the clerical and professional classes. It was not until the reforms of the Victorian era that the public schools became predominantly middle-class institutions, in terms of both their demographics and ethos. In the eighteenth century, by contrast, expectations about how boys should spend their free time, and to what standards of behaviour they should be held, were coloured by the wider culture of the aristocracy, a group not always known for its self-restraint, especially not in the bad old days before the Reform Bill of 1832, which extended the parliamentary franchise to middle-class property-owners. In this pre-democratic age, public schoolboys were born to rule in a sense that simply doesn't exist anymore. They came from a small network of elite families who exercised a near monopoly on political power.

The educational historian W. V. Wallbank has described the culture of 'combative learning' that prevailed under these conditions.[20] Public school education was based on a series of adversarial relationships – between masters and pupils, prefects and fags, public schoolboys and the local community – that encouraged young men to develop the qualities of masculine valour and ingenuity that would prepare them for the competitive worlds of parliamentary politics and public life. This combative ethos was expressed in many facets of school life, including the culture of political debate and speech making, the popularity of prize fights and blood sports and the frequent scrapes between boys and members of the local community.

There was also a highly theatrical element to the eighteenth-century public school. During Eton's triennial 'Montem' festival, pupils would dress up in elaborate, carnivalesque costumes and beg members of the local community for 'salt', or financial donations to pay for the head boy's first year at university. At other schools, the daily practice of reciting passages from memory before the class, end-of-term speech days, informal drama clubs and annual festivals, such as Westminster's Latin play, trained young men how to speak and act authoritatively in public. In this respect, public school served as a rite of passage in which privileged adolescent males engaged in what sociologists today would call 'role experimentation', or the playful adoption of unfamiliar personae during a period of rapid personal change.[21] Even schoolboy rebellions were sometimes understood as part of the process of experimental self-discovery that prepared young men for the world of affairs. In his autobiography Edward Gibbon noted in approving tones that in the nation's public schools, 'the mimic scene of rebellion has displayed, in their true colours, the ministers and patriots of the rising generation'.[22]

All of this ensured that life in an eighteenth-century boarding school was an often brutal and disorderly affair. The range of bullying techniques alone evinces a taste for bizarre forms of cruelty that rivals some of the more dissolute Roman emperors. At Eton, fags were marched out into the countryside, given a 10-yard head start and then pursued by prefects who took potshots at them with pistols. At Rugby, juniors were made to run the gauntlet between two lines of seniors, who whipped them with knotted handkerchiefs. At Winchester, juniors were toughened up for their fagging duties by being forced to wear 'tin gloves', produced by grabbing a sizzling branding stick that toughened their palms for carrying coffee pots, frying pans and other items of fag-labour. At Marlborough, an early form of bungee jumping was invented when junior boys were tied to knotted bed sheets and launched over the fifth-floor balustrade of the boarding house. The practice was discontinued when a boy crashed to his death on the stone floor below.

Domestic conditions were also very poor: indigestible rations, poorly heated boarding houses, overcrowding, fights and abuse of various kinds. Reminiscing about his days at Eton in the 1830s, Edward Thring described the 'Long Chamber' where Collegers slept as a 'land of misrule'.[23] With a single log fire to heat a hundred-foot-long chamber, boys often slept two or three to a bed, partly for warmth and partly for illicit recreation. Periodically, parties would be formed to deal with the continual infestation of rats that ran across the boys' faces as they slept. When the Long Chamber was cleaned out in 1854, two cartloads of rats' bones were extracted from beneath the floorboards.

Yet alongside the tales of servitude, bullying and physical privation that are a standard feature of the pre-Victorian public school memoir, we also encounter passages describing the delicious ease and freedom of life, the gay pageant of leisured pastimes, lavish boarding house feasts, the after-hours revels of play-acting, cards and storytelling, tramps across the surrounding fields, the ardent absorption in hobbies and private reading and the forging of lifelong friendships. Officially boys were kept to relatively narrow bounds around the school, but with low numbers of masters and a culture that viewed teacherly surveillance as a breach of honour, they enjoyed considerable liberty to roam free. Many school memoirs of the pre-Victorian age tell of poaching expeditions on local farms and estates, followed by late-night boarding house feasts of hare, pigeon or trout. A popular pastime at Harrow was 'toozling', which involved beating to death any wildlife found in the surrounding hedgerows. Boys at Marlborough carried what was known in school slang as a 'squaler', a light wooden stick, weighted with lead, for the killing of game encountered on their afternoon tramps across the Wiltshire countryside. There are also many tales of a less savoury nature. In his study of boarding school fiction, Jeffrey Richards observes that the 'dissolute' style of masculinity that was popular among the Regency aristocracy was shared with members of the 'rough' working class.[24] A taste for drinking, gambling, whoring, blood sports and prize fights encouraged an edgy solidarity between the highest and lowest echelons of society.

Schoolboy liberty came in both positive and negative forms: the freedom *from* teacherly surveillance and extracurricular commitments, and the freedom *to* self-government through the prefect-fagging system. These liberties seem to have been consciously cultivated by teachers, parents and boys alike. Recalling his time at Eton between 1811 and 1822, the writer William Hill Tucker observed that, 'the masters from Keate downwards never interfered or intervened in any way out of school. We were a self-governing community. People who have not known the system have objected.'[25] As Tucker suggests, boys were left to themselves precisely so that they could form a self-regulating society. This system was valued both for the liberty it granted and for the order that emerged as a result of that liberty. John Moultrie, who was a contemporary of Tucker's at Eton, describes the same system of order sprung from liberty in the florid tones of his verse memoir, *Dream of Life* (1843). Alongside his descriptions of the rigours of fagging, the 'interminable gloom' of the Long Chamber where scholarship boys slept and the 'mad riot' that erupted after lights out, Moultrie is keen to point out that,

> No robber-horde were we,
> Anarchical, self-willed, by force alone
> From mutual wrong and violence restrained;
> But a well-governed people, proud to own
> Legitimate control, and to maintain
> Our glorious constitutions unimpaired.[26]

Moultrie suggests that, when left to their own devices, upper-class schoolboys will institute an orderly and hierarchical system of authority. His reference to the boys' 'glorious constitutions' makes the political analogy clear: this is a vision of England in microcosm, a well-governed polity founded on ancient liberties and deep bonds of fealty among a noble elite.

Both supporters and critics of the system repeatedly identified the eighteenth-century public school as a miniature state of nature, a free space in which upper-class boys collectively encountered the harsh realities of life in the raw. In the *Edinburgh Review* in 1858, a time when the public schools faced significant pressure to reform, Sir James Fitzjames Stephen argued, 'we do not believe that any system was ever invented so real, so healthy and so bracing to the mind and body', and that this excellence stemmed from 'the entire absence of any restraint or supervision, except during the hours actually passed at lessons'.[27] For Stephen, public schooling constituted a kind of negative enlightenment. The rigours of school life prevented young men from 'forming illusions about the life which lies beyond their own observation'. The school liberated the student from the false consciousness of social relations, and brought him into contact with 'real men, real passions and real things' so that 'when he hears or speaks of them his associations are with realities and not with mere words or books'.[28] This pedagogical vision is both profoundly anti-domestic, with its association of false 'illusions' with the female space of the home, and anti-intellectual, with its promise of access to unvarnished reality rather than the abstractions encountered in books.

Unsurprisingly, aristocratic libertarians tended to cleave to Thomas Hobbes's account of pre-civilized life, rather than the more benign visions of John Locke, Jean-Jacques Rousseau and others. Hobbes famously described life in his hypothetical state of nature as 'solitary, poor, nasty, brutish and short' and a war of 'every man against every man'.[29] While Hobbes used his speculative history of pre-civilized man, a vision animated by his experience of the bloody strife of the English Civil War, to justify sovereign authority, public school libertarians enlisted it in the service of prefect rule. In both cases, a hierarchical system of governance was justified in comparison to a presumed natural state of poverty, weakness and brute physical struggle. Moultrie makes precisely this case for the system of prefect rule:

> And what if aristocracy, upheld
> By right prescriptive, ruled with feudal sway
> Her unenfranchised vassals – still her yoke
> Was milder and less grievous to be borne
> Than arbitrary bondage, forced elsewhere
> By strength of fist, on the reluctant necks

Of trembling urchins, all too weak to win
The freedoms which they sighed for.[30]

Moultrie justifies prefect rule by comparison with another, hypothetical state that lacks even this degree of 'unenfranchised' protection. He looks beyond the existing order of pupil self-governance to a terrifying state of outright war in which the physically strong subject the weak in 'arbitrary bondage'. In doing so, he draws on the same set of tropes that were often repeated in defences of pupil self-governance: 'robber hoardes', savage gangs and the 'anarchical' life of pre-civilized man.

This could be called the *Lord of the Flies* (1954) defence of public school discipline. William Golding's tale of schoolboy barbarism performs a similar mental exercise to that of Hobbes. By stranding his English schoolboys on a deserted Pacific island, Golding creates the fictional conditions for them to revert to a state of nature, free from the artificial institutions of the modern world. As readers, we watch with horrified glee as the boys' primal instincts emerge from beneath their tattered school uniforms. But once the initial flush of delight in the freedoms of natural life has passed, we are left with a profoundly pessimistic view of human civilization. The civilized world of schools, governments, law, authority – the whole gamut of 'houses an' streets, an' TV' for which the scientifically minded Piggy pines – is the only barrier keeping us from our original nature as fearful, aggressive, cannibalistic monsters.[31] *Lord of the Flies* ends with a vision of authority restored in the form of a British naval officer who arrives on the island just as Ralph is about to be speared by Jack's rampaging huntsmen. This is an implicit argument for the legitimacy of hierarchical institutions. Golding's book riffs on the same theme that recurred in the conservative defence of aristocratic libertarianism and Hall's later social scientific treatment of adolescence: that the turbulent transformation from childhood to adulthood involves a 'recapitulation' of mankind's own passage from barbarism to civilization. This is a characteristically modern fear that the youth among us are merely one step away from savagery.

For critics, however, the system of aristocratic libertarianism was a derogation of the public schools' responsibility to serve the interests of civilized society as a whole. By the turn of the nineteenth century, the public school had become a byword for juvenile delinquency and aristocratic excess. In 1810, in the pages of the reformist periodical the *Edinburgh Review*, Sidney Smith excoriated public schooling as 'a system of abuse, neglect, and vice'.[32] While apologists claimed that the prefect-fagging system curtailed the 'insolence' of the aristocracy, Smith argued the opposite – that it bred in the oldest and strongest boys 'an absurd and pernicious opinion of their own importance' that blinded them to the interests of others. In 1819, when the radical parliamentarian Henry Brougham introduced a Bill that would prevent abuses of public school scholarship funds originally intended for the poor, he blamed his defeat on 'the romantic attachment which English gentlemen feel towards the academic scenes of their early life'.[33] This was an early example of a complaint that would be voiced repeatedly in subsequent years: that the brutal rites of passage that defined public school life bred in the ruling class an irrational sense of loyalty to their almae matres that was an obstacle to progressive social reform. All too often, claimed Smith and Brougham, former public schoolboys felt greater kinship with the small number of men who had undergone the same formative adolescent experiences, than with society at large.

AT ETON COLLEGE in 1808, a loud explosion rang out from the garden of Dr Bethel, an assistant master at the school, and echoed across the main quadrangle. This was not, as had been the case at other public schools in the wake of the French Revolution, the beginning of a collective student uprising; nor was it an expression of tribal conservatism, a defensive measure to protect the rights of boys. Instead it was the work of a single boy, whose intentions were symbolic, aesthetic, psychological, spiritual and even magical. Earlier that afternoon the boy had laid a trail of gunpowder from the edge of his housemaster's garden to the trunk of an old tree in the centre of the lawn. Using a magnifying glass, he ignited the charge and watched as the powder fizzled across the grass and produced a loud explosion, which in turn produced a shocked response from the school authorities. In the young boy's richly symbolic imagination, the explosion was a riposte to the static forms of the institution, its unearned privilege, hierarchical authority and intellectual moribundity. The fissiparous energy of the gunpowder symbolized the creative powers of man and nature. These powers were the source of human freedom and perfectibility, but under the present conditions of society they lay everywhere in chains, warped and trammelled by vicious institutions that fostered tyranny, greed and subjugation.

The explosion was the work of Percy Bysshe Shelley, whose poems are now staples of undergraduate English Literature anthologies and whose recumbent form adorns an official monument in the Oxford college from which he was expelled. In 1808, however, Shelley was a lonely, disaffected public schoolboy. Throughout his first year at Eton he was mercilessly bullied, most likely because he refused to fag for his assigned prefect. He was sometimes set upon by as many as a hundred boys, all baying at the top of their lungs, 'the Shelley, the Shelley, the Shelley'. These persecutory mobs hounded him around the school grounds and into the town, tearing his clothes and kicking muddy footballs at him. One of the reasons that Shelley suffered so acutely was that he often attempted to fight back. He would descend into apoplectic rages, kicking and screaming at his tormentors. It was for this reason that throughout his early years at the school he was known as 'Mad Shelley', an easily riled pariah, whose ethereal good looks and dreamy nature made him all the easier a target.[34]

After he blew up his housemaster's tree, the young misfit was given a new nickname. 'Mad Shelley' became 'The Eton Atheist', not for any overt statement of unbelief, but for his willingness to challenge the authorities – the 'gods' – of the school. After his tormented early years, Shelley's schooldays improved. He was lucky to be a fee-paying Oppidan rather than a Colleger, and hence was free to lodge with a master away from the school grounds. Dr Bethel was a genial and liberal character who was tolerant of Shelley's idiosyncratic ways. Secreted away in his private room at the Doctor's house, Shelley was free to pursue his own intellectual interests, an alternative course of study that supplemented the school's official classical curriculum with ancient works of alchemy, witchcraft and magic; modern treatises on the new sciences of chemistry and electricity; and the radical political philosophies of Condorcet, Rousseau, Benjamin Franklin and William Godwin.

For Shelley, these were not merely academic texts. Instead they contained the same vital and unruly energies as the gunpowder charge he had set in his housemaster's garden. Like many disaffected schoolboys, he fled from the dull world of the institution into an alternative reality of his own creation. This more vivid and idealistic world was both a retreat from and a riposte to the official values of the school. Shelley converted his room at Dr Bethel's house into a makeshift laboratory, where he conducted experiments with a Galvanic battery, constructed kites designed to harness the power of electrical storms, mixed volatile chemical compounds and built hot air balloons, which he launched over the college grounds. On one occasion, he wired his battery up to the doorknob and gave Dr Bethel an almighty shock as the wary master looked in on his strange young pupil. In the first decade of the nineteenth century, the new sciences of chemistry and electricity were not recognized as official academic disciplines. The curriculum at both of England's ancient universities was dominated by classics, mathematics and theology. Any empirical science that was taught had to be fully compatible with 'natural theology', which interpreted scientific knowledge in the light of religious orthodoxy. Chemistry and electricity were still associated with atheism, the occult and philosophical radicalism. For Shelley, science was a visionary, almost psychedelic pursuit. The new sciences stripped away the dull surfaces of things and disrupted everyday habits of perception. They suggested that the world could be taken apart and re-made from its elementary building blocks. This was in direct contrast to the implied philosophy of the school, an ancient institution that drew its authority from a royal charter and hundreds of years of tradition. It was no wonder that Dr Bethel eventually confiscated his chemistry books.

Shelley also crafted for himself a flamboyant public identity as an eccentric radical. This new identity was bricolaged together from his youthful enthusiasms: Gothic novels, magic and the occult, spectacular science and radical philosophy. Shelley was once discovered in the grounds of his boarding house presiding over a circle of blue flame, attempting to summon the Devil. He wore dishevelled, loose-fitting clothes and ate only fruit and vegetables bought from lowly market stalls. In the school holidays he dressed as an agricultural labourer and sought work on a local farm. At the age of sixteen he became a minor celebrity among his schoolfellows when he published a sensationalist Gothic novel, *Zastrozzi*.[35] His choice of genre was itself an affront to the official values of the school. This was the most schlocky and disposable corner of the literary marketplace, a million miles away from the timeless verities of the classics. Even after he had left school for Oxford, former classmates would show up at his door in order to witness the 'Eton Atheist's' legendary feats of cursing, during which he would pour invective upon his father, the King and God himself. This was all part of a larger performance, in which he signalled his rejection of the culture of his parents, the school and the rigidly hierarchical society they represented.

Shelley's university friend and later biographer Thomas Jefferson Hogg framed his private reading as a cunning repurposing of the culture of aristocratic libertarianism.[36] In effect, Shelley turned the system of pupil liberty against itself, using the time that others would devote to gossip, drink and field sports to scientific and philosophical study. Finding himself a senior boy with time on his hands, and being more than capable of keeping up with his official lessons, he decided to train his heart and mind to a different discipline than that offered by the school.

In his later poetic works Shelley returned more than once to this moment of decision, the point at which a young man dedicates himself to an emancipatory course of study in opposition to a repressive institution. In his long poem *The Revolt of Islam* (1818), a symbolic re-imagining of the French Revolution, Shelley points to the decisive moment when his young protagonist (modelled largely on his own experience) sees through the corrupt school – 'a world of woes' filled with 'the harsh and grating strife of tyrants and of foes' – and fastens upon an alternative course of self-directed learning:

> And from that hour did I with earnest thought
> Heap knowledge from forbidden mines of lore;
> Yet nothing that my tyrants knew or taught
> I cared to learn, but from that secret store

Wrought linked armour for my soul, before
It might walk forth to war among mankind.[37]

Shelley describes his private studies at Eton and after as a kind of
'lore', quarried from 'forbidden mines'. This reading is transgressive
and dangerous. 'Lore' is a different type of thing to 'learning' or 'knowledge'. Shelley's language imbues his adolescent reading with magical
properties, ancient provenance and underground means of transmis-
sion. It communicates the rush of discovery, the sense of penetrating
beyond the everyday world into a secret community of like-minded
outsiders. This is a different mode of learning to the overbearingly
masculine, 'combative' culture of the school and a different form of
protest than the armed mutinies that took place around the same time.

After his death at the age of 29 in a boating accident in the Bay
of Spezia, Shelley was repeatedly cast, by both his supporters and
critics, as the archetypal schoolboy rebel, a young man whose identity
was forged in opposition to – and whose subsequent career as both
a poet and an advocate for radical causes such as democratic reform,
open marriage and vegetarianism was a doomed attempt to break free
from – the repressive institution of the school. Alongside Chatterton,
Keats and Rimbaud, Shelley has joined the tragic ranks of the eternally
young, cut short in his prime, still bristling with unfulfilled potential
and youthful energy. But while his early death prevented any possibility
of a middle-aged decline from rebellion to nostalgia, it also left him
trapped in the sickly sweet idealism of youth. It was Shelley's fate to
be mythologized by subsequent generations as a kind of radicalized
Peter Pan figure, caught in the suspended animation of adolescent
passions and jejune political idealism.

In the eyes of J. T. Coleridge, a contemporary of Shelley's at
Eton, the young poet's political radicalism stemmed from stalled
development, his inability to mature properly under the influence of
the school:

(Mr Shelley) speaks of his school as a 'world of woes', of his
masters as 'tyrants', of his school-fellows as 'enemies', – alas!
What is this, but evidence against himself? Everyone who

knows what a public school ordinarily must be, will only
trace in these lines the language of an insubordinate, a vain, a
mortified spirit.[38]

Coleridge uses a line of attack that would crop up repeatedly in later
denunciations of upper-class English radicals: that Shelley's political idealism sprang from his constitutional inability to submit to
the righteous authority of the school. There is a hint here of Cyril
Connolly's much later description of upper-class radicals in the 1930s
as 'psychological revolutionaries, people who adopt left wing for-
mulas because they hate their fathers or were unhappy at their public
schools'.[39] Political idealism becomes, in this reckoning, a kind of
pathology, a mental perversion that stems from character flaws that
can be traced to the individual's unwillingness to knuckle down to
school discipline.

　　Within the public schools themselves, Shelley became the poster
child for an alternative tradition that used avant-garde art and radical
politics as a means of critiquing the institution from within. Shelley's
poetry often featured in the kind of illicit, self-directed reading that
he himself had pursued as a boy. At Eton in the 1840s Algernon
Swinburne read Shelley's verse in defiance of an official school ban.
Rather than joining his fellows on the playing fields, the eccentric
Swinburne holed up in the school library and pored over Shelley's
radical verse. Swinburne was proud of the nickname assigned to him
by his bullies – 'Mad Swinburne' – as this was a direct echo of Shelley's
nickname at the school forty years earlier.[40] In *Goodbye to All That*
Robert Graves relates the story of a friend who was flogged for reading
Shelley at Denstone College in the early 1880s. 'When his schoolmaster beat him,' recalls Graves, 'he protested between the blows:
"Shelley is beautiful! Shelley is beautiful! Shelley is beautiful."'[41] At
Marlborough in the 1920s Louis MacNeice imbibed Shelley's 'utopias
of amethyst and star light' and believed in 'the Enfant Terrible as an
unacknowledged legislator'.[42] Shelley was part of the 'fashionable child
cult' worshipped by the aesthete rebels of the school, his works sitting
alongside those of Edward Lear, Aldous Huxley and the Sitwells as
part of a radical counter-canon.

But beyond Shelley's individual legacy as a rebel icon, it was the method and style of his dissent that had the longest afterlife within the world of the public school. With his carefully crafted bohemian identity and flair for rebellious stunts, Shelley engaged in a new mode of adolescent self-fashioning that was to become the template for subsequent generations of disaffected schoolboys and girls. In the more tightly scheduled and strictly disciplined world of the later nineteenth- and twentieth-century public schools, violent struggles between boys and masters gave way to new forms of subcultural dissent as the chief means of asserting adolescent liberty. Rather than taking up arms against their masters, disaffected schoolboys fabricated alternative worlds for themselves, private realms in which different kinds of identity and different systems of value could flourish. These worlds were pieced together through private reading, affectations of style and dress, the formation of clubs and cliques, verbal performances of slang, nonsense and swearing and the publication of dissident magazines. Even when they didn't namecheck Shelley himself, students who turned to art and culture as a means of escaping school discipline drew upon the same recipe for cultural resistance that Shelley had dramatized in his radical verse and put into action in his spectacular schoolboy pranks.

'Get up, there's a little fellow under you', illustration from Thomas Hughes,
*Tom Brown's School Days* (1857).

# TWO

# Thomas Arnold's Schooldays

The last of the great public school rebellions took place at Marlborough College in 1851. Unlike Winchester, Rugby and Eton, where pupils rioted amid the cloistral gloom of an ancient foundation, Marlborough was a new institution, founded in 1843 in order to provide affordable education for the sons of middle-class clergymen. Marlborough was part of the boom in public school-style education that took place in the Victorian era. This was the period in which the middle classes decided that they too would like their sons to acquire the classical learning, gentlemanly cultivation and powerful contacts that were assumed to be the products of elite education. Marlborough was founded at the very beginning of this process of reform, and in its early days it displayed all of the quirks and vicissitudes of the old world of the eighteenth-century public school. But the rebellion of 1851, and in particular the reforms enacted by the new headmaster, George Cotton, helped to usher into existence the new world of managed adolescence that was to characterize the Victorian boarding school.

One of the problems with Marlborough College in its early days was that it was too cheap. In their attempt to provide affordable education for the sons of penurious clergymen, the founders of the College set the fees too low and left the institution without adequate funds. The school grew very quickly in its early years, rising from 200 pupils in 1843 to 500 in 1848, and, as a result, conditions were very poor, even by the low standards of the traditional public school. The new school buildings were badly designed, with vast dormitories and a single oversized classroom that did nothing to facilitate discipline and order. To further compound the situation, school funds could not cover the salaries of enough masters to provide either adequate education or a minimal level of order. Right from the start, the school was beset by problems with bullying, fights and expulsions. In the months leading up to the rebellion of 1851, Marlborough was in a continuous state of low-level guerrilla warfare, in which boys intermittently damaged school property and attacked masters, while the besieged authorities flogged and expelled as many of the culprits as they could catch. As with many of the previous rebellions, the boys' anger was focused not on the masters but on a non-academic member of staff, Mr Peviar, the Gate Sergeant, who punished even the most minor breaches of school rules and kept a detailed record of the offences committed by each boy. This degree of punctilious monitoring would not have sat well with any notions of pupil self-governance that the boys of this new foundation may have adopted from their comrades at older institutions.[1]

The uprising itself was the result of detailed planning. Secret organizing committees were formed and stores of fireworks and gunpowder were gathered in advance. The rebellion began at 5 o'clock sharp on the evening of 5 November with a loud rocket explosion. The headmaster had already cancelled the annual fireworks celebrations in the fear that it would become a flashpoint for disorder. His fears were confirmed when the first rocket was followed by a veritable barrage of munitions. As the explosions sounded above the school, the rampaging students built bonfires, smashed windows and ransacked classrooms. On the third day of the rebellion, the school authorities attempted to restore order when they captured five boys from the mob and immediately expelled them, but this limited incursion only served to pour oil on an already powerful fire. One of the expelled boys was a much-loved prefect and a charismatic leader of the rebellion. As he and his four comrades were driven from the school grounds, their carriage was followed by a crowd of students, who paraded through the local town, chanting the names of the expelled heroes and singing raucous songs. As it processed through the once sleepy Wiltshire town, the student mob was swelled by local townsmen and women who were drawn to its energy and noise. When the mob made its circuitous way back to the school, it proceeded to smash the headmaster's windows and set fire to the racket courts. Pausing by the school gates, it belched forth the imposing figure of the school's champion boxer, who chased down and thrashed Mr Peviar to the great delight of all assembled. They then raided the headmaster's study, burning his collection of birches, the ledger in which student crimes were recorded and his recently completed manuscript on Sophocles, which was ready to be sent to his publishers in London.

After a week of fighting, teachers and students agreed to a truce. The terms were highly favourable to the students, as they effectively abolished all of the reforms enacted by masters over the preceding four years. In addition to six expulsions, the headmaster managed to extract only the merest concessions from the rebels: they wrote a letter of apology and paid 15 pounds in damages. There was another outbreak of rioting a week after the truce was agreed, but this was only a localized, unplanned affair and order was quickly restored. The School's governors did not officially sanction the headmaster, Rev. Matthew Wilkinson, but after an appropriate period of time had elapsed, he was quietly ushered out of the school.

With the appointment of a new headmaster, George Cotton, conditions at Marlborough began to change in subtle but important ways. One of Cotton's first acts as headmaster was to enlist an elite group of senior prefects to enforce discipline within the boarding houses and playing fields. Shortly after the new headmaster's arrival, a junior boy recorded his excitement in his diary: 'capital speech from Cotton. The Sixth form are to govern the school.'[2] By making the prefect-fagging system an official part of the school's chain of command, Cotton sought to remove it from its roots in ancient tradition and divest it of its tribal ethos. His aim was not, however, entirely to abolish the liberties enjoyed by students under the old system of self-governance, but rather to shape that liberty into forms that served the ends of the institution as a whole. The prefect elite enforced order and exercised discipline when required, but their primary role was to set an example for the lower ranks to emulate. These senior boys, poised on the verge of adulthood, would embody the values of self-discipline, piety and community spirit that Cotton wished to spread throughout the school.

Cotton rebuffed the attempts of his board of governors to institute an official system of surveillance, which would have required all boys leaving school grounds to be accompanied by a master. He insisted that boys 'must either submit to the prefects, or be reduced to the level of a private school, and have their freedom ignominiously curtailed'.[3] With this statement, Cotton seems to express the sentiments of aristocratic libertarianism – the belief in the radical autonomy of upper-class boys – but the crucial difference is that he makes this statement in the knowledge that the senior prefects are the creatures of his will. Under Cotton's new regime, Marlborough boys would enjoy the freedom to act as they pleased, so long as they did so within the bounds set by a moral framework that was ratified by the institution, exemplified by the prefects and emulated by the boys themselves.

Cotton also encouraged more friendly relations between pupils and masters. This was another attempt to break with the tribalism of the previous era, the assumption that boys and masters occupied separate spheres within the school and pursued their own conflicting interests. He made sure to recruit young, energetic masters, many of whom had recently graduated from Oxbridge and public schools. The aim was to bridge the no-man's-land that had grown up in the previous generations between childhood and adulthood. Indeed, just as the figure of the rowdy adolescent came to prominence in Britain in the late eighteenth-century public schools, so too did the sympathetic pedagogue emerge in the early Victorian era as a response to that earlier bugbear. Cotton and his young assistant masters promoted cricket, rugby and other organized sports as official school pursuits, rather than the rowdy and disorganized practices that they were in most schools. Games were another means of capturing and channelling the tribal sentiments of boy society. In the 'Circular to Parents', which he penned on assuming command of the school, Cotton stated his aim to bring students 'as much as possible together in one body in the college itself and in the playground'.[4] For Cotton, as for many subsequent headmasters, organized games were an explicitly counter-revolutionary tool, a means of redirecting the energies of youth into collective forms that served the institution as a whole.

BEFORE HIS APPOINTMENT as the headmaster of Marlborough, Cotton had spent the previous fifteen years as a housemaster at Rugby School, where he had been a protégé of Thomas Arnold, the school's reforming headmaster. By 1852, the year that Cotton took charge at war-torn Marlborough, the deceased Arnold was well on his way to the legendary status that he would enjoy for the next half-century and more. The legend of 'Doctor Arnold', the great figurehead of Victorian reform, was erected upon the twin foundations of Arnold's *Sermons*, of which he published multiple volumes between 1834 and 1844, and Arthur Penrhyn Stanley's biography, which was first published in 1844. In spite of the air of worthiness that accompanied the genre, Arnold's *Sermons* sold well and were highly regarded. Queen Victoria was reputed to have kept a copy at her bedside for nightly perusal.[5] Stanley's *Life and Correspondence of Thomas Arnold* further cemented the Doctor's status by performing a characteristically Victorian canonization of the author's former headmaster: rather than converting Arnold into a saint, Stanley transformed him into an institution. 'Whatever peculiarity of character was impressed on the scholars whom [Rugby] sent forth,' writes Stanley, 'was derived not from the genius of the place, but from the genius of the man. Throughout the whole, whether in the school itself, or in its after effects, the one image that we have before us is not Rugby, but Arnold.'[6] Stanley's biography merged the existence of the school with the character of the man in charge: the *genius loci* of an almost three-hundred-year-old institution was quashed by the monumental figure of the Doctor.

Arnold's renown was further cemented by the work of the men whom he had influenced either as schoolboys or fellow masters at Rugby. He possessed a powerful capacity to inculcate in his protégés the same sense of moral and religious mission that he himself brought to his work. Alongside Cotton, who after his time at Marlborough went on to become Bishop of Madras, where he promoted organized sports as a means of healing the divisions of the Indian Mutiny of 1857, and Arthur Stanley, who in addition to his hagiography of the Doctor became Dean of Westminster, his disciples included Charles Vaughan, the headmaster of Harrow School, William Lake, the Dean of Durham Cathedral, James Prince Lee, the headmaster of King Edward's School in Birmingham, and the poet Arthur Hugh Clough.

Arnold and his protégés saw the public school as a fundamentally religious institution in which the pursuit of moral and intellectual excellence were part of the same holistic spiritual discipline. This sense of moral purpose was most famously expressed when Arnold stated the order of priorities for a public school teacher: '1st, religious and moral principles; 2ndly, gentlemanly conduct; 3rdly, intellectual ability.'[7] His teachings were among the first to install the ideal of 'character' at the heart of public school education. According to Arnold, it was not the 'combative', theatrical flair prized by eighteenth-century schoolmasters that should be at the heart of elite education, but instead the moral values of the Christian gentleman. In some cases, however, the sheer intensity of the Doctor's dedication to his disciples not only inspired lifelong devotion but sowed the seeds for their later existential breakdown, when the precocious youth, trained to an exacting standard of moral excellency, came into contact with the real world beyond the sheltered domains of school and university. Stanley, Clough and the Doctor's own son, the poet and educationalist Matthew Arnold, underwent what the historians Edward Mack and W.H.G. Armytage called 'soul-shattering experiences' when their ideals came into contact with the world at large.[8]

Cotton's strategy at Marlborough for reforming the school was taken straight from his old mentor's playbook. Arnold's reforms at Rugby had little to do with curriculum and almost everything to do with the tone and texture of school life. He was an evangelist, who sought to transform the public school from a state of nature into a community of Christian souls. He pursued these goals not through authoritarian means, but through the soft power of speechifying and moral suasion. From his pulpit, Arnold exhorted his young charges to be constantly on the watch for the presence of evil; from his study, he empowered a hand-selected corps of prefects to spread the word and lead by example within the little world of the school. Arnold's great strategic gambit – the same one that Cotton adopted at Marlborough – was to infiltrate the system of pupil self-governance and thereby to extend his spiritual influence through his prefect-surrogates into the unruly and dangerous community of adolescents. The key to controlling hyperprivileged adolescent males, he claimed, was to 'govern them through their governors'.[9]

The cult of personality that built up around Arnold ensured that his actual influence on the development of the Victorian public school system has often been overstated. In reality, there was a world of difference between the predominantly religious pedagogy that he developed at Rugby in the 1830s and '40s – what the historian David Newsome called 'godliness and good learning' – and the various kinds of organized sports, physical discipline, surveillance, militarism and nationalism that would characterize many schools later in the century.[10] At Rugby, in addition to taming the old system of pupil self-governance, Arnold centralized boarding houses on school grounds to facilitate community cohesion, raised enrolments, stressed the importance of winning university scholarships and refocused the life of the school on the chapel. Yet there were many aspects of school life that he left untouched. Classics retained their almost complete dominance of the curriculum. Flogging remained a central part of the school's disciplinary system, although its use was now extended to the prefects as well as the headmaster. Many ancient school rituals continued, such as 'Singing in the Hall' (juniors boys had to sing songs while holding a lit candle in each hand and being pelted with lumps of stale bread) and 'Cocktail Club' (an evening of bingeing on saved-up beer rations mixed with smuggled spirits).[11] Unlike Cotton and many later Victorian headmasters, Arnold was almost entirely uninterested in organized sports; he saw no connection between the playing fields and the cultivation of moral character.

But if the disciplinary value of house matches and cold showers was not one of the lessons that later headmasters learned from the Doctor, a fear of youth and rebellion most certainly was. Arnold symbolizes a shift in attitudes towards privileged adolescent males that would have a lasting influence throughout the Victorian era and after. In place of the eighteenth-century doctrine of aristocratic laissez-faire, he stressed the need for careful adult guidance in order to ensure healthy and normalized maturity. His moral pedagogy was designed to shuttle adolescents as quickly as possible from childhood into manhood. In his sermons, Arnold warned his youthful congregation that, 'we do not grow in general fast enough', and that, when combined with the all-too-rapid physical development of puberty, this mental immaturity could only produce 'derangement and deformity in the system'.[12] In the same sermon, he speculated about how far it was possible to 'hasten' the passage to maturity 'without exhausting prematurely the faculties of either body or mind'.[13] He concluded that this was quite possible, as the loss of youthful vigour would be accompanied by commensurate gains in self-discipline and rational autonomy. According to Stanley, the Doctor's first comment on being appointed to the headmastership of Rugby was to the effect that, 'My object will be, if possible, to form Christian men, for Christian boys I can scarcely hope to make.'[14] The great danger, for Arnold, was adolescence itself, the tumultuous period between childish innocence and adult self-possession, during which the developing soul was acutely susceptible to sin.

Arnold had himself been educated at Winchester in the first decade of the nineteenth century and had first-hand experience of the tribal culture of public schoolboys. On his first night at the school when he knelt to say his prayers he was attacked by his fellow pupils and publicly goaded for his piety. In a letter to a friend in 1827 he remarked that, 'my own school experience has taught me the monstrous evil of a state of low principle prevailing among those who set the tone to the rest'.[15] At Winchester Arnold avoided the worst forms of bullying that might be aimed at a pious, withdrawn, excessively scholarly boy due to his love of outdoor activities, such as fishing, tree climbing and swimming. From time to time he even joined in with some of the 'ragging' and practical jokes in the dormitories after-hours. He also passed through a youthful phase of political radicalism, recalling later that during his time at Winchester he was 'well nigh a Jacobin'.[16] After a flirtation with ultra-Toryism while at university, however, he eventually settled on the amalgam of political liberalism and broad church Anglicanism that would define his mature beliefs. In short, Arnold had direct experience of the tempestuous fluctuations of youth, the way in which the embryonic, developing self could easily be swayed to adopt radically divergent beliefs in quick succession.

In a letter of 1835 to the *Quarterly Journal of Education*, 'On the Discipline of Public Schools', Arnold listed six sins endemic among schoolboys: profligacy, systematic falsehood, cruelty and bullying, active disobedience, idleness and the 'bond of evil'. Of these six vices, all of which were widely practised under the system of aristocratic libertarianism, it was the bond of evil that troubled him most. The 'old feelings' of tribal attachment led public schoolboys to assume that it was 'their business, by all sorts of means, – combination amongst themselves, concealment, trick, open falsehood, or open disobedience, – to baffle [their master's] watchfulness, and escape his severity'.[17] Schoolboys were united by 'this accomplice spirit, this brotherhood of wickedness' in opposition to their masters. It was when boys gathered together in groups that Arnold feared most for their souls. In his biography, Arthur Stanley described how his one-time headmaster could not pass by a group of boys talking at a fireplace on a winter's evening without seeing the Devil standing among them.[18] For Arnold, individual boys remained at least partially attuned to their moral consciences, but when leagued together they exhibited a devilish tendency to conspire against their elders and plot sinful acts of rebellion.

The word 'combination' recurs throughout Arnold's sermons and essays and marks an important departure from Cowper's earlier alarm at the 'mob of boys'. A mob is irrational, chaotic, anarchic. It sublimates the agency of the individual in the mindless energy of the mass. A combination, by contrast, is planned, organized, structured. It augments the power of the individual through strategic membership of a collective. Instead of the irrational mob, Arnold fears the cunning and guile of a coordinated cabal. His use of the term evokes the same quasi-military organization that was on display during many of the armed rebellions that had taken place at public schools in the preceding decades. 'Combination' was also one of the names given to the earliest trade unions, which were the objects of fierce political struggle throughout the nineteenth century. Arnold's use of this politically resonant term plays on the same anxiety voiced in *A Sketch of the Rights of Boys and Girls* about the cascading effects of public school rebellion, the fear that the dangerous autonomy granted to upper-class boys might spread beyond the microcosm of the school to the 'Hackney men' and other social groups who would like to claim the same rights for themselves. Arnold's lucubrations on the 'old feelings' among boys, their 'bonds of evil' and their tendency to form 'combinations' express a deep-seated fear of adolescence, a paranoiac sense of the unknowability of young minds and their resistance to adult responsibility.

Both Arnold's pedagogical theories and his practical reforms were inspired by the wider political culture of the time, which was defined in large measure by the first Reform Bill of 1832 and its extension of the democratic franchise to middle-class property owners, a provision that Arnold publicly supported in a pair of articles published in the *Sheffield Herald*. Arnold's biographers have repeatedly painted him as a frustrated statesman who instituted his prescriptions for national politics in the microcosm of the school. By improving public school education, he hoped to exert a wider influence on the nation's ruling elite. One of his chief concerns was to rejuvenate what he saw as a decadent and enervated aristocracy so as better to equip it for leadership in a time of widespread agitation for further democratic reform. This was the logic of 'govern them through their governors' applied at the national scale: the senior prefects whom Arnold cultivated at Rugby were to be the new leadership class of a rejuvenated national polity. The old aristocratic mode of privilege and entitlement, so brutally on display in the unreformed public schools, would be replaced by a new ethic of governance that was based on Christian piety and moral self-discipline. Many of Arnold's signature reforms – sympathetic teachers, centralized boarding, invitations to senior boys to take tea with the Doctor and his wife in their private apartment – sought to cultivate a gentler, more domestic atmosphere within the school. The previously unchecked instincts of hyperprivileged adolescent boys were to be tempered by the civilizing influence of the middle-class home. This was a supremely bourgeois school revolution, which sought to align a previously aristocratic institution with the middle-class values of domesticity, piety and professional vocation, and, by doing so, to avoid the revolutionary horrors that had befallen France and America at the end of the previous century.

In his writings Arnold makes the same connection between aristocratic libertarianism and Jacobinism that we saw in the earlier response to public school rebellions. In his essay on public school discipline, he defends the use of corporal punishment both on the basis of its being an effective means of correcting behaviour and also because it runs counter to dangerous contemporary philosophies of individual rights. The opposition to corporal punishment, he claims, stems from

> that proud notion of personal independence which is neither reasonable nor Christian, but essentially barbarian. It visited Europe in former times with all the curses of the age of chivalry, and is threatening us now with those of Jacobinism. For so it is, that the evils of ultra-aristocracy and ultra-popular principles spring precisely from the same source – namely from selfish pride – from an idolatry of personal honour and dignity in the aristocratical form of the disease – of personal independence in its modern and popular form.[19]

For Arnold, aristocratic libertarianism and natural rights were symptoms of the same 'disease'. 'Ultra-aristocracy' and 'ultra-popular principles' both express a faith in personal independence and the right of the individual to determine his or her own social destiny. From Arnold's Christian moralist perspective, this is simply 'selfish pride'. He believed in the objective and impersonal law of divine authority. This faith in an implacably objective moral law found its expression in the system of moral pedagogy that Arnold instituted at Rugby. He may have been a rather distant presence at the school, focusing his attention on the exalted members of the sixth form rather than on the lower ranks, but through his diffuse influence Arnold sought to guide his charges towards a single destination: Christian manhood. In the language of today's pedagogy, the 'learning outcome' of his teaching was neither a set of transferable skills nor a body of knowledge, but instead a new kind of identity. Beyond the formal mechanism of prefect rule, this was Arnold's most lasting influence on public school discipline – the new sense of moral seriousness and spiritual vocation that was directed towards moulding the characters of adolescent boys.

ARNOLD'S ROLE IN reforming the public school system may have been overstated by his disciples and hagiographers, but his status as a Victorian cultural icon is indisputable. The capstone upon the Arnold legend was laid in 1857 by Thomas Hughes's *Tom Brown's Schooldays*, a hyper-romantic novel about life at Rugby in the early years of Arnold's headmastership. There had been stories set in public schools prior to Hughes's novel – Maria Edgeworth's 'The Barring Out' (1796) and her play *Eton Montem* (1799) were two early examples – but it was the success of *Tom Brown* that paved the way for the emergence of a whole new genre of writing. The novel was an instant hit, running through five editions and 11,000 copies in its first year alone, and 52 editions by 1892.[20] By the end of the nineteenth century, the public school story was one of the most popular and instantly recognizable literary genres. Nested within public school fiction were several subgenres, including prep school stories, sports stories, friendship stories, misty-eyed romances of lost youth, stories of reforming headmasters, narratives of schools at war and, in the years following the First World War, a handful of debunking exposés. At its heart, however, the school story was a drama of limit and transgression. It described a closed world in which the hero could test the limits of authority, only to find his errant way back into the embrace of house, school, class and nation. This was the genre's lasting inheritance from the legendary figure of Arnold, as mediated by the romantic idealism of Hughes. Arnold's mission to reform the dissolute world of the eighteenth-century school and to inculcate a new sense of moral self-discipline in English schoolboys was continued in the fictional worlds of Greyfriars, St Dominic's, Whitminster and Rosslyn.

The success of public school fiction was in part due to the emergence in the second half of the nineteenth century of a new market for boys' newspapers and magazines, most of which relied on the school story for their staple fare. One of the earliest examples of the form, *Beeton's Boys' Annual* (owned and run by the husband of Mrs Beeton, the famous Victorian cookbook author), was founded in 1855 and ran extracts from *Tom Brown's Schooldays* shortly after the novel's first publication. The true giant of the form, however, was the *Boys' Own Paper*, founded in 1879 by the directors of the Religious Tract

Society, which boasted a circulation of 250,000 copies at the height of its popularity.[21] The genre flourished during the heyday of the public school system in the late nineteenth and early twentieth centuries, a time when many other institutions, including Boys' Brigades, scout troops, borstals and state-funded 'board' schools, drew their inspiration from the character-building ethos of the public schools. The success of the genre was enabled both by rising levels of literacy among working-class children, who after 1870 were educated in government-run elementary schools, and by very cheap prices. An issue of *Gem* or *Magnet*, the most popular boys' papers, cost two pennies and were available from almost all news-stands. In his history of working-class literacy, Jonathan Rose describes the 'common schoolboy culture' that was fostered among readers of public school stories from radically different social classes.[22] The school story was one of the vehicles that helped to spread the public school ethos beyond the exclusive precincts of Rugby, Eton, Harrow and Winchester. Even as it shed Hughes's pious tone, the school story remained a fundamentally conservative genre, one that encouraged readers to adopt a nostalgic and idealized view of an educational institution that most never had the opportunity to attend.

In his 1943 essay on boys' newspapers, George Orwell went so far as to argue that the prevalence of the public school story was the result of a deliberate strategy by conservative press barons to bewitch working-class children with fantasies of an idealized public school world and thus to deflect any allegiance they might bear to the political interests of their own class. Orwell notes the way in which school stories play up the 'glamour' of the institution for all it is worth – the haunting Gothic architecture, the venerable traditions, the heroic feats of athleticism and the cosy moments of repose while toasting sausages in front of a dormitory fire.[23] He also runs through a long list of racial and ethnic stereotypes that the genre relied upon for its bogeymen: excitable Frenchmen, sinister Spaniards, treacherous Arabs, shifty, inscrutable Chinamen, dunderheaded but loyal Danes and Swedes, benighted and primitive Africans. Orwell's essay drew a stern rebuke from Charles Hamilton, who, under the pseudonym Frank Richards, penned the enormously popular Billy Bunter series of public school stories. Hamilton dismissed Orwell as a *bien pensant* liberal, whose intellectual pretensions rendered him blind to the virtues of plain speech and good, old-fashioned storytelling. But quite apart from his misunderstanding of Orwell's literary style, which was nothing if not plain and direct, Hamilton's blustering self-defence only served to further incriminate himself as a dyed-in-the-wool reactionary. In addition to his unreconstructed views on adolescent sexuality (best ignored or repressed), foreigners (uniformly worse than Brits) and class (the higher the better), his tone was fatally out of date in the post-Second World War era: 'If Mr Orwell supposes that the average Sixth-Form boy cuddles a parlour-maid as often as he handles a cricket bat, Mr Orwell is in error.'[24] And yet, as Frank Richards, he continued to sell vast numbers of stories and novels to an eager reading public. The *Guinness Book of World Records*, which estimates his lifetime output at more than one hundred million words, lists him as the world's most prolific author.

While later public school stories may have sold more copies, none had as long-lasting a cultural impact as Hughes's *Tom Brown's Schooldays*. This influence was measured less in terms of raw sales figures and more through the profound impression the book made upon adult as well as juvenile readers. In the eyes of its most dedicated fans, *Tom Brown's Schooldays* was more than just an entertaining piece of popular fiction; instead, it was a book to live by, a model for how to rejuvenate both the individual self and society as a whole through the transformative effects of moral pedagogy. Chester McNaghten, the headmaster of Rajkumar College, an English-style boarding school in Raipur, India, which was founded in 1870 in order to anglicize the native elite, read the sporting passages from *Tom Brown's Schooldays* at school assemblies instead of a sermon. In 1911 the British Board of Education recommended that every elementary school in the land should have a copy of the book in its library. Baron Pierre de Coubertin, the founder of the modern Olympic Games, carried the book with him as a kind of spiritual Baedeker when he toured the English public schools during the 1880s in his attempt to understand what he called 'the powerful figure of Thomas Arnold and the glorious contour of his incomparable work'.[25] It was from this visit that he dated his lifelong quest to introduce *la pedagogie sportive* to his native France and resuscitate the Olympic spirit for the modern world.

*Tom Brown's Schooldays* is a thinly veiled sermon on the Arnoldian values of piety, self-discipline and school spirit. We see the drama of limit and transgression in Hughes's novel when Tom, the promising bloom of young English manhood, loses his way in the cut and thrust of school life and ends up turning to the bad. Along with his partner in crime, 'Scud' East, he cribs his prep, fights with other boys, cuts out of bounds to poach birds' eggs and swims in the farmer's pool. Tom and his friend become 'outlaws, ticket-of-leave men ... in short, dangerous parties'.[26] Outside the law of the school the boys lead 'the sort of hand-to-mouth, wild, reckless life which such parties generally have to put up with'. They fall into the habit of 'doing things which were forbidden, as a matter of adventure', and begin to look upon the rules as 'a sort of challenge from the rule-makers'.[27] Hughes would certainly have read Arnold's *Sermons,* and his phraseology here echoes the Doctor's brooding fears of the 'old feelings' and 'spirit of combination' fostered by the tribal allegiance of schoolboys against their masters.

But in Tom Brown's case – and in the cases of the genre's most famous boy heroes: Stalky, Mike, Billy Bunter, William Brown and Harry Potter – benign authority wins the game and guides the transgressor back into the fold. The Doctor is an almost supernatural figure within the novel, distinguished not only by his higher learning but by the magical qualities of his vision and voice. Early in the novel as the School House celebrate a doughty footballing victory over the rest of the school (this is before the rules of the game were codified to limit the sides to eleven players each), Tom notices the headmaster, who surveys their revels:

> He knows better than anyone when to look, and when to see nothing. Tonight is singing night, and there's been lots of noise and no harm done – nothing but beer drunk, and nobody the worse for it, though some of them do look hot and excited. So the Doctor sees nothing, but fascinates Tom in a horrible manner as he stands there, and reads out the psalm, in that deep, ringing, searching voice of his.[28]

The Doctor sees everything, but he knows when to take official notice and when to let things slide. When Tom and his friends turn to the bad, the Head's all-seeing eye tracks their errant way: 'his eye, which was everywhere, was upon them'.[29] This strafing searchlight is accompanied by the most far-reaching public address system available in a pre-electronic media age. That 'deep, ringing, searching voice of his' works its way into the hearts and minds of the boys. His sermons bypass their cynicism and the false walls of their inauthentic adolescent selves. He knows more about his pupils than they themselves do. He knows them to be, in essence, good Christian Englishmen.

The tone in which Hughes presents Tom's conversion is almost impossibly pious. The shift between Book One, with its hearty enjoyment of poaching expeditions, dormitory feasts and the fags' rebellion, and Book Two, with its hand-wringing pietism and improving moral message, was satirized by P. G. Wodehouse in his 1903 article, 'The Tom Brown Question', which propounded the tongue-in-cheek theory that Hughes was coerced into rewriting the second half of the novel by the 'Secret Society For Putting Wholesome Literature Within the Reach of Every Boy, And Seeing That He Gets It', or the S.S.F.P.W.L. W.T.R.O.E.B.A.S.T.H.G.I. for short (most likely a satire on the Religious Tract Society, which published the *Boys' Own Paper*).[30] This stern group of moral reformers relents only to allow Hughes to add his account of Tom's heroic boxing match against Slogger Williams in Book 2, Chapter Five. This is the only reasonable way, claims Wodehouse, in which Tom's transformation from hearty scamp to quavering prig could possibly be explained.

But accusations of sermonizing did not trouble Hughes in the slightest. The author made his intentions abundantly clear when he revealed after the novel's barnstorming success that, 'my whole object in writing at all was to get the chance of preaching!'[31] Many of Arnold's disciples went on to have more distinguished careers than Hughes, but with its vast sales figures and countless imitators it was in the fictional form of *Tom Brown's Schooldays* that the Doctor's image and ideals were most effectively spread around the world. Indeed, the novel itself can be read as a prophetic allegory of the reform of the public school system as a whole. Tom's individual conversion from rebellious malcontent to Christian gentleman foreshadowed the systematic expansion and reform of Britain's public school system that took place over the course of the second half of the nineteenth century. When Wodehouse and other readers complained about Tom's unlikely conversion, they expressed their discomfort with the system of managed adolescence that had emerged in the wake of Arnold's reforms, with all of its moral sententiousness and petty discipline. Many commentators found something unnatural or inauthentic about the prodigies of moral seriousness turned out at the end of public school novels. Wodehouse's own school stories often parodied the heavy-handed didacticism of the genre's less able proponents. In Wodehouse's 1909 public school novel, *Mike*, two new boys greet one another in their shared study. On exchanging names, Psmith, the monocle-sporting aristocrat who has recently been expelled from Eton, asks Mike, 'Are you the Bully, the Pride of the School, or the Boy who is Led Astray and takes to drink in Chapter Sixteen?'[32] Wodehouse pokes fun at the conventions of a genre that, by the beginning of the twentieth century, had congealed into a sticky mess of cliché and didacticism. Wodehouse's heroes, Mike and Psmith, remain unregenerate scamps, enjoying a series of madcap capers and scrapes with authority but never really challenging the values of the institution. For Wodehouse, adolescence was a time of charming gameplay, something to be prolonged and enjoyed in fictional form, rather than a morally fraught progress towards maturity.

Like Cotton, Hughes had himself been a pupil at Rugby under the Doctor, although not as a member of the inner circle of prefect-disciples. In later life he was a lawyer and Liberal MP rather than a schoolteacher, but he bore the stamp of Arnold's influence for the rest of his life. In 1880, dissatisfied with his limited victories as a parliamentarian and social reformer, Hughes left Britain to found a utopian society in the backwoods of Tennessee. This was a small-scale farming community, equipped with its own library, inn, croquet lawns and newspaper, where all land was owned and worked collectively. The community was designed to empower the second sons of the English upper classes who had been disinherited under the system of primogeniture (the inheritance of all money, land and titles by the first-born male heir of a family). Despite his best efforts, the 'colony' lasted less than ten years, its members sorely tested by a typhoid epidemic, legal confusion over land titles and the difficulty of life in the rough and ready American South. The name that Hughes gave to his quixotic utopia, however, made the source of his inspiration abundantly clear: Rugby, Tennessee.[33]

As a public campaigner for working-class education, Hughes was associated with the Muscular Christianity movement, a loosely affiliated group of pedagogues, journalists, churchmen and MPs, who promoted a mixture of physical strength and Christian piety as the antidote to the ills of the age. Muscular Christianity was a second-generation outgrowth from Arnold's educational philosophy, a more robustly physical and socially engaged version of the Doctor's pre-scriptions for the moral training of adolescent boys. Throughout the latter half of the nineteenth century Muscular Christianity became a global phenomenon that was adopted in various hybridized forms around the world, including in colonial boarding schools, American universities, British workingmen's associations, Papua New Guinean rugby leagues and Japanese youth organizations.

With its focus on the values of community spirit and self-discipline, the doctrine seems almost purpose-built for the new institutional world that emerged in the later nineteenth century in order to manage the minds and bodies of potentially disruptive groups of young people. Hughes delivered sermons on Muscular Christian themes to Working Men's Associations in northern towns, advo-cating for the formation of a 'Christian Guild' of manual labourers who would resist the sins of drunkenness and brawling that beset such communities. The Christian Guild was conceived as a kind of prefect-elite for the urban working class, a cadre of Muscular Christian paragons who would exert a tempering influence on a demographic group that was viewed by many as a potential source of political and social unrest. To contemporary readers, the Muscular Christian belief that organized sports and evangelical religion could heal the acute social divisions wrought by industry and empire seems naive in the extreme; and yet, as the editor of a recent volume on the history of the movement points out, we live with its secularized legacy today in the form of the language of fair play, service and team spirit that pervades educational institutions of all types.[34]

In Hughes's writings, 'manliness' became the new watchword for the ideal character of the Muscular Christian youth. Hughes explored the concept in his published lectures, *The Manliness of Christ* (1879), in which he re-cast the life of Jesus in terms of the masculine values of courage, strength, compassion and self-discipline. As in Arnold's *Sermons*, Hughes casts adolescence and youth as a fraught moral training ground in which the individual's essential character, his durable and authentic 'manliness', has to be forged against the backdrop of weakness and temptation. Hughes offers Christ as the model upon which his listeners should mould their own characters: 'it is thus through mastery of [Christ's] own meaning and position from the first ... upon which we should fix our thoughts if we want to understand, or to get any notion at all, of what must have been the training of those eighteen years.'[35] This description of the necessary 'training' of the adolescent self sounds less like the story of a humble childhood in ancient Nazareth and more like a prescription for public school education in Victorian Britain, a sense that is confirmed by an early chapter title: 'The Holy Land A.D. 30 – the Battlefield of the Great Captain'.[36] Both in ancient Nazareth and Victorian Britain, claims Hughes, the key to manliness is the paradoxical ability to train oneself to act without guile or pretentiousness. It is only through the vigorous effort of self-discipline that one's true moral nature will emerge from behind the false walls of the self.

This was the ground on which the struggle over the moral character of adolescent boys was to be waged throughout the later nineteenth and early twentieth centuries. The central narrative pivot of *Tom Brown's Schooldays*, and many of the public school stories that followed in its wake, is the protagonist's conversion from rebellious outsider to establishment insider. Crucially, however, this conversion hinges not only on the hero's external behaviour – his newfound readiness to abide by the official rules of the institution – but on a complete moral transformation at the deepest level of his being. In the early stages of the narrative, the schoolboy hero plays a series of daring games against the authorities, cunning ruses by which he seeks to evade his seniors and indulge his wayward desires. He may perform the part of the pious schoolboy for his superiors, but this facade is merely part of the game of wits he plays in order to experiment with his unformed self. Over the course of the narrative, this talent for outlaw cunning is replaced by the hero's mature moral character, an authentic self that has been latent within him but unexpressed throughout the early stages of the novel. The narrative moves from rebellion to loyalty and from theatrical performance to authentic being.

What Wodehouse pointed out, however, was the instability of the boundary between the two halves of the narrative, between Tom Brown before and after his moral transformation. With his whimsical tale of authorial sabotage by a coercive gang of moral reformers, Wodehouse highlights the inauthenticity of the novel's moralistic conclusion and the unconvincing nature of Tom's new self. Indeed, having witnessed young Tom's impish capacity for cunning and gameplay, why should we believe that the mature identity that he adopts at the end of the novel is not itself an elaborate performance designed to further his career and ensure his prosperity? Is not the persona of the Muscular Christian gentleman itself an elaborately crafted mask, one that requires years of hard work and school discipline to fashion? After all, authenticity is the gold standard against which the most accomplished forms of performance are measured. Perhaps, then, Arnold and Hughes's greatest innovation was not a new culture of moral earnestness, but instead a better kind of method acting.

In his famous takedown of Arnold in *Eminent Victorians* (1918), Lytton Strachey focused on precisely this aspect of the Doctor's persona: its fabricated nature. He inverts Hughes's image of the headmaster as a distant yet benign controlling force to produce the counter-image of Arnold as a self-fashioned Old Testament God:

> He himself, involved in awful grandeur, ruled remotely, through his chosen instruments, from an inaccessible heaven. Remotely – and yet with an omnipresent force. As the Israelite of old knew that his almighty Lawgiver might at any moment thunder to him from the whirlwind, or appear before his very eyes, the invisible embodiment of power or wrath, so the

Rugby schoolboy walked in holy dread of some sudden manifestation of the sweeping gown, the majestic tone, the piercing
glance, of Dr Arnold.[37]

This was the nub of Strachey's critique: that the Doctor's persona was
an elaborately got-up shtick. The legendary Arnold is little more than
a collection of theatrical tricks: 'the sweeping gown, the majestic tone,
the piercing glance'. Published shortly after the conclusion of the First
World War, *Eminent Victorians* was part of a new cultural moment
that rejected the moral certainties of the Victorian institutions that
had helped to promote that conflict. Cyril Connolly referred to it as
a 'revolutionary book' and dubbed its author the 'great anarch', who
cursed the institutions of school, church, army and empire in their
own mandarin tongue.[38] In this passage, Strachey converts Arnold into
a figure of high camp, got up in his scholastic robes and thundering
forth in his fruity, self-satisfied tones. Strachey's supreme act of rebellion against Victorian values was to reveal the performative nature of
an identity that had for decades been wrapped in a heavy mantle of
reverent essentialism. And yet, ironically, his attack ultimately confirmed the Doctor's standing as the embodiment of the ideals of the
Victorian age. Strachey may have scrawled elegant graffiti upon the
Arnold monument, but the edifice remained in place.

Perhaps the most unlikely keeper of the Arnoldian flame, however,
was the great Trinidadian historian C.L.R. James, who recalled how
his 1910s schooldays at Queen's Royal College in Port of Spain helped
to convert him into 'an alien in my own environment among my own
people'.[39] James and his schoolfellows imbibed the public school ethos
both from their masters and from their avid perusal of the *Boys' Own
Paper*, *The Captain*, *Tom Brown's Schooldays* and Wodehouse's *Mike*
stories. In *Beyond a Boundary* (1963), his rumination on the system of
values he learnt from his love of English literature and cricket, James
recalls how 'from the eight years of school life this code became the
moral framework of my existence. It has never left me. I learnt it as
a boy, I have obeyed it as a man and now I can no longer laugh at
it.'[40] James was a Marxist historian, a campaigner for West Indian
independence and a staunch opponent of British imperial rule, yet

in *Beyond a Boundary* he contributed as much to the romantic idealization of Thomas Arnold as any of the Doctor's earlier acolytes. He casts Arnold's legacy as 'one of the most fantastic transformations in the history of education and of culture', situating it alongside the ancient Greek Olympics as an authentic expression of humankind's capacity for justice and reason.[41]

Yet the glory of James's book is that it reveals both the utopian ideal and the hypocritical contradictions of the public school ethos that he imbibed as a boy. James is, after all, a Caribbean boy who is taught the values of moral self-government in a land that is denied national self-government by its colonial rulers. It is only in later life that he realizes 'the limitation on spirit, vision, and self-respect' that was the product of an educational system geared exclusively towards the veneration of someone else's culture.[42] James points out how, in spite of all of his hard work and inherent skill, the system was rigged against him. Each year the two boys who gained the highest marks in the national exam competition were awarded scholarships to study at Oxford. This was the first rung on a career ladder that could lead, at its highest point, to a seat on Trinidad's Governing Council. Even as a *Tom Brown*-obsessed schoolboy, however, James recognized this system for what it was: rank tokenism, designed to appease nationalist sentiment and maintain British rule in the Caribbean. Instead of climbing the ladder, James disappointed his teachers and parents by devoting himself to cricket, literature and left-wing politics. He used his elite English education not as a means of securing his own place at the top table, but instead as a platform from which to advocate for national self-determination and freedom for all. Crucially, however, he presented this as a logical extension of the public school ethos of fair play, rather than its repudiation.

Central to James's writing in *Beyond a Boundary* is the notion of style, which encompasses both the physical grace of the cricketer as he shapes to make a stroke and the intellectual brio of the author as he crafts sentences upon the page. In his supple prose, James creates for himself a hybrid identity as a Caribbean-socialist-Arnoldian-aesthete. He is a walking contradiction – a 'strange fruit' produced by a highly fraught process of cultural 'transplantation' – who nevertheless exhibits such poise and self-possession that the contradictions seem unimportant.[43] Just as Wodehouse and Strachey fan their readers' doubts about the authenticity of the Arnoldian pose, James confirms that gentlemanly identity is as much a matter of skill and gameplay as the execution of a successful cover drive on a sticky wicket.

THE PUBLIC SCHOOL novel may have been a fundamentally conservative genre, yet it is in the unlikely form of Harry Flashman, the fifth-form bully of *Tom Brown's Schooldays*, that we find the most strident rebuttal of the Arnoldian creed. Hughes casts Flashman as a low-down, self-interested coward, the antithesis of the honest team player that Tom will eventually become. Flashman's role in the novel is brief: he terrorizes the third form, roasts Tom in front of an open fire, is defeated by the fags' rebellion and is eventually expelled by the Doctor for drunkenness. But this minor character of Victorian children's literature was rescued from ignominy in 1969 by George MacDonald Fraser, who reimagined him as the anti-hero of what became a best-selling series of novels. Over the course of twelve hugely popular books, Flashman's picaresque adventures take him from the first Anglo-Afghan War of 1839–42 to Bismarck's Prussia in 1848, from the Charge of the Light Brigade in the Crimea in 1854–5 to the Indian 'Mutiny' of 1857, and from the Chinese opium war of 1860 to the battles of Isandlwana and Rorke's Drift in Southern Africa in 1879. Along the way, he rises to the very peak of the Victorian establishment, winning for his feats of bravery a knighthood, the Victoria Cross, invitations to speak at Rugby speech days and a seat in the House of Lords. Throughout his adventures, he acts with an impeccably consistent moral character, comprising equal parts cowardice, dishonesty, self-interest, lust and greed.

The narrative is framed as the contents of Flashman's memoirs, penned before his death in 1915 and discovered in 1965 at an auction of household furniture. Right from page one, Flashman lays into Arnold, Rugby and the Victorian public school ethos with enormous gusto. 'Hughes got it wrong, in one important detail,' he claims in the opening line of the novel,

You will have read, in Tom Brown, how I was expelled from Rugby School for drunkenness, which is true enough, but when Hughes alleges this was the result of my deliberately pouring beer on top of gin punch, he is in error. I knew better than to mix my drinks, even at seventeen.[44]

The tone is at once bluff, comic, righteous, bawdy and unillusioned, a heady antidote to Hughes's high-minded idealism.

Flashman applies his rough wit to all aspects of the Rugby myth, including Arnold's sermons, the dull classical curriculum ('I'd have got more classics from an hour's wrestling with a Greek wench than I did in four years from Arnold') and the 'sturdy fools' churned out under the system of Muscular Christianity.[45] When he recalls the speech that Arnold delivered on the sins of drunkenness before he was expelled, Flashman observes:

I haven't a good memory for sermons, and he went on like this for some time, like the pious old hypocrite that he was. For he was a hypocrite, I think, like most of his generation. Either that or he was more foolish than he looked, for he was wasting his piety on me. But he never realised it.[46]

This is the most serious charge that Flashman lays against Arnold and the Victorian public school ethos: hypocrisy, or the inability to acknowledge the true motivations for one's behaviour. The rhetoric of godliness and good-learning makes a mockery of what Flashman sees as the true constituents of human nature: lust, appetite, an instinct for self-preservation and the desire for an easy-going, comfortable ride through life. In this passage, Fraser betrays his debt to Strachey's earlier portrait of the Doctor as a hammy actor, who used his fabricated headmasterly persona to terrorize impressionable young boys. Fraser imparted a distinct air of theatricality to his own anti-hero, whose globetrotting adventures are often driven forward by acts of disguise and performance. In *Flashman at the Charge* (1973), Flashman remarks, 'I am an actor, I suppose.'[47] But if Arnold is a method actor, then Flashman is more classical. He alters his external appearance and behaviour in order to get what he wants, but he never falls for his own shtick.

Flashman is a survivor from the bad old days of aristocratic libertarianism. He sticks bullishly to the traditions of the eighteenth-century public school, in which fags were roasted before fires, the strong survived and high-born gentlemen took their pleasures where they pleased. In the first of the novels, Fraser draws our attention to Flashman's roots in the pre-Arnoldian world when his protagonist, recently enlisted in Lord Cardigan's Hussars and shipped out to the subcontinent, delivers a letter to General Sir Willoughby Cotton in Kabul. On recognizing Flashman for a fellow Rugby man, Cotton observes that he was expelled from the old school. When Flashman confesses that he too was kicked out for drunkenness, the General launches into the following tirade: 'No! Well, damme! Who'd have believed they would kick you out for that? They'll be expellin' for rape next. Wouldn't have done in my time. I was expelled for mutiny, sir – yes, mutiny! Led the whole school in revolt. Splendid! Well, here's to your health, sir!'[48] As with many of the characters in the series, General Sir Willoughby Cotton is a real-life figure taken from Fraser's wide reading in nineteenth-century history. In his youth, Cotton was one of the ringleaders of Rugby's 'great rebellion' of 1794, when senior boys rose up in protest against the brutal style of the then headmaster, Doctor Henry Ingles, known to his students as the 'black tiger'.[49] As is made clear in the novel, however, Cotton did not suffer unduly from the stigma of his rebellious schooldays. His illustrious career included several positions of high command within the British Army, including a stint as commander of the troops in Jamaica, during which time he suppressed a slave rebellion, and a steady rise to the rank of General. Cotton was living proof that the right kind of public school rebellion served not as a barrier to entry, but rather as a positive credential for membership of the ruling elite.

The meeting with Cotton reveals Flashman as an essentially nostalgic figure, whose behaviour and attitudes hark back to the era before Arnold's reforms. He is a man out of time, an aristocratic rake in a world of bourgeois prigs and moral reformers. And yet Flashman is also the product of post-1960s popular culture. Fraser published his first novel in 1969 and quickly followed it with *Royal Flash* in 1970, *Flash for Freedom!* in 1971, *Flashman at the Charge* in 1973, *Flashman in the Great Game* in 1975 and then new instalments every four or five years until the final novel, *Flashman on the March*, appeared in 2005. The success of the series was due, at least in part, to the way in which it subtly reflected the mores of its own time. Flashman refuses all moralizing cant, has a complete disregard for the proprieties of institutions such as the public school, the army and the civil service and displays a steadfast commitment to the pursuit of his own pleasures. These traits are both remnants of the culture of aristocratic libertarianism and reflections of the hedonistic popular culture of the 1960s and after. Flashman's cowardice and fear of violence even echo the anti-war sentiment of the post-1968 generation. Fraser's Flashman is a man for all seasons, a relic of the lost world of eighteenth-century libertinage and an avatar of popular culture's ethos of individual freedom.

Flashman's pop cultural status was confirmed in 1975 when United Artists bankrolled a big budget film adaptation of Fraser's second novel, *Royal Flash*, directed by Richard Lester and starring Malcolm McDowell as Flashman and Oliver Reed as Otto von Bismarck, in which McDowell capers around nineteenth-century Europe in a high-sheen military uniform – all bright red coat and glistening medals – that mirrors the emerging glam style of Elton John, Freddie Mercury and Gary Glitter. His lusty misadventures in whorehouses, taverns and country houses echo the tour bus antics of a travelling rock group. He may be a soft, cowardly everyman, but the fabulous uniform and rakish ways impart a kind of rock star cachet to the character. This is in sharp contrast to the film adaptations of *Tom Brown's Schooldays* that appeared in 1940, 1951 and 2005, all of which echo the sentimentality of Hughes's original and play up the status of the public school as a venerable site of national heritage and tradition. The casting of McDowell in the lead role added another layer of pop sheen to the Flashman persona. Malcolm McDowell was *the* cinematic face of youth culture in the late 1960s and '70s. Before playing Flashman, he played Mick Travis, the public school revolutionary in Lindsay Anderson's *if. . .* (1968), and Alex, the aesthete sociopath in

Stanley Kubrick's film adaptation of *A Clockwork Orange* (1971). In the space of seven years McDowell embodied three archetypal figures of adolescent masculinity: the idealist radical, the guttersnipe hooligan and the committed hedonist.

Flashman's pop-cultural afterlife confirms, 150 years after the fact, Thomas Arnold's worst fears about the connection between aristocratic libertarianism and radical democracy. Arnold's letter 'On the Discipline of Public Schools' identified the 'proud notion of personal independence' as the invisible thread that connected 'ultra-aristocracy' with 'ultra-popular principles'. He and his disciples' reforms sought to cut that thread by installing the middle-class values of self-discipline and team spirit in the hearts and minds of the nation's ruling elite. The legacy of those reforms was an educational system that often fostered conformity and class feeling, rather than independence and open-mindedness. Flashman's aristocratic hedonism cuts right against the grain of this conformism. But the man responsible for Flashman's resurrection from the ashes of Victorian fiction would surely be wary of this alliance between his anti-hero and the glossy youth culture of the last fifty years. George MacDonald Fraser was a self-proclaimed Tory bigot of the old school. The enormous success of his novels enabled him to retire from the cut and thrust of multicultural Britain to his bolthole on the Isle of Man, an offshore haven that he glowingly described as retaining the atmosphere of Britain before the post-war era of immigration and the welfare state. In his later years Fraser was given to grumbling in interviews about political correctness 'gone mad' and lamenting the decline of Britain's once great empire. Another reason for the success of the Flashman series was the opportunity it afforded for the vicarious enjoyment of its protagonist's thoroughly unreconstructed attitudes towards women, the lower classes and colonial subjects. In an interview with the *Daily Mail* in 2008, Fraser put the series's success down to the 'unsparing honesty' with which Flashman not only admitted to, but actively revelled in his own unsavoury attitudes.[50] These are the conflicting materials from which the Flashman phenomenon was constructed: the hedonism of post-1968 youth culture combined with a red-in-tooth-and-claw view of human nature.

'A Public School Birching', from R. G. Van Yelr's *The Whip and The Rod* (1941).

# THREE

# The Secret Life
# of the Victorian Schoolboy

In his 1961 work *Asylums*, the Canadian sociologist Erving Goffman included British public schools alongside prisons, mental asylums, army training camps, naval vessels, juvenile detention centres and monasteries as examples of what he called 'total institutions'. Goffman defined a 'total institution' as 'a place of residence and work where a large number of like-situated individuals, cut off from the wider society for an appreciable period of time, together lead an enclosed, formally administered round of life'.[1] Total institutions are self-contained worlds, often set apart from mainstream society by geographical location and architectural enclosure, where life follows a detailed and rigid routine. There is an extensive system of surveillance. Access to the outside world is controlled and monitored. All of the subject's material and spiritual needs – food, companionship, exercise, pastoral care – are provided for within the formal structures of the institution.

The purpose of this unflinching discipline, claimed Goffman, is to mould the characters of 'inmates'. Total institutions are 'forcing houses for changing persons; each is a natural experiment on what can be done to the self'.[2] Through the minute organization of everyday life – wake-up routine, meal times, hygiene, work schedules, recreational activities, communication with the outside world, and so on – the institution trains its members to adopt particular forms of behaviour and belief. In the monastery, the inmate becomes a monk, in the barracks he becomes a soldier, in the asylum he becomes a patient and in the public school he becomes a gentleman. The total institution exerts upon its charges what Goffman called 'a discipline of being – an obligation to be of a given character and to dwell in a given world'.[3]

Today it might seem strange that Goffman would analyse elite fee-paying schools in the same terms as prisons and mental asylums, but, writing at the beginning of the 1960s, he was in effect looking back on the system of elite education that operated in Britain roughly between the middle of the nineteenth century and the middle of the twentieth. For much of his data Goffman drew on the memoirs of George Orwell, Robert Graves and other critics of the high-imperialist public schools, and it was not until the later 1960s and '70s that the last vestiges of Victorian pedagogy gave way to the new focus on academic results, lavish facilities and liberal discipline that survives today. Goffman has been criticized for ignoring the differences between the various kinds of institution he analysed in *Asylums*, but he was always clear that the total institution was what Max Weber called an 'ideal type', an intellectual diagram composed of characteristic features abstracted from many different institutions, rather than an empirical description of a specific place.[4] When he cast the English public school as an 'asylum', he had in mind a kind of utopian – or more accurately, dystopian – Victorian boarding school that encompassed all of the most salient features of the places he had studied. This ideal institution may not have been built from bricks and mortar, but its abstract form could be detected in many actual schools throughout the country.

Over the course of the second half of the nineteenth century the public school evolved into a different kind of institution than the one that emerged at Rugby, Marlborough and elsewhere in the wake of Arnold and his disciples' reforms. As the century progressed, the religious idealism of the first flush of reform gave way to a more systematic and worldly approach to the practical task of forging the souls of English gentlemen. This was the era of the school as disciplinary machine, a complete system of regulations and routine that mass-produced the imperial ruling class. The public school became, more than ever, a miniature world, an enclosed space cut off from society at large, which revolved around its own rarefied set of rules and traditions, fetishes and taboos. The aristocratic libertarian conception of the school as a state of nature, open to the surrounding country-side but free from the constraints of domestic and civic life, gave way to a new vision of the school as an immersive environment, a wrap-around alternative reality that moulded the character of the pupil by subsuming him within what Goffman called a 'discipline of being'.

When it was released in 1961 *Asylums* became a surprise popular hit, acquiring a mass readership beyond the university lecture hall. The book resonated with readers in industrialized societies that were on the brink of profound change, in which the authoritarian institutional style inherited from the Victorian era was being challenged by new forms of popular democracy and individual rights. Indeed, the success of *Asylums* was due less to its account of how authority functioned in the total institution, and more to its description of the myriad ways in which inmates resisted or evaded that authority. Goffman repeatedly stressed that, 'whenever worlds are laid on, under-lives develop'.[5] Even in the most rigidly disciplinarian institutions, inmates find ways to signal their dissent and express their individuality. Rather than spec-tacular displays of outright rebellion, however, dissent more often took the form of the subtle acts of 'absenteeism' or 'secondary adjust-ments' that signalled the individual's self-proclaimed distance from the ideals of the institution. In the case of the public school, this could be something as seemingly mundane as dawdling on a compulsory cross-country run, skimping on homework to make time for a hobby or smuggling a novel into class under the covers of a Latin grammar. Under the strict regime of the total institution, overt acts of rebellion bore severe sanctions. Refusal to fag for a prefect or join in house sports would likely result in a painful and humiliating beating. But subtler means of opposition – ones that remained close to the official rules yet signalled a difference in personal taste or identity – might be just as effective and less painful. Goffman's great insight was that even the simplest forms of adolescent goofing off – from daydreaming to dawdling to doodling – could be seen as attempts to assert personal identity in the face of the official culture of the institution.

Goffman's analysis can also help to explain what happened to the riotous energies of the eighteenth-century schoolboy in the newly con-strained world of the Victorian public school. In the total institution, violent struggles between boys and masters gave way to new forms of subcultural dissent as the chief means of asserting adolescent liberty. Alongside the official forms of everyday life there flourished a shadow system of workarounds and cheats that enabled individuals to indulge in behaviours and experiment with identities that were disallowed by the official machinery of the institution. Sometimes these were minute acts of self-assertion, such as afterhours banter in the dormitory or tricking a teacher into a digression by mentioning his pet interests, but in other cases the Victorian public school was home to a more full-blooded sexual under-life that included homosexual affairs, individual and mutual masturbation, the circulation of pornography and obscene books, violent sexual bullying and pederastic relationships between masters and boys.

When news of this secret world did make its way into the public domain, it often provoked moral panic similar to that which had followed the armed rebellions of the later eighteenth and early nineteenth centuries. Concerned headmasters, parents, doctors, politicians and public moralists of all sorts believed that schoolboy vice was a threat to the well-being of the nation. The central mission of the Victorian public school was to train the leadership class that would administer the machinery of empire. At the heart of this pedagogical mission was the all-important ideal of 'character'. Latin, Greek, mathematics, history, science, rugby, cricket and rowing all had their place in the curriculum, but these were means rather than ends in themselves. The ultimate goal of the total institution was to form the character of its inmates, to instil in them the habits of self-discipline, loyalty and disinterested judgement that would enable them to secure and extend Britain's geopolitical might. The secret sexual under-life of the boarding house thus had a significance that resonated well beyond the behaviours of individual pupils within the enclosed space of the school. If the nation's future leaders could so easily succumb to vice, then the health of the body politic as a whole was under threat. Wanking schoolboys spelled national decline. This logic was made plain in the early 1890s when a group of headmasters from the nation's leading public schools appealed to the Home Office for help in their efforts to rid their boarding houses of pornographic books imported from the Continent.[6] Whitehall officials treated this as an important matter of state, sending diplomatic delegates to various European capitals in an attempt to halt the traffic in obscene publications at its source. Victorian fears about adolescent sexuality gave a new meaning to the familiar term 'body politic'. In the minds of worried headmasters and Whitehall officials, what adolescent boys did with their hands and genitals in their dormitories at night had an indirect, but still frighteningly real, bearing on the fate of the Empire.

THE NINETEENTH CENTURY was a period of enormous growth in educational provision for the middle classes. Existing institutions expanded and new ones were founded in order to meet demand from affluent parents who wished to equip their sons with the training and connections that would help them to succeed in the modern professional world. This dense thicket of institutions included charitable foundations on the model of the original public schools, such as Radley (1847), Lancing (1848) and Ardingly (1858), in which power was split between boards of governors and the headmaster and his staff; endowed grammar schools that rewrote their charters to enable them to take paying students and modernize their curricula (Sherborne, 1550; Repton, 1557; Uppingham, 1584); schools for particular constituencies, such as the sons of clergymen (Marlborough, 1843; Rossall, 1844), soldiers (Cheltenham, 1841; Wellington College, 1859) and religious nonconformists (Mill Hill, 1807; Caterham, 1811; Silcoates, 1820); prep schools to coach pupils to pass the entrance exams for public schools; and day schools and 'crammers' for boys who flunked out of boarding schools and had to scrabble to prepare for exams.

In spite of their myriad differences, these schools formed a loose network of institutions that catered to families at the upper end of the social scale. A great many of them, but by no means all, adopted the organizational forms of what we would now recognize as the 'traditional' public school: strict discipline, narrow bounds, moral character, organized sports, exam preparation, *esprit de corps*, colours and uniforms, old boys' clubs to feed the mood of nostalgia and solicit financial donations in later life, and a national organizing body to oversee the system as a whole (the Headmasters' Conference, founded in 1869).

This system became a central component – perhaps *the* central component – of British imperial society, the training ground for an elite leadership class that went on to administer the machinery of empire, from the judiciary to the civil service, from parliament to the military, and from business to education.

This institutional identity was also fostered by successive government reports that treated the nation's elite schools as a single, two-tiered system that should be encouraged to reform itself in line with the strategic interests of the state. The Clarendon Commission of 1861 was founded in order to investigate abuses of the nine 'great' schools' original endowments, while the Taunton Commission of 1864 investigated the new foundations and grammar schools. Both Commissions made recommendations that were intended to restructure the system along modern organizational lines. They suggested that schools teach more up-to-date subjects, including science, engineering and modern languages, in order to keep pace with Britain's powerful competitor nations, such as France and Prussia.[7] They also prompted schools to improve domestic conditions and guard against the worst excesses of the system of pupil self-governance. Rather than transforming the public schools into an efficient modern educational system along the lines of the German gymnasium or the French lycée, however, the real outcome of the two Commissions was to entrench their status as conservative bastions of English heritage. The authors of the Clarendon Report painted a highly idealistic picture of the relationship between the ancient public schools and English national identity:

> The English people are indebted to these schools for the qualities on which they pique themselves most – for their capacity to govern others and control themselves, their aptitude for combining freedom with order, their public spirit, their vigour and manliness of character, their strong but not slavish respect for public opinion, their love of healthy sports and exercise.[8]

This is yet another example of the trope of the public school as national microcosm. The report cast the public schools as the fountainheads of a national tradition of enlightened leadership that guaranteed the order and prosperity of the nation as a whole. It was in part this new conception of the school as a hallowed portal of Englishness that prevented the commissioners from enacting more far-reaching reforms. If you convince yourself that an institution emerges from the wellspring of an organic tradition, rather than the political realm of competing interests and contested values, then you will be less disposed to straighten its kinks and iron out its inequities.

The Taunton Commission also focused public attention on the small but growing network of middle- and upper-class girls' schools that had emerged by the mid-Victorian period. The Commissioners originally intended only to investigate endowed schools for boys, but at the behest of Emily Davies, a leading voice in the Victorian campaign for women's education, they extended their purview to include twelve girls' schools as well as the 820 boys' schools already under consideration. The Commissioners heard evidence from Frances Buss, the headmistress of North London Collegiate School, and Dorothea Beale, the headmistress of Cheltenham Ladies' College, about the challenges facing female educators. Buss and Beale were representatives of what would become the two main strands within middle-class girls' education in the later nineteenth and twentieth centuries: the metropolitan day school and the boarding school on the model of the boys' public school. While they criticized the general state of disorganization within girls' schools, so impressed were the Taunton Commissioners with Buss's testimony – one remarked, with evident surprise, that 'we were all so much struck by [her] perfect womanliness' – that they recommended that a girls' high school should be established in every large town throughout Britain.[9] It would be a long time before anything like this came to pass, but by the end of the nineteenth century the Girls' Public School Trust had a network of thirty schools with more than 7,000 pupils, including flagship institutions in Chelsea, Notting Hill, Croydon and Oxford. Cheltenham Ladies' College, which was modelled on its male counterpart, Cheltenham College, was the template for many of the new girls' boarding schools that sprang up around the country, from St Leonard's in Fifeshire to Downe House in Kent and Roedean on the Sussex Downs.[10]

While the aim of both types of school was to extend to middle-
and upper-class girls an academically rigorous education similar to
the one enjoyed by young boys of the same class, these new institutions operated within a wider society that placed little intrinsic value
on female intelligence and afforded very few career opportunities
for educated women. Boys' public schools prepared their charges for
the worlds of work and power. Their focus on classical languages
and organized sports was non-utilitarian in character, but the formal
properties of self-discipline, respect for authority and disinterested
judgement that these activities were thought to foster were seen as
the ideal qualities for public life. Schools segregated by gender were
an integral part of a social system in which political and administrative power were exclusively masculine properties. Indeed, boys' prep
and public schools were only the first stages within a wider network
of ruling-class institutions that were inhabited exclusively by men.
The norms of masculine behaviour and speech that were first learned
at school prepared young men for the similarly hermetic and rule-
bound worlds of the Oxbridge college, the Whitehall department,
the officers' mess, the colonial secretary's office, the gentlemen's club
and the bar of the MCC.

While the new girls' schools adopted many features of the education that had previously been monopolized by boys – classical
languages, modern science, competitive examinations, organized sports
– traditional male rites of passage were adapted to meet what were
assumed to be the needs of young women. The ethic of leadership
became one of 'service'. The study of Latin and Greek was supplemented with lessons in drawing and music. Bounds were narrower,
social interactions more closely monitored, the sense of enclosure more
complete. In place of corporal punishment, school authorities relied on
the withholding of privileges and elaborate forms of public shaming as
the chief means of maintaining discipline. Even the value of organized
sports was subtly revised to suit feminine natures. Louisa Lumsden,
the headmistress of St Leonard's, one of the grandest of the new girls'
boarding schools, outlined the character-forming values of different
team sports: lacrosse for grace; hockey for cheerful endurance; cricket
for gentleness and courtesy.[11] Just as the boys' public schools became,

in W. H. Auden's words, factories for the 'mass production of English gentlemen', so too did the girls' schools seek to equip their charges with a standardized feminine identity.[12] This identity may have been a departure from the homebound angel of the previous epoch, but girls' schools nevertheless inherited from their masculine counterparts their role as character-forming and gender-managing institutions.

Many of the new boys' schools founded in the nineteenth and early twentieth centuries were located in remote areas of the countryside – from Marlborough (1843) on the Wiltshire plains to Gordonstoun (1934) in the remote Scottish Highlands. The natural fortifications of sea cliffs and highland moors facilitated the enclosure of the school and helped to create the sense of being in a *locus solus*, a mythological space outside of modern society. A number of older institutions re-located from urban to rural surroundings. Shrewsbury School moved from its cramped quarters in the town up to a lofty perch atop the banks of the River Severn. This was an opportunity not only to house more pupils but to adopt a whole new aesthetic, with the open vistas of the top common, the creamy red stone of the chapel and the impos-ing facade of the main school buildings. At about the same time, Charterhouse moved from its central London location to Godalming in Surrey, where it rolled out endless new playing fields and nestled into the Arcadian repose of outer suburbia.

One architectural historian has referred to the period from 1840 to 1870 as the 'heroic age' of public school building, much of which was in the 'scholastic' and then the 'ecclesiastical' Gothic styles.[13] The misty-eyed medievalism of Victorian public school architecture was designed to drown out the hum of the Industrial Revolution and to insulate the members of this elite community in the tones and tex-tures of an older, supposedly simpler time. Some schools even laid on extracurricular activities such as carpentry and handicrafts in order to cultivate the sense of medieval sodality and retreat from the modern world. Many also built museums, installed art collections and adorned their grounds with statuary and gardens. One of the less heralded functions of the post-Victorian boarding school was to curate the sensory experiences of its pupils. It was through environment and atmosphere as well as classical languages and organized sports that public schools sought to mould the characters of their pupils. The Gothic revival style was so loaded with conservative political significance that many progressive and nonconformist schools consciously chose Classical or Renaissance architectural styles as a riposte to the gloomy Gothicism of the orthodox mainstream. A speaker at the opening ceremony for the Nonconformist Proprietary School at Leicester in 1837 argued that the Gothic style was favoured only by those pedagogues 'whose associations fondly [cling] to the dark Monastic exploded institutions of our country, who love to dwell rather on the gloomy periods of our history, than to contemplate the blaze of light and knowledge which has since burst on the scene'.[14] The speaker's comments recognize the way in which the architecture of the school subtly insinuates upon the pupil an essentially static and hierarchical model of English history.

Somewhat ironically, however, the growth of the public school system was enabled by the Victorian railway boom. A rapidly expanding railway network enabled parents to dispatch their sons to the far corners of the country for their education. The very structure of the school year changed with the new railway technology: instead of two long terms, the year could now be divided into three shorter portions, as the journey back and forth between school and home was quicker and less arduous. For most pupils, the atavistic Gothicism of public school architecture was accessed through the vast industrial portals of the new urban railway terminals, which were themselves often adorned with similarly medieval trappings. One of the staple scenes of the public school novel sees the young hero packed onto a train by his parents on a bustling, steamy railway platform. He receives kisses from his mother, words of wisdom from his father and promises to write from his brothers and sisters. After a long, expectant journey, he arrives at the end of a distant branch line, from where he is driven by horse and trap through the lowering gates of the school. The pupil's forthcoming moral transformation is prefigured by his spatio-temporal removal from the everyday domestic world to the Gothic retreat of the school. This stock scene was most recently replayed in J. K. Rowling's *Harry Potter*, in which our young hero departs from platform nine and three-quarters for the magical elsewhere of Hogwarts.

The sense of monastic isolation was further emphasized by the elaborate system of privileges and traditions that prevailed in both new and old schools. Rigid and minute rules applied to all of the most mundane aspects of everyday life, including dress, fagging, chapel attendance, dining hall etiquette, access to gardens, playing fields and different parts of the school grounds, library privileges, home visits, morning ablutions and evening recreation. In his fictionalized account of life at Harrow in the years leading up to the First World War, Arnold Lunn described the school as 'a network of traditions designed to curb the arrogance of the newcomer. You may not walk down the middle of the road, wear your hat on one side, nor carry your umbrella furled unless you are an established "blood".'[15]

In the Victorian era this 'network of traditions', a body of informal yet binding laws that were passed down between generations of schoolboys, was incorporated within the official life of the institution in the form of the 'colours test'. At some schools, new boys were given a two-week grace period before they had to sit an oral exam, administered by their house prefects. The price for failure: a beating. The content of this exam was not Latin and Greek grammar but instead the minutiae of the history, rules and slang of the school itself. The colours test revealed the true purpose of Victorian public school education: to become a public school man. Boys were sent away to school not simply to acquire knowledge and skills that would be useful in later life, but instead as a kind of initiatory rite.

Yet the tribal mystique of the Victorian public school went hand-in-hand with a hyper-rational approach to the organization of time and space. The leisured ease of eighteenth-century school life gave way to a much more tightly scheduled, rigorously disciplined and closely monitored environment. Inspired by Arnold's reforms at Rugby in the 1830s, many Victorian headmasters pursued the tactic of including the prefect-fagging hierarchy within the official structures of the school. This was government by the boys themselves, under the close direction of the school authorities and the community spirit of the institution. Prefectorial privileges, which in many cases included the right to beat junior boys, were often given to the captains of sports teams, heads of house and members of the sixth form, all positions of authority and glamour within the world of the school. In the 1850s when George Cotton introduced prefect-rule as part of his efforts to suppress the riotous energies unleashed by the Marlborough rebellion, he retained a strong allegiance to the old values of pupil autonomy and self-governance. But as the century progressed, Cotton's reservations were increasingly ignored as masters and prefects alike relied on overt forms of surveillance to ensure the moral probity of their charges: nightly patrols by housemasters, bedtime supervision by prefects, health inspections by matrons and doctors, even the encouragement of sneaking and 'honourable spying' among the boys themselves.

This new system of discipline was enabled by the centralization of boarding houses and dining services within school grounds. Before the Victorian era large numbers of pupils lodged off-site in the homes of masters or 'dames', private citizens who earned extra money by housing and feeding schoolboys. Over the course of the nineteenth century this practice died out; eventually all pupils were housed on-site in boarding houses, which were owned by the school and run by individual masters. Within the boarding house, dormitories became smaller, better lit, their beds more uniformly spaced and their inhabitants segregated by age. The centralization of boarding was accompanied in many cases by the narrowing of bounds. The wanderings of the eighteenth-century schoolboy across the surrounding countryside were now contained within the hermetic world of the school. Special permission from a master or special status within the hierarchy of the institution (prefect, house captain, first eleven member and so on) was required for any unsupervised trip out of bounds. Towards the end of the century, when the system was at its most rigid and disciplinarian, many schools forbade friendships between boys in different age groups and boarding houses. At some institutions, it was forbidden to move around the school alone or in a pair. Groups had to contain three or more boys, as this would enable them to exercise collective self-discipline in the face of the potential dangers of unsupervised adolescent masculinity. At others, the measures used to contain sexual urges extended to restrictions on diet, compulsory cross-country runs and daily cold showers. Some pedagogical experts even suggested that dining halls should serve no meats, cheeses or beer at dinner, as these might enflame the animal spirits of impressionable young boys just before they were confined to their dormitories for the night.

The historian Patrick Joyce has described how many Victorian public schools adopted a 'cellular organization' that enclosed the everyday experiences of pupils within a series of tightly controlled physical spaces. The cellular structure radiated outwards from the most intimate spaces of the individual cubicle or study to more public spaces such as common rooms, dormitories, classrooms, playing fields, the chapel and assembly hall. According to Joyce, these were the 'cellular divisions within which individual subjectivity was nurtured'.[16] As they rose through the ranks of the school, pupils were granted gradually more private space and free time. The cubicle gave way to the study; the harried life of the fag gave way to the ease and autonomy of the prefect. This was part of the public schools' ethos of leadership training. The ultimate aim of the Victorian public school was to prepare its charges for membership of the governing elite. The goal, in short, was to teach young men how to govern others; but before they were deemed capable of this, they were given extensive training in how to govern themselves.

And yet self-government was not an explicit part of the school's formal curriculum. There were no lectures on the theory and practice of self-discipline – no classes on continence, no tutorials on temperance. Instead the spatial structure of the built environment and the temporal structure of the timetable were designed to inculcate in junior boys habits of regularity and discipline that would enable them as adults to govern both themselves and others in the absence of overt constraints. In spite of their increasingly rigorous organization, elite public schools continued to hew to the classical ideal of liberal education, which was concerned with the training of free men, as opposed to slaves. In the Victorian era, however, the pathway to freedom lay not through the self-governing tribes of boys, as it had done in the previous epoch, but via the minutely detailed labyrinth of rules and regulations, spaces and zones, that governed everyday life in the school. It was only once the individual pupil had internalized the structure of the labyrinth – or at the very least could present a plausible appearance of having done so – that he was deemed to be a mature member of the tribe.

The school's machinery of character formation was also accompanied by an unspoken, yet powerfully effective code of emotional reserve. The physical and temporal structures that organized the bodies of schoolboys were supplemented by the immaterial, yet no less palpable, structures that organized the expression of thoughts and feelings. John Galsworthy, best-selling author of *The Forsyte Saga* and a pupil at Harrow in the 1880s, described the 'unwritten rules of suppression', which dictated that no strong emotion should be shown at school except in praise of a successful cover drive or rugby charge.[17] This is what E. M. Forster had in mind when he described the 'under-developed hearts' of public schoolboys.[18] It is also the source of that hoary old stereotype of the repressed English gentleman. Emotional reserve became the cornerstone for a whole new civic code, which was inculcated first in the boarding school and later reinforced as the prized quality sought by examiners for positions of authority in the civil service, the army and the church. A certain quality of unemotional detachment was considered the most important attribute for leadership. This is what the Clarendon commissioners referred to when they praised the public schools as the source of an Englishman's 'ability to govern [himself] as well as others'. There is no doubt that the qualities of discipline, disinterest and detachment are essential for good judgement in many walks of life. But when they are enshrined as institutional dogma and exercised in the absence of sympathy and humour, they can harden into something cruel and unusual. In the late nineteenth- and early twentieth-century public schools, alienation was all too often elevated into a principle of ethics.

It is a striking fact of modern British history that the great majority of its most privileged men experienced the same emotional wrench at the same point in their young lives. In no other advanced nation was boarding as prevalent as it was in Britain between the mid-Victorian period and the later twentieth century. At the age of seven or eight the sons of affluent families were extracted from their homes and sent away to the hermetic world of the prep school. The sharp break with the child's familiar sources of comfort and identity was integral to how the boarding school functioned: rip away the old ties and you can more easily mould young characters into useful shapes. Nathaniel Woodard, founder of a network of schools at Lancing, Hurstpierpoint, Ardingly and Denstone in the mid-nineteenth century, explicitly stated that 'the chief thing to be desired is to remove children from the noxious influence of the home.'[19] Deprived of the contaminating influence of their families, boys quite naturally transferred their affections to the institutional mechanisms of the school and the values it represented.

The historian Vyvyen Brendon has shown how, for many boys and girls, being sent away to school was a rite of passage that came as a profound shock, one that was not assuaged by the fact that it was simply part of the furniture of middle- and upper-class existence. Drawing on childhood letters, as well as memoirs and novels written in adulthood, Brendon explores 'the experience of separated children', reconstructing an emotional penumbra that included feelings of abandonment, resentment, fear, bafflement, self-loathing and profound sadness.[20] Over time these initial feelings of devastation often gave way to habituation to and even enjoyment of school life; but, as Brendon points out, this did not negate their original existence, nor did it assuage their lingering after-effects. It is wrong to impose one's own values on the past, to see history only through the lens of one's own intellectual categories and moral standards. To do so is a form of self-regard that insulates the individual from the radical difference of the past – from what the past can teach us about the contingency of all historically situated lives. But the responsible attempt to avoid anachronism should not blind us to the atmosphere of sadness and repression that hovers in the background of so many accounts of boarding school life.

IF THE NEW forms of discipline instituted by Arnold and Cotton were born of the fear of armed uprisings, then the later Victorian obsession with the minute details of everyday life was fuelled by a late-breaking obsession with sex. When Arnold enjoined his pupils to guard against the temptations of 'vice' he was referring to the endemic sins of drunkenness, laziness, practical jokes and armed rebellions, and not to sexual impropriety.[21] The fear of adolescent sexuality that came to colour so much of boarding school life only really came into effect in the 1850s and after. It was around this time that headmasters and parents started to worry about what one authority called the 'solitary vice' and the 'dual vice', or individual and mutual masturbation. These fears were further enflamed in the later nineteenth century by a new concern with homosexuality, especially in the wake of the criminalization of sodomy in 1885 and the furore surrounding the Oscar Wilde trial in 1895. While the enclosure of the Victorian public school was first prompted by the threat of armed rebellion, it quickly morphed into an institutional architecture for the containment of adolescent sexuality. The segregated, surveilled and scheduled life of the Victorian schoolboy was designed to provide as little time as possible for wandering attentions and dangerous desires.

One of the most influential Victorian writers on sex was William Acton, whose 1857 treatise *The Functions and Disorders of Reproductive Organs, in Childhood, Youth, Adult-age, and Advanced Life, Considered in the Physiological, Social, and Moral Relations* inspired a whole subgenre of quasi-scientific writings on sexuality. Acton's work focused almost exclusively on male sexuality, and in particular on the development of 'normal' sexual behaviour in the different stages of life. Acton believed that the human body functioned as a closed system, which possessed a finite store of vital energy. This precious vitality had to be conserved through abstinence, exercise and healthy living, otherwise it would be frittered away before the subject reached his prime and entered into a 'normal' and productive marriage. The two great evils against which Acton warned his readers were masturbation and prostitution; these practices were unhealthy precisely because they frittered away precious semen, and with it the vigour of the nation's male population.

Acton's treatise helped to install the figure of the schoolboy masturbator, or 'onanist' (named after the Old Testament figure, Onan, who spilled his seed on the ground rather than inseminating Tamar, the widowed wife of his brother), within the increasingly fevered imaginations of teachers and parents. Some of the most lurid passages were devoted to lengthy descriptions of the effects of masturbation. In the onanist, we learn, 'the frame is stunted and weak, the muscles underdeveloped, the eye is sunken and heavy, the complexion is sallow, pasty or covered with spots of acne, the hands are damp and cold, the skin moist'.[22] Masturbation was at once a spiritual and a physical disease, one that sapped the moral will at the same time that it wasted the vital energies.

For many commentators, it was the solitary, antisocial nature of the practice that was troublesome. The psychologist Henry Maudsley lamented the 'offensive egotism' of the masturbator and the way he seemed to retreat from contact with parents, teachers and school-fellows.[23] The headmaster of Uppingham, Edward Thring, inveighed against 'secret acts' and 'hidden pleasures'.[24] The spurious medical discourse on masturbation was itself a register of popular fears about unsupervised adolescents, their capacity for mercurial shifts of mood and their fluid, unformed personalities. In his cultural history of masturbation, Thomas Laqueur points out that the medico-moral discourse on self-abuse was a product of the European Enlightenment (the first treatise on the subject was published in 1712), which cast masturbation as the 'dark side' of reason and progress. Masturbation was troubling to schoolmasters and psychologists precisely because it was 'a secret in a world in which transparency was of a premium'.[25] It existed beyond the limits of the capacity of adult authorities to control young boys' bodies. It was a private, endlessly renewable source of self-gratification that was fuelled by imaginative fantasies that floated free of the disciplinary system of the school.

In reality, housemasters and prefects were doomed to failure from the start. At the moment of his arrival at sexual maturity, the Victorian public schoolboy was ensconced within the hothouse world of the institution, with its physical proximity to hundreds of other warm male bodies and its complete absence of female company. The culture of athletic hero-worship that flourished in the latter part of the century encouraged an appreciation of the male form, which could easily slip over from the purely aesthetic into the more fulsomely erotic. In many schools there was a semi-official culture of romantic friendships between boys, in which young men would develop crushes on one another and send syrupy letters back and forth between boarding houses. Robert Graves explained how his headmaster at Charterhouse tolerated these relationships on the proviso that, 'My boys are often amorous, but seldom erotic.'[26] This is an example of how a total institution might tolerate, or indeed welcome, certain elements of the under-life as a defence against more threatening forms of disorder. In many schools homosexual crushes and banter were seen as a useful pressure valve for adolescent sexuality, a kind of ersatz romantic play that released tensions in a harmless way before a young man's arrival at mature heterosexuality.

Many later nineteenth- and early twentieth-century schoolmasters actively encouraged intimacy with their pupils as part of what they saw as a holistic educational process that cultivated aesthetic and intellectual refinement, as well as moral character and athletic prowess. For intellectually precocious boys, individual tutorials, private corres-pondence, holiday reading parties and informal social gatherings with masters were an integral part of the educational experience. For the most part these informal arrangements were treated as natural outgrowths of the institution's humanist pedagogy, but later in the nineteenth century, in an increasingly shrill atmosphere of moral panic over the threat of homosexuality, some schools introduced measures to guard against potential impropriety.[27] At Eton a tension emerged between a group of dissident Socratic teachers, who cultivated poten-tially dangerous intimacies with their most promising pupils, and more orthodox masters, many of whom doubted the value of excessive intelligence as well as the intentions of their colleagues.[28] In some quarters the virtues of Platonic love between masters and pupils were openly celebrated. William Cory, a charismatic master and composer of the 'Eton Boating Song', wrote *Ionica* (1857), a collection of poems in celebration of (chaste) homosexual love as an enabling balm to the educational process. Although it seems that Cory refrained from physical contact with his pupils, his openly emotional attachment to his chosen favourites caused disquiet among his fellow teachers, and eventually the headmaster demanded his resignation.[29]

It is impossible to gauge accurately the scale of the sexual under-life of the Victorian public school. Written accounts from the period were governed by a strict code of decorum and reserve. Even the scien-tifically minded Acton, who has been cast by historians as an exemplar of the new empirical approach to the study of human sexuality that would later flourish in the work of Henry Havelock-Ellis, Sigmund Freud and Alfred Kinsey, couched his discussion of masturbation in terms of secrecy and restraint.[30] Although he stated that his aim was to produce the most accurate account possible, Acton also admitted that he refrained from disclosing the full testimony of his public school correspondents due to its troubling nature. For all of his readiness to address sexuality directly, Acton remained bound by a powerful sense of reserve that was closely allied with the institution of the public school. The same torturous conflict between the desire to reveal and conceal schoolboy sexuality is to be found in Edward Lyttelton's 1887 manual *The Causes and Prevention of Immorality in Schools,* in which Lyttelton reports a headmaster's fear that,

> If you speak plainly to [boys] you will rudely tear the scales from their eyes, and rouse them to a sense of a world of impure horrors they never dreamt of before. If, on the other hand, you speak in veiled language, you will only stimulate their curiosity, the most fruitful source of evil in the young.[31]

Both Acton and Lyttelton's correspondents found themselves in a double bind, caught between irreconcilable impulses towards frank disclosure and obfuscatory concealment.

Fictional accounts of school life exhibited a similar rhetorical tension. Behind a dense thicket of euphemism – 'vice', 'beastliness', 'impurity' – it is possible to detect a thriving sexual under-life in the background of many a Victorian school story. The most notorious example is Frederick Farrar's *Eric; or, Little by Little,* a novel that was inspired in part by Acton's treatise on masturbation. Eric's steep moral decline begins when he engages in the sin of 'Kibbroth-Hataavah' in the dormitory late at night.[32] This is a biblical allusion to Numbers 11:34–5, in which the Israelites pass through a place named Kibbroth-Hataavah, which means 'the graves of lust', on their journey to the Promised Land. Scholars of biblical Hebrew will know that this refers to the sin of gluttony, rather than the wasting of semen, which is described in the Genesis story of Onan; but, equally, readers of Victorian children's literature will understand that representations of food often stand in for youthful sexual desires. In short, this is a very roundabout way of letting informed readers know that young Eric was wanking. Yet the novel is suffused with doom-laden references to Kibbroth-Hataavah, which is clearly central to Eric's physical and moral disintegration. Like the vice itself within the minds of doctors and pedagogues, in Farrar's novel references to masturbation are carefully concealed but everywhere apparent.

What we can glean from these sources is that the Victorian public school was a delicately balanced system of disavowal and half-knowledge, a miniature world in which the official discourse of self-denial and temperance was matched by an informal shadow life of desire and gratification. The prevalence of these illicit practices no doubt varied based on the specific subcultures that existed in different schools at different times. In many cases we can detect this erotic underworld by inferring it from the measures put in place to contain it. At Sherborne, for example, the authorities developed an official protocol for how to deal with alleged cases of sleepwalking. As it turns out, the school was not in fact suffering from an outbreak of mass somnambulism, but rather sleepwalking was the most plausible excuse available to boys who were caught out of bed in the dead of night, no doubt on their way to or from the comforts of some other boy's bed. Likewise, at Eton in the 1860s heavy bars were placed over dormitory doors to prevent after-hours wanderings. The presence of the metal bar over the lintel proves the existence of the very escapades that it was designed to frustrate. Lyttelton, who was the headmaster of the school, admitted as much when he said that the new dormitory architecture would merely spur boys on to greater 'ingenuity' in their night-time perambulations.[33]

Without a doubt, the most astonishing record of the sexual under-life of the Victorian boarding school comes from John Addington Symonds, who was at Harrow from 1854 to 1858 under the headmastership of Charles Vaughan, one of Thomas Arnold's most respected protégés. In later life Symonds became an eminent man of letters and one of the first public campaigners for gay rights, but as a young man he became embroiled in what would today make headlines as a sexual abuse scandal in one of the nation's most prestigious schools. Symonds's account of his experiences at Harrow eschews the rhetorical contortions that characterized so much Victorian discourse on sexuality; his writing is clear, direct and, by the standards of any historical era, sexually explicit. Yet the liberty of expression that he achieved in writing his life story did not entirely escape the dampening effects of the public school code. For all of their honest reckoning, Symonds's memoirs were kept secret. He refrained from publishing the text during his lifetime and instructed his literary executor to maintain the embargo after his death. In fact, *The Memoirs of John Addington Symonds* were not published until 1984, almost a century after his death, in an era that had adopted an entirely new set of norms about the public discussion of sexuality.

Symonds was a dreamy and imaginative child who was raised in an atmosphere of high moral seriousness in his Unitarian father's household in Bristol. Home life was morally exacting, but also comfortable, nourishing and stable, providing plenty of time and space for young John to retreat into the vivid private world of his imagination. Little surprise, then, that his first term at Harrow came as a brutal shock to the system. Physically slight and emotionally high-strung, he found it difficult to adapt to the school's rough and ready culture of prefect-fagging and outdoor sports, although he was eventually excused from both due to his academic brilliance and weak constitution. Symonds would later explain that, 'I accepted life at Harrow as a discipline to be gone through. It was not what I wanted. But being prescribed, it had its utility. Thus from the commencement of my schooling I assumed an attitude of resistance and abeyance.'[34] This is precisely the kind of response that Goffman discerned in the behaviour of disaffected inmates. Rather than pushing violently back against the institution, Symonds retreated into himself, maintaining an inner kernel of detachment from the communal life that unfolded around him.

But Harrow's culture of manly philistinism turned out to be the least of Symonds's worries. Alongside the official curriculum of lessons and games, the school also harboured a complex shadow world of sexual relationships between boys. In his *Memoirs*, Symonds describes the widespread practice of senior boys adopting juniors as their 'tarts'. As soon as they entered the school, all of the most attractive new boys were given female names and appraised for their erotic comeliness by the seniors. Older boys might adopt one of the juniors as his 'bitch' and receive sexual favours in exchange for safety and comfort within the boarding house. In some cases, these relationships seem to have been fairly tame and more or less consensual; in others, they were openly carnal. Symonds relates how, 'here and there one could not avoid seeing acts of onanism, mutual masturbation, the sports of naked boys in bed together'.[35]

Symonds's sexual trouble reached its peak during his senior year, when his closest friend, Alfred Pretor, confided to him that he had been having a romantic affair with the headmaster. At first Symonds refused to credit his friend's story, but when Pretor revealed a collection of empurpled love letters from Vaughan, his disbelief was overcome. Symonds felt compelled to remain silent out of loyalty to his friend and duty to the institution, but he now recoiled in horror whenever Vaughan's hand came to rest on his thigh during private tutorials in the headmaster's study. Charles Vaughan was a prodigy of Arnoldian pedagogy. He had been a disciple of the Doctor's at Rugby, won a string of prizes at Trinity College, Cambridge, and landed the headmastership of Harrow at the tender age of 28. Once installed on Harrow Hill, he set about reforming an institution that had fallen into seemingly terminal decline. Between 1844 and 1859 Vaughan increased student numbers from sixty to 469, and in the process improved academic standards, increased the number of university scholarships won by Harrovians each year and gradually raised the school's reputation among the public-school-attending classes.[36] At the height of his powers in 1859, Vaughan was tipped by many as future Archbishop material, perhaps even in with a chance of the very top job within the Church. And now John Addington Symonds, repressed schoolboy homosexual, was in possession of the dirty secret that revealed the colossal hypocrisy of it all.

Symonds's initial turmoil abated when he left for Oxford that summer, departing a year early on account of his academic brilliance and desire to escape the institution. But during an undergraduate reading party at Whitby the following spring, he confided his story to his new mentor, John Connington, Professor of Latin at Trinity College. Symonds's tutor advised him to inform his father, who in turn wrote to Vaughan demanding that he resign his post immediately and agree never to accept another position of high office, in exchange for an assurance that the affair would never be made public. After his wife travelled to Bristol in vain to plead with Mr Symonds for leniency, Vaughan submitted to the blackmail and resigned the headmastership of Harrow.

Without ever divulging the cause of his retirement from public life, Vaughan delivered a passionate leaving speech that described his solemn sense of Christian duty and abiding commitment to the values of the institution. His retirement, he claimed, was prompted by his deep-held conviction that fifteen years of public service was enough for any man, and that he must withdraw into the shadows to avoid the worldly sins of vanity and self-interest. Vaughan toiled away for decades in relative obscurity as a parish priest in Doncaster, repeatedly turning down offers of prestigious appointments and a route back into the bosom of the establishment. It was more than twenty years later, after Mr Symonds finally passed away, that Vaughan accepted a position as Bishop of Llandaff and finally left the shadows behind.

This was a startlingly abrupt and yet curiously composed retreat from public life. In his memoir Symonds claims that Vaughan resigned with 'consummate skill', as though the graceful cover-up of a pederasty scandal was one of the key abilities of a Victorian headmaster. He also claims that his father's blackmail was motivated by his abiding respect for 'Harrow, for English society, and the Established Church'.[37] In short, this was an act of institutional good faith: secrecy and discretion, rather than transparency and redress, were seen as the appropriate means of dealing with an unpleasant affair of this sort. This was a cosy establishment cover-up of what in today's society would make lurid headlines as a paedophilia scandal in one of the nation's leading schools.

AT CHARTERHOUSE BOYS were beaten with a 1.5-metre-long (5-ft) bunch of birch switches with a handle at one end. During springtime, at the tip of the switches were large, hard buds, left in place by masters for extra bite against the buttocks. Custom stated that the master was allowed to take a new bundle of switches after every sixth stroke.

The favoured instrument at Stonyhurst was the 'tolly', a solid piece of rubber the size of a shoe. This could cause the hand of the victim to swell up to the size of a woollen glove and turn a livid yellowy-green colour. At Rugby, it was a thin wooden cane, with a lead-weighted tip for increased accuracy and impact. At Eton, as at many schools, beatings took place at a specially constructed 'flogging block', a kind of wooden altar over which the victim bent with his clothed buttocks presented to the assembled congregation. In addition to the master or senior boy who wielded the birch, proceedings were aided by two 'holders down', who lifted the victim's shirt tails and fixed him in place when he recoiled from the pain. At other schools the victim was 'horsed' on the back of a master or boy (held aloft with the arms around the neck) so that his rear presented to the executioner at the most convenient height.

Whether in the hands of masters or prefects, flogging was a highly ritualized feature of school life. At Lancing the victim had to walk from his boarding house to present himself for punishment in the main school building. When the boy arrived, the school captain would lean out of the window and shout 'under school' across the courtyard. The offender then had to knock, enter and stand directly behind the closed door. The prefect who was to administer the beating would then enumerate the boy's crimes, before the offender was ordered to assume the position and receive his strokes. At Marlborough the announcement of a beating took place at a raised dais with a prefect stationed at either side. The headmaster announced the boy's crime to the assembled school, then led prefects and pupil into the sixth-form common room. The unmistakable sounds of the flogging would then emanate from the other side of the closed door. One early headmaster was renowned for carrying a large set of keys in his pocket, which would jangle in gothic fashion as he led the offender to his doom.

The orderly sequence, the formulaic pronouncements, the consistent sound effects, the public display: these are the elements of a sacred ritual. Many Victorian school memoirs describe the sense of hushed reverence that would accompany a beating. At Eton the boys would line the staircase to the headmaster's study and watch as the victim ascended to receive the school's most severe punishment

– a licking from the headmaster. School memoirs return again and again to the indelible sensory memories that these experiences leave in later life. James Brinsley-Richards, who was at Eton from 1857 to 1864, remarks that:

> I never quite believed the stories I heard until I actually saw a boy flogged, and I can never forget the impression which the sight produced in me . . . Several dozen fellows clambered upon forms and desks to see Neville corrected, and I got a front place, my heart thumping and seeming to make great leaps within me. Next moment, when he knelt on the step of the block and when the lower master inflicted upon his person six cuts that sounded like the splashings of so many buckets of water, I turned almost faint.[38]

The ritual was designed to leave an impression on the mind that would last longer than the cuts on the flesh of the victim. In this brief passage, Brinsley-Richards refers to the oral legend of his classmates, the 'sight' or spectacle of the act itself, the bodily sensation of the quickened pulse, and the gruesome sound of the 'splashing' of the blood as the birch bites into the flesh. This is a sensory feast, a moment of intensity and immediacy that stands out sharply against the dull routine of school life.

A number of historians have suggested that birching became less common over the course of the nineteenth century.[39] With the new focus on the moral character of adolescent males, discipline was more often focused on the schoolboy's capacity to govern himself, rather than on physical punishment. The new conception of childhood and adolescence as distinct phases of life with their own developmental rhythms also lessened the use of the rod. Boys should be cajoled towards moral goodness through the soft power of emulation, shame and the collective pressures of school culture, rather than physical threat. But if caning became less frequent in the Victorian era, it also became more significant. Caning was part of a public ritual of shame and guilt that was freighted with a new psychological depth. Rather than simply correcting behaviour, the cane bit right through the flesh into the depths of the offender's character. It carried a sharp moral sting, the expiation of which required that the offender assume not only the right behaviour, but also the right *identity*. Heather Ellis has recently argued, however, that after a dip in frequency in the middle of the century, flogging in fact seems to have increased again towards the century's end.[40] The period roughly between 1880 and the First World War constituted the height of Britain's imperial phase, a time when public schools were seen as bulwarks against national decline, which fortified the minds and bodies of the imperial ruling class through rigorous institutional discipline. In an atmosphere of public anxiety about Britain's ability to maintain its position of global dominance, argues Ellis, teachers and prefects reached more frequently for their canes, unconvinced that moral sense alone could spur the nation's schoolboys to the required level of manly vigour.

The flogging ritual was a central part of the school's culture of masculinity. A good flogger might become renowned for his strength and skill among pupils and masters alike. The skill with which a teacher caned was analogous to the skill with which a Latin scholar teased out the metrical patterns of a verse composition, or a first eleven cricketer dispatched a cover drive to the boundary. The rhythm of the stroke, the accuracy of the positioning, the bite of the impact, the phrasing of the rebuke: these were the component parts of a technical craft, which had its own recondite standards of excellence. There was also a masculine ethic attached to the passive side of the ritual. To take your beating like a man, to avoid flinching, to stem the flow of tears, to stand up to the ordeal: this was a way of proving yourself in the eyes of the institution. The ritual was designed to induce powerful feelings of shame and guilt, but when the ordeal was done the subject could also congratulate himself on his strength of will and hardy moral fibre.

The ritualistic intensity of flogging also ensured that it was a powerful element in the under-life of the institution. Flogging became part of the schoolboy's shadow culture, a staple of the oral legends and salacious stories that circulated first in the boarding house and later at gentlemen's clubs and other old boys' gatherings. Tales of heroic resistance on the part of plucky rebels, strategies for outwitting authority and legends of overzealous masters who took too keen a pleasure in the quivering flesh of their charges were sources of fascination and wonder in the underground world of boarding school gossip. New boys would exchange tips on how to lessen the pain of flogging. Trousers could be padded with newspaper or some other dampening material, but if the offender was caught this would certainly mean more strokes in recompense.

During Edmund Keate's reign as headmaster of Eton in the 1820s, a group of seven boys known as the 'howling dervishes' earned themselves a glamorous reputation among their school fellows for their rebellious high jinks and scorn for the pains of the birch. In his memoir Charles Wilkinson describes the dervishes as 'fine, hearty, high-spirited boys, who hated verses and lessons in general'.[41] These 'out of bounds' characters would run wild across the local countryside, milking cows' udders into one another's mouths, joyriding on farmers' horses and dressing up in false moustaches 'a la dandy officer' to drive a tandem carriage through college for a bet. They were known as the 'howling dervishes' for the way they would roar and scream during their almost daily beatings, not out of suffering but as an affront to the authorities. As Wilkinson tells it, they 'howled from sheer impudence, for the fun of the thing'.[42]

These feats of evasion and trickery were holdovers from the days of aristocratic libertarianism, but as discipline tightened and surveillance spread in the Victorian period, the under-life of flogging found a new outlet in the form of the secret craze for flagellation pornography. One historian has estimated that roughly 50 per cent of all pornographic works published in Britain between 1840 and 1880 contained flagellation as a major theme.[43] Former public schoolboys who retained an erotic fascination with their youthful punishments could stoke their fantasies with a wide range of titles, readily available from certain discreet metropolitan booksellers. These titles included *The Mysteries of Flagellation, Quintessence of Birch Discipline, The History of the Rod: Curiosities of Flagellation* and *The Yellow Rod: Fashionable Lectures Composed and Delivered with Birch Discipline by Certain Beautiful Ladies*. Many of these titles suggest works of didactic value or historical-ethnographic interest, a form of generic misdirection that served as convenient cover for the delights that lay within. The pedagogical theme was continued in the texts themselves with the oft-repeated scenography of the schoolroom and the cloister, the cast of characters, which included sadistic schoolmasters, governesses and other authority figures, and detailed descriptions of the implements of torture, including birches, canes, cat-o'-nine-tails, battledores and leather straps.

These works were predominantly consumed by wealthy, upper-class men who could afford to pay as much as three or four guineas for a single work, the equivalent of two weeks' wages for the average mid-Victorian British worker.[44] The most sought-after works were opulently produced luxury items that often ran to a mere 150 copies per edition. Flagellomaniacs formed an elite bibliophilic sub-culture, the members of which shared books, stories and other birchen arcana at private dinners and visits to each other's libraries. One of the most celebrated groups of pornographic connoisseurs centred on the parliamentarian Richard Monckton Milnes, and his vast library of erotica at Fryston Hall, his country house near Castleford, West Yorkshire, known to its denizens as 'Aphrodisiopolis'. Members of the loose network included the explorer Sir Richard Burton, the dealer in obscene books Sir Richard Hankey and the radical poet Algernon Swinburne. Swinburne's letters to Milnes expatiated on his own experiences of being flogged by his housemaster, James Leigh Joynes, at Eton. Swinburne describes how Joynes would choose picturesque sites outdoors for his chastisements, pour eau de cologne on his face, call him 'pepper bottom' and marvel at the lush red blood on the verdant green grass.[45] As a housemaster, Joynes was not in fact empowered to beat his pupils, and behaviour of this sort would likely have got him sacked. Swinburne's letters are pornographic fantasies, which combine the sensory immediacy of Brinsley-Richards's eyewitness account of the flogging ritual with a new layer of perverse imagination, all of which is conducted under the cover of his and Milnes's gentlemanly personae as bibliophilic men of letters.

For the more adventurous Victorian gentleman, literary delights such as *Experimental Lecture by Colonel Spanker* (1878) could be supplemented with personal visits to one of London's many flagellation brothels. George Cannon, a publisher of pornographic books in the early part of the Victorian era, estimated that there were at least twenty flagellation brothels in the capital at the time.[46] Cannon was quite clear that flagellation brothels were the resort of old boys who had learned the taste for birching at boarding school: 'hundreds of young men through having been educated at institutions where the masters were fond of administering birch discipline, and recollecting certain sensations produced by it, have imbibed a passion for it, and have longed to receive the same chastisement from the hands of a fine woman.'[47] For many of its denizens, the flagellant underworld functioned as a kind of virtual reality machine, an erotic heterotopia that existed alongside but just out of sight of the everyday world of schools, churches, offices, homes and gardens. From Mrs Berkley's establishment in Portland Place to the Verbena Grove 'schoolroom' in St John's Wood, London contained a secret geography of perversion that existed in the interstices of daily life. By stepping out of the real world and into this alternative realm, grown men could be transported back in time to the vivid experiences of their childhood in the total institution. Under the strict attentions of the governess, those experiences were aestheticized and eroticized, converted from troubling memories into pleasurable fantasies.

The archive of Victorian flagellation pornography is far too extensive to survey in any great detail, but even within this frequently repetitive, prolix, disorderly and haphazard mass of writing a consistent theme emerges: that a secret world of flagellants exists behind the facade of respectable society, especially within the enclosed world of the boarding school. Many of these works seem to derive their most exquisite enjoyment not only from the act of flagellation itself, but from the revelation of this practice to a select audience of undercover connoisseurs. They indulge in both a physical and an intellectual eroticism, both the pleasure-pain of the birch against the flesh and the pleasure-knowledge that such practices exist in the darker corners of everyday life. You could even say that Victorian flagellation pornography makes erotic sport with the public school code itself, deliciously teasing out the suppressed enjoyment that nestles beneath the English gentleman's reserved exterior.

*The Mysteries of Verbena House: or, Miss Bellasis Birched for Thieving* (1882) is one of the more readable works of Victorian flagellation pornography, perhaps because it was partly authored by George Augustus Sala, a respectable journalist and sometime contributor to Charles Dickens's periodical *Household Words*. Verbena House is an exclusive girls' boarding school in Brighton, which, as only the most clued-in readers would have known, shares a name with the London flagellation brothel that was patronized by such luminaries as Swinburne and Milnes. The narrative, such as it is, hinges on the discovery that Miss Catherine Belassis, 'the belle of the school', has stolen a golden doubloon from Miss Montis, the daughter of a Cuban plantation owner. The severity of the crime requires that Miss Sinclair, the headmistress, depart from her customarily lax discipline and inflict corporal punishment on the offender. Lacking expertise, she seeks advice from the Reverend Calvedon, whose 'public school experience' makes him an authority on birchen discipline, 'than whom no more inveterate, and no more scientific, flagellant existed'.[48] Under the reverend's erotic tutelage, the once staid Miss Sinclair is converted into a crazed flagellant, who pursues her own erotic satisfaction while also improving the moral conduct of her school.

In addition to the numerous scenes of flagellation, *Verbena House* positively revels in exposing the gap between the school's public facade and its hidden life of erotic enjoyment, or between the 'smiling faces' and 'aching bottoms' of its pupils.[49] The text occupies the same rhetorical space as Acton's *Functions and Disorders of the Reproductive Organs* and Symonds's *Memoirs*, but here the tension between secrecy and disclosure, or under-life and institution, is played entirely for erotic effect. For instance, when Miss Montis's golden doubloon is first discovered to be missing, all of the school's pupils are 'searched to the skin' and their private desks and workboxes turned out. This act of surveillance reveals the secret trade in contraband that operates beneath the surface of the institution. One girl keeps a bottle of gin in her desk, another a copy of John Cleland's infamous pornographic novel *Fanny Hill*. These passages might lack overt sexual content, but they nevertheless gratify the reader's cynical enjoyment of the revelation of the school's secret desires. Earlier in the text, when the narrator describes Miss Sinclair's attitudes towards corporal punishment, he plays upon the same delicious tension between public performance and secret knowledge. 'Had any inquisitive commissioner of middle-class education forwarded her a form to fill up,' he claims, 'she would probably have left in black the space headed, "What punishments do you make use of?" or else inserted the discreet answer, "Such as I deem suited to the offence."'[50] This is one of the more astonishing moments in Victorian fiction, the point at which the narrator of a pornographic novel refers to the 1868 Schools Inquiry Committee in order to mix bureaucracy and flagellation, public scrutiny and secret perversion, administrative reason and erotic enjoyment.

The glancing allusion to the official, public world of bureaucracy and government administration was in fact one of the genre's repeated tropes. In their private flagellant correspondence, Swinburne often addressed Milnes as 'Rodin, l'inspecteur des écoles'.[51] An 1870 compendium of flagellatory tales and poems, *The Romance of Chatisement; Or, Revelations of the School and Bedroom*, repeatedly refers to cases of excessive corporal punishment in schools that have been reported in *The Times* and parliamentary debates. The author takes evident glee in imagining the contents of the parliamentary reports: 'For once the blue book must have had a piquant page.'[52] The preponderance of bureaucratic allusions within Victorian flagellation pornography confirms its status as the in-house genre of the governing class. By placing parliamentary blue books and school inspectors' reports alongside more graphic depictions of bare buttocks and swishing canes, upper-class flagellomaniacs derived the exquisite satisfaction of being party to secret knowledge inaccessible even to the highest authorities in the land.

In many ways Victorian flagellation pornography was an elaborate exercise in perpetual adolescence, which enabled readers to suspend the demands of middle-class masculinity, with its stifling code of self-possession and heteronormativity, and enter a pre-rational world of juvenile enjoyment. This world was filled not only with quivering schoolboys and stern masters, but extravagant female presences such as the buxom governess, the cruel schoolmistress and the debauched adventuress. Over the course of a single narrative, many iterations and recombinations of the flagellation scene might be tried, with different characters adopting different positions in the geometry of vice. This was a world, in short, of sexual polymorphousness, in which the boundaries of the self were loosened and readers might explore a range of identities and experiences. It was also a world that embraced limitation, repetition and juvenility as positive principles, means of escape from the adult world of reason and self-possession. In his pioneering study of Victorian male sexuality, Stephen Marcus arrived at the conclusion that for the English upper classes flagellation pornography and brothels functioned as 'a kind of last ditch compromise with and defence against homosexuality'.[53] Indeed, there is a long history of conflicted, sado-masochistic masculinity among the British ruling class: W. E. Gladstone, T. E. Lawrence, A. E. Housman, T. H. White and Wilfred Thesiger are among the most well-known examples of public school-educated flagellants, all of whom seem to have sublimated barely acknowledged sexual desires into the scourging practice of flagellation.

But looked at from a different perspective, flagellation porn and brothels also functioned as a form of forbidden knowledge about the nature of the school as an institution. In the introduction to his 1914 play, *Misalliance*, George Bernard Shaw remarked that: 'we are tainted with flagellomania from our childhood. When will we realise that the fact that we can become accustomed to anything, however disgusting at first, makes it necessary for us to examine carefully everything we have become accustomed to?'[54] What Shaw is describing here is a kind of collective amnesia, the wilful forgetting by a whole swathe of society of the pain and damage done by corporal punishment. This kind of blindness is the product of what Goffman called 'institutionalization': the adoption of institutional norms and behaviours to the point of unconscious habituation, or even dependency. Of course, the Victorian upper classes were not institutionalized in the same way that the inmates of mental hospitals and monasteries might be. After all, a man's schooldays lasted only from the ages of seven to eighteen, with a few years of easeful 'varsity life to follow. After that he was free to enjoy the enormous privileges attendant upon his social class. And yet, even as a mature, self-possessed, classically educated gentleman, the former public schoolboy often bore with him the mental stamp of his time in the institution. In many ways, the most important aspect of Victorian public school discipline was what young men forgot, or supressed, or simply didn't care to remember, in the process of growing up.

Set against this background of collective amnesia, Victorian flagellation pornography looks more like a positive form of knowledge than an escape from the troubling reality of sexual desire. The paraphernalia of birches, flogging blocks and jangling keys were important elements of the material culture of the school, symbolic manifestations of the same hierarchical order that was articulated in the seating arrangements in chapel, the sartorial display of colours and uniforms and the minute system of rules and privileges that governed access to different parts of the school grounds. They were the physical manifestation of the immaterial will of the institution, public school identity in material form. By incorporating the rod and its attendant rituals within erotic fantasies, by converting them into fetish objects and elevating them to the status of totemic presences to be worshipped and enjoyed, flagellation pornography revealed the symbolic function that these items performed within the life of the school. In *Asylums*, Goffman noted the close ties between authority and transgression in the total institution. 'In order to work a system effectively,' he observed, 'one must have an intimate knowledge of it.'[55] For a significant number of Victorian public school men, that intimacy and knowledge were to be found in the secret world of the flagellant underground.

'Toffs and Toughs', photograph by Jimmy Sime, 1937.

# FOUR

# Classics and Nonsense

James Brinsley-Richards's *Seven Years at Eton* is a characteristic example of the Victorian public school memoir. Written in 1883, long before the time of Robert Graves and George Orwell, when the genre became a favourite vehicle for critiquing the mores of the ruling class, Brinsley-Richards's memoirs are good-humoured, nostalgic and tolerant of both the privations and idiosyncrasies of the British boarding school tradition. The narrative begins with an account of the author's return to Eton in adulthood, during which he visits a local tobacconist to purchase a cigar, presumably to aid the pleasant flow of memories that such a visit would likely stimulate. But this unremarkable event in the everyday life of a Victorian gentleman is the occasion for a remarkable moment of personal discovery. 'The other day being at Eton,' recalls Brinsley-Richards, 'and calling in for a cigar at a tobacconist's in the High Street, I came there upon a copy of verses I had written years before whilst a boy at the school.'[1] Having made this astonishing discovery, the author moves briskly on to describe his youthful travails in mastering ancient Latin and Greek and the illicit collection of 'convenient verses' from which he copied lines in order to complete his weekly composition exercise. In his good-humoured way, he jokes that it is the discovery of his old verses in the tobacconist's shop that has prompted him to write his memoirs, 'for it set me thinking on all the years I spent at school, enjoying myself so much, and learning so little'.[2]

It is worth pausing for a moment to consider just how this piece of serendipity comes about. The 37-year-old author returns to Windsor and purchases a cigar, which he discovers is wrapped in the tattered manuscript of some Greek verses he penned for a school exercise more than twenty years earlier. He informs us that Mrs Fraser, the tobacconist, was in the habit of purchasing old verse compositions from Eton schoolboys in order to use as 'screws' for her tobacco. Presumably she bought a job lot of the author's old verses when he left the school and, at this later date, randomly selected one of his manuscript sheets from the jumble of wastepaper she keeps on hand. In spite of Brinsley-Richards's deadpan delivery, this is a powerful moment of chance and revelation. Rather than the sensory richness of Marcel Proust's madeleine, for Brinsley-Richards it is the dry and dusty tactility of the manuscript page, plucked by chance from a disorderly pile, that transports him back into the past.

If the morocco-bound edition of Homer symbolized the sacred source of European culture, the highest ideals to which the institution aspired, then Brinsley-Richards's 'convenient verses' were the embodiment of the school's under-life, the shadow system that enabled public schoolboys to cheat their masters and steal time for their own interests. Rather than the chance occurrence of finding his old verses in a tobacconist's shop, perhaps the most striking thing about Brinsley-Richards's school memoir is that the first thing he remembers is not the content of his classical education – the lines of Horace that stuck in his memory, say, or the elegant Latin speech he delivered on Founder's Day – but rather its empty centre. In place of the well-formed sentences and civilized ideals we might expect, Brinsley-Richards describes how he used to crib his work and the nonsense verse he produced as a result. 'As I read the queer jumble of dactyls and spondees which had once passed muster for versification,' he observes, 'the recollection of how I used to do my Latin verses came upon me with a sense of sudden humour which was irresistible.'[3]

This 'queer jumble' of half-understood language is the product of a pedagogical system that valued metrical form over semantic content and grammatical accuracy over intellectual comprehension. The two chief tasks of the eighteenth- and nineteenth-century public schoolboy were to memorize large chunks of Greek and Latin texts and produce original verse compositions in the accepted classical metres.

Brinsley-Richards relates how his fifth form teacher, Mr Elliot, would fly into a rage if his pupils produced 'false quantities' in their verses, but 'was largely tolerant as to the sense of our verses so long as they would scan'.[4] This is a roundabout way of saying that Mr Elliot did not mind if his pupils wrote nonsense, so long as it was elegant and metrically accurate nonsense. This is a common refrain within Victorian public school memoirs, a minor key theme that plays in counterpoint against the major key themes of classical pedagogy, ancient tradition and nostalgic reverie. Grown men, many of whom occupy positions of high authority within the institutions of government, look back on their schooldays with a quizzical sense of wonder at the absurdities of the system. They revel in the forms of nonsense language and verbal play that this system produced as its unintended by-products, and they take nostalgic delight in the solidarity this engendered among young boys who sought to outwit their masters through ingenious feats of cribbing.

Nonsense is the inverse image of classical pedagogy, the silky lining to its sow's ear. Schoolboy nonsense took myriad forms: the nonsense of literal translations of English phrases into Greek and Latin, and vice versa; the nonsense of shoehorning juvenile sentences into ancient poetic metres; the nonsense of adolescent chatter, gossip, banter, slang and profanity; the nonsense of daydreams, flights of fancy and moments of mental vagrancy in the midst of the daily grind of boarding school life. It would be a mistake, however, to dismiss these forms of verbal and conceptual play as *mere* nonsense, as mindless, immature outbursts, without value or significance. In the flights of nonsense that emanated from the pens and mouths of schoolboys, language became a toy to be played with, a gift to be enjoyed, rather than an extension of the school's wider system of discipline and order. Nonsense also served as a momentary escape from the strictures of ruling-class masculinity, a pastoral elsewhere beyond the reach of classical pedagogy and character training. It is also one of the more unexpected ways in which the public school system has exerted its influence on British popular culture. The delirious chatter of schoolboy nonsense has been a staple of British comedy throughout the later nineteenth and twentieth centuries, from Lewis Carroll to *Beyond the Fringe*, and from Rudyard Kipling to *Monty Python*.

THE CLASSICAL CURRICULUM of the Victorian public school had its origins in the Early Modern grammar schools, hundreds of which were founded by public charter over the course of the fifteenth, sixteenth and seventeenth centuries. The purpose of the grammar school was to instruct young boys, predominantly from the middling and merchant classes, in the classical languages that were essential for careers in law, government and the church, and, in doing so, to impart to them the gentlemanly qualities of judgement and taste. The most prestigious of the new grammar schools became centres of scholarship and clerical culture in their own right. The curriculum of St Paul's School in London, for instance, was partly written by the Dutch Humanist scholar Erasmus. This in turn influenced the curriculum and methods of older institutions, such as Winchester and Eton. These elite schools, many of which developed links to the ancient universities through the endowment of colleges and scholarships, were part of the pan-European spread of Humanist culture that revived classical learning throughout the Early Modern period.

By the middle of the eighteenth century a clear distinction had emerged within Britain's publicly endowed schools. On the one hand were the myriad town and country grammar schools that provided an often quite rudimentary classical education to members of their local communities; and on the other was a select group of public schools, which attracted a wealthy and sometimes noble clientele from far and wide. These latter schools were bastions of an elite clerical culture that permeated the ancient universities and the established church, which prized classical learning, High Church theology and Tory politics.[5]

The great majority of endowed schools were legally bound to teach Latin and Greek by the terms of their original charters. For many smaller institutions, the binding words of the charter stifled their ability to adapt to the changing needs and desires of the communities they served. Over the course of the eighteenth and nineteenth centuries many middle-class families deserted the grammar schools in favour of private academies that might have lacked a certain prestige, but nevertheless offered an up-to-date curriculum that had practical use in the worlds of trade and commerce. For elite public schools, however, the legal stipulation to teach classical languages remained in close accordance with the ethos of the institution as it developed over time. Before the reforms of the Victorian era, public schools hewed unselfconsciously to the grooves of tradition, happy to inhabit what they took to be a continuous intellectual culture that stretched all the way back to the classical world. As one historian puts it, 'an Etonian under Keate would have felt quite at home in the schools of the time of Quintilian or Ausonius.'[6]

The public schoolboy's daily routine may have been dominated by the memorization of passages and the composition of original verses, but the ultimate aim of this unflinching linguistic discipline was to train future statesmen and civic leaders in the art of eloquence. The most gifted scholars were selected to present speeches in Greek and Latin on festival days; their verse compositions were sometimes collected in printed editions and sold by London booksellers. This was part of their preparation for the oratorical displays that they would later make in the Houses of Parliament, often in a highly Latinate English larded with copious classical allusions and quotations. The tradition continues today in the form of public school and university debating clubs, which might lack classical finesse, but continue the task of training future leaders in the persuasive arts.

Greek and Latin were to remain central to the educational treadmill that led from the public schools through Oxford and Cambridge universities and into the upper echelons of government until well into the twentieth century. It was not until 1960, for instance, that Oxbridge finally scrapped its Latin entry requirements. Yet over the course of the Victorian era both the method and ethos of classical education underwent significant changes. The predominance of Greek waned in favour of the supposedly more martial and masculine Latin; and the unreflective embrace of tradition gave way to a new pedagogical culture that was geared towards mental conditioning, moral character-building and exam preparation, all of which was closely interwoven with the reformed professional institutions at the heart of Britain's expanding empire.

In 1864 the Clarendon Commission praised the 'traditional' mode of classical education in the nine 'great' public schools, but also recommended that Greek and Latin should be limited to three-fifths of the curriculum (only!), in order to make room for more modern subjects. In the subsequent decades many elite schools introduced 'Modern Sides', where students could study history, literature, modern languages, geography and the sciences, but for the most part these were low-status subjects, and the Modern Side was regarded as a convenient place to park low-achieving students and eccentrics. The Taunton Commission, which investigated the remaining eight hundred endowed schools, was more circumspect about the value of classics. In its report the commission suggested that Greek should be discarded entirely as a hindrance to effective teaching, and they made legal provision for endowed schools to rewrite their founding charters in order to change their curricula and teach more modern subjects. By the end of the nineteenth century a new hierarchy had emerged within British schools. At the top of the pile were a select group of elite institutions, including the nine great schools and the most prestigious new foundations, which taught a full curriculum of both Greek and Latin. The middle tranche included regional grammar schools, newly founded private schools and minor public schools, which taught predominantly Latin and modern academic subjects. And at the bottom of the pile were the new state elementary and secondary schools, which taught utilitarian subjects and vernacular English.

This stratified education system reflected the inverse ratio between the use value and cultural prestige of classical learning. By the middle of the nineteenth century Latin and Greek were emphatically dead languages. But as the practical utility of classics declined, their fetish value soared. In the busy, busy world of nineteenth-century Britain, Greek and Latin were prized more than ever as emblems of cultural capital, social prestige and personal glamour. Families who made their money in trade and industry began to send their sons away to public schools in the hope that they could convert some of their hard-earned brass into the more fleeting value of culture. This was the social alchemy performed by the public school in the age of industrialization: the conversion of steam engines into textbooks, cotton mills into Catullus. In his 1833 survey of English national characteristics, *England and the English*, Edward Bulwer-Lytton gave the lie to the high-minded hypocrisy of parents who claimed to send their sons to public school in order to imbibe the eternal verities of the classics. 'Bosh,' claimed Bulwer. What we would today call 'aspirational' parents, those who scrimp and save to send their children to expensive schools, 'secretly meditate other advantages besides those of intellectual improvement'.[7] 'We speak of educating the boy,' he continued, while 'they speak of advancing the man' by placing him in close proximity with the sons of the nobility.[8] In short, social climbing began at school.

But even within the rarefied precincts of the public schools, there was a clear distinction between the classical sixth form, where talented boys studied a wide range of Greek and Latin texts, and the more prosaic work of the lower forms, which focused on the grammatical and syntactic rules of the ancient languages. The most talented students flourished into 'classically educated gentlemen' and went on to enjoy a lifelong love of the ancient canon. Christopher Stray has pointed out how, for a select group of upper-class males, a love of Greek and Latin literature formed the basis of an elite gentlemanly culture that flourished in London clubs, Oxbridge colleges, Whitehall departments and literary periodicals throughout the nineteenth century.[9] Latin and Greek helped to forge bonds of solidarity among a hermetic ruling class, as well as providing a source of individual solace in the midst of the tribulations of the modern world.

This elite form of classical pedagogy was closely aligned with the new exam culture that emerged in the mid-Victorian era. In 1854 the Northcote-Trevelyan Report recommended that entry to the higher orders of the Civil Service should be governed by a new system of merit-based exams, rather than the old practices of patronage and personal connections. Shortly afterwards, the Roebuck Commission, which investigated the logistical failures that had bedevilled the British army during the Crimean War, put an end to the practice of purchasing commissions. Soon merit-based exams were the accepted gateway to Oxford and Cambridge Universities, the civil service, the Church and other prestigious professional institutions. While the content of these exams often required candidates to display a wide range of general knowledge, the formal qualities of mind that they promoted were closely aligned with the style of classical learning practised in public school sixth forms and Oxbridge colleges.

Patrick Joyce has shown how Victorian classical pedagogy promoted a peculiar form of Olympian detachment in its most gifted students.[10] In place of emotional response, concrete judgements and creative thought, classics foregrounded formal analysis, dialectical sophistication and personal disinterest. In tutorials, high-achieving students were taught to assimilate large bodies of textual information and form synoptic judgements from a number of different perspectives. Rather than adopting a specific position, the aim was to cultivate flexibility of thought and detachment of perspective. It is this pedagogical system that lies behind the famously aloof, mandarin style of the stereotypical British civil servant, a figure familiar to many of us from the classic television sitcoms *Yes Minister* (1980–84) and *Yes, Prime Minister* (1986–8). As Joyce makes clear, it is a style of thought that is not only geared towards the efficient management of an imperial bureaucracy, but one that covertly excludes other ways of thinking and governing.

For the most part, however, this form of pedagogy was reserved for the upper echelons of the public school system. For the lower forms, beyond which many boys never progressed, the business of classics lay in the rote learning of grammatical formulae. A gifted student might appreciate the more refined facets of the works he studied, but they were of secondary importance in comparison to the formal tasks of preparing exercises and construing sentences in class. With the expansion of the public school system over the course of the nineteenth century and the increasingly disciplinarian ethos of many institutions, this grammatical practice came to look more and more like a mechanistic routine. 'Grammar grinding' was the colloquial phrase used by schoolboys and masters alike to describe the inflexible, machine-like and frequently mindless routine of classical study.

Thus many Victorian schoolmasters valued classics not for their explicit content but as a kind of intellectual gymnasium that toughened the mind and sharpened the will. The Latin and Greek languages were taught as much for their formal properties as abstract systems as for their usefulness as means of communication. Lord Plumer famously observed of his Victorian schooldays that, 'we are often told that they taught us nothing at Eton. It may be so, but I think they taught it very well.'[11] Plumer jokes about what Stray calls the 'content-free discipline' of nineteenth-century classical education.[12] For many boys who never made it anywhere near the rarefied atmosphere of the classical sixth form, Greek and Latin existed on the same plane as compulsory cross-country runs, cold showers and fagging duties: part of the institutional grind that was meant to convert callow youths into stout English gentlemen.

IT WAS FROM this seedbed that the strange blooms of nonsense grew. Due to poor teaching, lack of interest, infrequent opportunities for continued use beyond the school and the myriad distractions of adolescence, many public schoolboys barely mastered, then promptly forgot, their Greek and Latin. Cribbing was a strictly prohibited but widespread feature of the school's under-life, a thriving shadow system with its own material forms, institutional memory and ethical norms. In his autobiography, Charles Darwin recalled how classics were 'to me simply a blank'. Rather than struggling to master Latin and Greek, Darwin had recourse to 'a grand collection of old verses, which by patching together, sometimes aided by other boys, I could work into any subject' in order to complete each week's assignment.[13] A historian of Winchester College describes how students kept a 'capital of vulguses' stored in the dormitory in an old hatbox, into which any boy in need of some lines could dip his hands and 'draw dividends'.[14] At Eton tattered collections of old exercises were known as 'Old Copies' and were often handed down to new boys when seniors left the school. The most prized collections were indexed by subject for ease of use. In his memoir Charles Wilkinson, who was at the school in the 1820s, recalls how pupils secretly passed around the classroom 'a little round paper pellet with a few moderate verses done with judicious mistakes'.[15] These anecdotes highlight both the scrappy materiality and the essentially chancy nature of the boarding house cribbing system. These illicit bibliographic tools functioned like linguistic tombolas, into which errant pupils could dip their hands to select an appropriate verse without troubling to understand its meaning or grammatical form. Rather than complex semantic systems, the Latin and Greek languages became cut-and-paste troves of useable gobbets.

In spite of its outlaw status, cribbing seems to have been governed by a tacit system of ethics. In E. F. Benson's 1916 novel *David Blaize*, the protagonist explains to a friend that cribbing is perfectly fine, so long as it is done only to maintain one's position in the class and thus avoid public humiliation or corporal punishment.[16] Cribbing for personal advancement, however, is wrong and goes against the schoolboy's code of honour. But the honour code is itself subject to the vagaries of local custom. The narrator notes that in some forms cribbing is widespread and highly organized, while in others it doesn't happen at all. This is how illicit institutional subcultures work: they are informal, secretive and rarely codified in official forms of writing and speech; hence they often vary widely in practice.

As a result of the imperfectly articulated ethics of cribbing, David experiences a quandary as to whether or not he should cheat. He knows in his honest schoolboy's heart that cheating is wrong, yet if he doesn't cheat, while everyone else continues to do so, he will incur the wrath of his teachers and lose status among his peers. Like many public school novels, *David Blaize* was written by an adult who was himself a public school headmaster and scion of a large family of educators and scholars. David's tribulations throughout the novel – from cribbing to cricket, and from queer desire to his fraught relationship with his widowed father – are kept in check by a narrative structure that is heavily inflected by the author's own nostalgia and idealism. David's moral quandary about cribbing is resolved when he receives a stern warning from Maddox, a handsome senior prefect for whom David has a strong sexual crush and who acts as a surrogate for the author's own values. Maddox tells his young friend that in reality cribbing is 'an utterly rotten game', the punishment for which is a sound beating.[17] In this way, the novel exposes the ethical norms of the cribbing under-world, only to quash them with the absolute moral authority of the school itself.

Cribbing also frequently took the form of organized, collective labour, which gave expression to the sense of solidarity among adolescent boys who pitted their wits against their masters. In George Melly's fictionalized memoir, *School Experiences of a Fag* (1854), the narrator recalls the illegal methods he and his classmates used to pass their exams. Rather than diligently learning their lessons throughout the year, the entire boarding house clubs together in the week before the exam to collectively learn just enough to earn a creditable pass. Melly describes how the boys form themselves into 'gangs' and work through the night in coordinated shifts, taking turns to translate passages from Aeschylus and Demosthenes. He uses an extended military metaphor to describe their strategic 'councils' and coordinated 'campaign', as though this was an armed uprising rather than an end-of-term Greek test:

> We formed ourselves into gangs; the first was to work from bed-time till 3 a.m., the second was to be waked at that hour, and to work on till first lesson at seven. It was a most dangerous game to play, as both servants and masters were determined to put it down; but where there is a will there is a way, and we generally triumphed over both.[18]

The sense of being locked in a game of wits with the authorities is further emphasized by the precautions the boys take to avoid detection, including building a covert fire and muffling the windows to avoid the attention of the school wardens as they patrol at night. The end product of these secret labours is not only the useable lines that will enable each boy to pass the exam, but the sense of adventure and solidarity that accompanies the work.

In *Tom Brown's Schooldays* Hughes describes the range of different methods that boys use to prepare their verses. The saintly Arthur, who lacks physical strength but is a paragon of scholarly dedication and spiritual purity, uses the 'artistic method', which entails working diligently to produce a seamless composition that displays his sure grasp of both the Greek language and the assigned theme. 'Madman' Martin, the school's eccentric genius who converts his study into a menagerie and conducts electro-chemical experiments in his spare time, uses the 'prosaic method': first he writes down eight 'matter-of-fact' lines of English prose, then he translates these lines word for word into metrically accurate Greek without any concern for 'whether the words were apt, or what the sense was'.[19] The as-yet-unreformed Tom has recourse to the 'traditionary method', by which he copies out old exercises that are contained in a secret dormitory scrapbook.[20] The final method, used by 'big boys of lazy or bullying habits', is called the 'vicarious' and involves simply thrashing a smaller boy until he does your Greek lines for you.[21]

While Tom and his friends use different methods to complete their assignment, they all rush through their work with the same object in mind: to make time to see the rare birds' eggs that Martin keeps in his study. By the time they leave his study, Tom and Arthur have 'learned the names of at least twenty sorts [of eggs]' and are now dedicated naturalists, who look forward to future expeditions roaming the surrounding fields and climbing trees to look for interesting specimens.[22] In short, Tom and friends rush through or cheat on their classical studies in order to make time for their own interests. Beyond avoiding a beating for failing to complete an assignment, cribbing was a way to defeat the demands of the curriculum so that pupils could focus on private reading, entomological collections, chemical experiments, amateur dramatics, poetry or whatever took their fancy. 'Madman' Martin is the patron saint of that marginalized public school figure, the scientist, who is relegated to the status of the scruffy eccentric by the school's official curriculum. The spirit of gentlemanly amateurism that is often cited as a feature of English intellectual life in the nineteenth century was not simply a matter of cultural temperament; it was also an institutional by-product of classical education at public schools and universities. Modern subjects like science, history and English were, by definition, amateur pursuits with no official position within the nation's elite seats of learning.

But if the purpose of cribbing may have been time theft, then its by-product was often nonsense. Henry Salt, an eccentric Eton master and social campaigner in the later Victorian period, recalled how as a boy he and his school friends clubbed together to crib their work. He calls this collective labour a 'Latin verse manufactory; for it was in truth as much a manual as a mental occupation, consisting largely, as it did, in collecting and copying stray scraps and fragments of verse, and old hackneyed phrases, which were then patched together in what was dignified with the name of "composition".[23] In the underworld of the boarding house, schoolboys dealt with Latin and Greek as material objects emptied of significance, which could be physically manipulated into abstract patterns that pleased their masters. This is a linguistic alienation as radical in its way as that performed by the Dadaists and collage artists of the twentieth-century avant-garde.

Salt lamented the absurdity of forcing students to write original poetic compositions in a dead language that none of them understood. The end products of this empty pedagogy were what he called 'nonsensical effusions' that emptied language of its meaning and purpose. Indeed, Victorian schoolmasters regularly complained about the 'nonsense' of their pupils' poorly understood and hastily cribbed compositions. The classical scholar W.H.D. Rouse lamented that his students 'had no literary conscience, took no pride in being right, wrote nonsense with contentment, and expected generally to be wrong'.[24] These complaints have added piquancy due to the fact that pupils were supposed to be mastering languages that embodied the logical rigour and imperial authority of two mighty civilizations. 'Nonsensical effusions' were an affront not only to the incompetent schoolmaster, but to the principles of reason and authority that underpinned the whole public school ethos.

Nonsense was a phase that well-drilled schoolboys were meant to grow out of, not just in the sense of maturing under the behavioural discipline of the school, but also within the linguistic structure of the curriculum. At Eton, one of the lower forms was explicitly called the 'nonsense' form. Here, junior boys would learn to produce metrically accurate sentences without worrying about their strict semantic sense. Once they had mastered the formal patterns of the ancient metres, they would then advance to the 'sense' form, where they would now be required to fill their metrical forms with meaningful phrases.

But while cribbing created the impression that a pupil was progressing through the stages of the curriculum, in reality he might be learning nothing at all. Charles Wilkinson relates the story of a contemporary at Eton in the 1820s, who cribbed his way up to the fifth form, while remaining at the intellectual level of the junior nonsense class. For this hearty athletic type, the inability to write meaningful Latin and Greek was no hindrance to his later professional advancement. This was before the Army adopted the merit-based exam system, so when he left Eton his father was able to purchase a commission for him in the Dragoons, 'where no such thing as verses were wanted'.[25] As Wilkinson puts it, 'his good sense and common sense, and undaunted bravery and great skill as a swordsman, carried him, as a cavalry officer, to the top of the tree.'[26] For the purposes of the Dragoon, all of Latin and Greek are 'nonsense'; they make no sense, either as linguistic systems or as means of professional advancement. This is in stark contrast to the rarefied, even metaphysical, notions of sense and reason that schoolmasters attached to the higher reaches of the classical curriculum. The anecdote serves to relativize the distinction that the school enforces between 'sense' and 'nonsense'.

Even after pupils had progressed to the higher forms, however, nonsense kept on bubbling up in the classroom. In his history of classical education in Britain, M. L. Clarke describes the method whereby pupils would separately translate each word of a Greek sentence into English before producing a continuous translation. This piecemeal method introduced an intermediate stage in the process of translation in which words were strung together without any attention to syntax or global sense as a complete sentence. The products, claims Clarke, were often 'ludicrous exhibitions of bald phraseology', which no doubt prompted outbreaks of mirth from pupils and stern warnings from their masters.[27] The sense of linguistic derangement was further entrenched by the bibliographic aids granted to schoolboys in their attempts to master Latin and Greek. Until the middle of the nineteenth century, it was standard practice to write Latin and Greek grammars in their original languages, thus presenting to junior scholars what Stray calls 'an account of the unknown in the unknown'.[28] Grammatical inflections and styles of pronunciation varied according to local custom. As boys were often transferred between schools, frequently to a more expensive institution towards the end of their schooldays in order to acquire polish before university, many found themselves schooled in incongruent, contradictory systems. Samuel Butler, the grandson of the legendary Shrewsbury headmaster of the same name and author of the early science-fiction novel *Erewhon* (1872), was moved from a private school that used the Eton Grammars, which his father Thomas Butler had previously thrashed into him, to Shrewsbury at the age of twelve. Here the school instead used Kennedy's Grammar and he was beaten for failing to switch between their respective grammatical systems.[29]

While nonsense as a literary form dates back at least to the medieval period and maybe beyond, Jean-Jacques Lecercle points out that it was the spread of formal education in the nineteenth century that turned it into a mainstream genre with wide popular appeal.[30] For Lecercle, nonsense is the uncanny by-product of the school, the dark mirror of irrationality and chance that distorts the institution's official values of reason and order. While classics masters foregrounded grammatical accuracy and rule-bound linguistic discipline, Victorian nonsense delighted in logical conundrums, syntactical slippages and language bent out of shape. In the looking-glass world of Lewis Carroll's Alice stories and the jingly-jangly patterns of Edward Lear's verse, language was allowed a brief holiday from the rigours of the classroom. The mental discipline fostered by classical syntax gave way to the more vagrant cogitations of the punster, the daydreamer and the recalcitrant child.

There is very little mention in Lewis Carroll's papers of his time at Rugby School, shortly after Thomas Arnold's tenure as headmaster. Nor does the public school feature explicitly in the Alice tales, which represent adult authority in the form of the demented Queen of Hearts and the many popular nursery rhymes that echo throughout the text, their moralistic messages turned on their heads. Indeed, it seems that Carroll was keen to forget his schooldays. At the age of 23 he confided to his diary, 'I cannot say that I look back upon my life at a Public school with any sensation of pleasure, or that any earthly considerations would induce me to go through my three years again.'[31] On visiting Radley College in the 1850s he admired the cubicles that had recently been installed for junior boys and mused that, 'from my own experience of school life at Rugby I can say that if I had been thus secure from annoyance at night, the hardships of daily life would have been comparative trifles to bear.'[32] It would be pointless to speculate on precisely what kinds of night-time annoyance Carroll might have suffered, although we do know that bullying, both sexual and otherwise, occurred in many institutions.

But in spite of Carroll's reticence about his unhappy schooldays, the institution is nevertheless present in the Alice books in what Lecercle characterizes as an 'indirect fashion'.[33] Alice's circuitous progress through the looking-glass world eschews the demands of linearity and reason imposed by adult society in general and the school in particular. Nonsense was an escape from the enforced maturity that pervaded middle-class Victorian culture. So much Victorian nonsense verse tries to evade the world of masculine maturity by fleeing to a playful, innocent world of feminized immaturity. In upper-middle-class Victorian society, the very early stages of childhood were coded as feminine. This was a time when both boys and girls were raised in the home, a female space presided over by mothers and nannies, and both sexes were dressed in frocks and their hair was allowed to grow long. It wasn't until a young man left for school that he entered the world of clearly defined masculinity. Now he would put on his breeches, associate with masters and schoolfellows and submit to the rigours of classical syntax, prefect-fagging and the rough order of the boarding house.

Against this backdrop, the figure of the young girl became a highly romanticized emblem of the lost youth of the adult male. The literary critic Catherine Robson has shown how this figure – present everywhere in Victorian culture from Carroll's adventuresome Alice to Dickens's sentimentalized orphan girls – stood in for a lost childhood that preceded the discipline of the school and the identity it conferred.[34] In one sense, Carroll's whimsical escape into the world of the little girl echoes the flagellant's fascination with erotic submission and the allure of the dominatrix. In spite of what seems at first an unbridgeable gulf between Carroll's mild fantasias and flagellation pornography's compulsive obscenity, the two forms sprang from the same pressures on masculine identity: both were the inverse products of school discipline, both were an escape from maturity and both undid the manly ideal that was forged on the playing fields and in the classroom.

Carroll's writing also tapped into the predominantly oral culture of childhood. If we sharpen our hearing and listen between the lines, we can pick up the tumbling babble of jokes, rhymes, wordplay, profanity, gossip and above all nonsense that formed the everyday speech of the schoolboy freed from lessons. In their pioneering 1959 study of children's folk culture and oral tradition, Iona and Peter Opie insisted that these forms of childhood speech were always 'more than mere playthings'.[35] Childhood rhymes and songs forge bonds of community that do not extend to the adult world. They serve as a magical currency that is passed back and forth within this secret community. This is a tripping, rhythmical gift economy, a form of juvenile aesthetics that relishes the pure sound of language, the freedom from the responsibilities of meaning and reason, the joy of play.

We hear snippets of this oral culture in the elaborate systems of slang that emerged in most public schools. School slang is the product of centuries of juvenile chatter. It bubbles up from the mulch of tradition, originating in the culture of pupil self-governance that operated throughout the seventeenth and eighteenth centuries. These arcane vocabularies – divs, beaks, groise, volski, cadger, lout, impotens, firk, purl, pussy, thoke, zephyr (you could make your own Edward Lear poem from this list) – are formed by the silt and sift of centuries spent in the mouths of boys. Unsurprisingly, the most extensive and refined school slang emerged at Winchester College, the oldest of the public schools. Known as Winchester 'notions', this elaborate vocabulary, often recorded in dictionaries and lexicons compiled by pupils in their spare time, was a palimpsest of language scraps imported into schoolboy speech during different epochs of the school's history. If you drill down into the deep strata of Winchester notions, you find traces of Old English ('thoke', 'cud'), Latin ('socius', 'sum'), Victorian slang ('quill') and local dialect.[36] Notions also had a pattern of inflections – modifications to the beginnings and ends of words – similar to those of ancient Latin and Greek. Thus 'thoke', which meant idle, became 'thokester', which meant idler. The oral culture of slang may have been a private language forged within the self-governing tribe of schoolboys, but in its etymological roots and inflected forms it also mirrored the wider disciplinary system of the school. Indeed, over the course of the Victorian era many schools incorporated slang into their official rules and regulations. Just as Thomas Arnold co-opted the culture of pupil self-governance to serve the ends of authority, school slang became part of the system of rules and customs that governed everyday life in the total institution and were recorded in the semi-official handbooks that new boys had to learn in order to pass their 'colour test'.

The attempt to incorporate the verbal play of the schoolboy within the official system of authority also extended to the fictional realms of stories and novels, which often relied heavily on the 'whizz-bang', 'ripper, old boy' formulations that adult authors imputed to their juvenile heroes. This was a sanitized version of the schoolboy's verbal dexterity, safely corralled into inoffensive formulae, shorn of its threat to adult norms of propriety. Arnold Lunn's 1913 novel *The Harrovians*, adapted from his school diaries shortly after he left Harrow, exposed the gap between this idealized vision and the reality of schoolboy profanity. To our contemporary ears, *The Harrovians* is tame stuff indeed, but in 1913 its depiction of pupils deriding the public school ethos and engaging in gleeful flights of profanity caused a minor scandal. Critics slammed Lunn's cynical vision of public school life and he was forced to resign from no fewer than five London clubs.[37] Lunn argued that swearing gave expression to the artistic temperaments of disaffected schoolboys. 'It is sometimes forgotten by those who attempt to suppress swearing in public schools,' he observed, 'that this art is often the one outlet for the literary instincts of youth. Imagination, dramatic instinct, and a knowledge of hagiology are indispensable to a past-master of the game.'[38]

Early in the novel, a group of senior boys stands on the sidelines of a rugby match, an enterprise that the boys deem to be 'utter[ly] useless', and engages in what the narrator calls an 'intellectual feast' of swearing.[39] The sheer artistic verve of the boys' profanity is a rebellious counterpoint to the empty order of the rugby match. But even in their gestures of dissent, the foul-mouthed boys display the same mental qualities required for success as a classicist. In *England and the English*,

Bulwer-Lytton noted that classical pedagogy encouraged a particular kind of mental 'knack' in pupils, a tricksy capacity to work language as a grammatical code, rather than as a deep set of meanings.[40] The 'intellectual feast' of swearing that Lunn depicts exhibits a similar kind of knack. In this sense, profanity was a public school infraculture, one that was in tension with but never independent of the framework of the school's disciplinary system. Indeed, like Thomas Hughes before him, Lunn was a reformist not a revolutionary. His aim was not to raze Harrow and the public school system to the ground, but instead to render it more flexible and accommodating. Lunn's argument is that the creative instincts expressed through swearing should be catered for within the official curriculum. The answer to schoolboy profanity, he suggests, is less classics and more English Literature.

The author with both the sharpest ear for schoolboy nonsense and the keenest instinct for channelling that nonsense for authoritarian ends, however, was Rudyard Kipling. In his *Stalky and Co.* series, which depicts the escapades of a group of renegade pupils at a Devonshire boarding school based on the author's own alma mater, United Services College, Kipling suggests that his protagonists' verbal play is both a part of their charm and a sign of their fitness for future careers in the imperial administration. In 'An Unsavoury Interlude', Stalky, Beetle and McTurk engage in an extended struggle with a rival boarding house as a result of a perceived insult about their uncleanliness. As ever, the high jinks are charming and the escapades are engrossing, especially the climax of the story in which the trio secrete the rotting corpse of a cat in the eaves of their rivals' dormitory. More than just a charming narrative, however, the tale is a veritable feast of wordplay, witticisms, allusions and verbal sallies. The boys' virtuoso glossolalia weaves together a vast range of different registers and types of speech, including thick Devonshire dialect ('Her runs under the 'ang of the heaves'), pompous headmasterly discourse ('You are futile – look out for my tie! – futile burblers'), polyglot nonsense ('Pomposo Stinkadore'), the louche tones of 1890s aestheticism ('Beetle, de-ah'), Franglais babble ('Jevaisgloater. Jevaisgloatertoutle blessed afternoon'), garbled Latin tags ('privatimetseriatim'), and snippets of Carroll ('come to my arms, my beamish boy ... Oh, frabjous day! Calloo, callay!').[41]

This is Kipling's own idealized version of the schoolboy's oral culture: robust, heteroglot, inventive, expressive of the inherent spark and danger of youth, but also anchored in the traditions of Shakespeare, the King James Bible and the classical curriculum. Indeed, the boys' ability to mock and mimic different kinds of language is part of their more general capacity for cunning and guile. It is part of the repertoire of skills they exhibit during their out of bounds adventures, including military tactics, disguise, local knowledge and elaborate forms of gameplay and performance. In this respect, *Stalky and Co.*'s verbal play mirrors the performative plasticity of Kipling's other, more famous, boy heroes, Kim and Mowgli, who can adopt at will the outward appearance of different ethnicities and species, while remaining at their core loyal British subjects. Indeed, Kipling's ideal colonial servant was always the enterprising colonel rather than the distant general. He favoured the charismatic renegade who could adapt to different cultures and ways of speaking, rather than the narrow parochialism of both the school and the colonial administration. In the *Stalky and Co.* tales, nonsense, parody and wordplay were part of his wider aim to enchant the imperial project, to imbue Britain's vast machinery of state with a sense of play and a sprinkling of magic.

WHY DID CLASSICS remain at the heart of elite education in Great Britain for so long? Why, in spite of repeated calls for reform and a rapidly shifting set of intellectual, technological, social and cultural contexts, did public school masters stick so doggedly to the classical curriculum? There is, one has to admit, a certain quixotic nobility to the endeavour, a laudable devotion to ideals other than the immediately useful, which seems all the more praiseworthy from the perspective of today's relentlessly market-driven and utilitarian education sector. During their long imperial heyday, Britain's public schools were devoted to an ideal of classical scholarship that gloriously – and in the end, perhaps, fatally – insulated them from the concerns of the everyday world. Public schools may have competed against one another in the marketplace, and they may have prepared their pupils for careers in the imperial administration, but much of their ethos and curriculum was designed to stem the lapping tides of commerce and politics that emanated from the world beyond.

Yet for many young men who underwent the rigours of public school classics this noble ideal remained entirely notional. Especially in the early stages of the curriculum, the lived experience of classics was as yet another part of the school's disciplinary system. Prefect-fagging, sumptuary laws, access to forbidden parts of the grounds and buildings, the order of seating in the dining hall and chapel, organized sports and inter-house competition, flogging and the profound linguistic alienation of classical study formed a complex network of rules and regulations that subsumed the individual within the collective life of the institution. In 1959 the literary historian Walter Ong noted how this strange process shared many features with the puberty rites of tribal societies: the separation from the everyday world; the violent transition to maturity; the mystical community of men; the enchantment of a secret language divested of its connection to stable meanings in the everyday world.[42] The Latin and Greek languages functioned in this context as intellectual trials of strength, their recondite lexical forms toughening the young man's mind just as the lash of the cane toughened his will.

Ong's theory also helps to explain the curious persistence of classics through the ages. Old boys remained sentimentally attached to classics throughout their lives not only because they were enchanted by the metrical niceties of Greek verse, but because they bore the indelible stamp of the public school initiation rite. Latin and Greek were tools for identity formation as much as they were bodies of knowledge. For many, their appeal lay in a realm beyond the rational and utilitarian concerns of educational progressives. Just as Edmund Burke defended the unwritten British constitution on the basis of 'presumption', a kind of pre-rational faith in the rightness of long-practised customs and institutions, classics were valued precisely because they had been around for so long and thus bound individuals into the deep traditions of the school and the caste it formed. A large part of their appeal emanated from the murky inner world of childhood memory and tribal initiation, rather than the clear blue skies of reason and progress.

Over the course of the twentieth century, as classics migrated from the centre to the margins of the curriculum, the tenor of public school nonsense changed. In place of Brinsley-Richards's jovial recollections or Lewis Carroll's pastoral escapism, a new strain of gothic surrealism began to feature in both autobiographical and fictional treatments of boarding school life. This bitter surrealist mode crops up everywhere, from inter-war memoirs by the likes of George Orwell and Winston Churchill, to the outlandish caricatures of *Beyond the Fringe* and *Monty Python*. The principal focus of this new, harder-edged surrealism was no longer classical pedagogy, although Latin and Greek continued to feature in many cases, but rather the sheer absurdity of the boarding school system – its bizarre institutional forms and the way it warped the characters of both pupils and masters. This was a kind of off-kilter, absurdist, close-to-the-bone humour that explored childhood alienation from the inside out.

In the gothic surrealist mode, the authority of the school manifests itself as a groundless power that seems to emanate from a place beyond meaning or reason. In his essay 'Such, Such Were the Joys', published posthumously in 1952, George Orwell describes his childhood sense of living in an 'underwater world' at his shabby little prep school, St Cyprian's. When the seven-year-old Orwell is repeatedly beaten for wetting the bed, he comes to realize that 'sin was not necessarily something that you did: it might be something that happened to you'.[43] Orwell's short memoir is justly famous today for its grim vision of boarding school life. The longevity of that vision is due in large part to the acuity with which he describes the collision between the cold logic of the school and the fragile, non-linear imagination of the child. The young Orwell's disorientation arises from his inability to understand the language of the adult authorities who determine his fate. He mishears the headmaster's wife's statement that he will be beaten in the 'sixth form' as the altogether more humiliating fate of being beaten by 'Mrs Form'. This linguistic slippage conjures for him the surreal vision of an all-English Valkyrie in tweeds and leather riding crop, who will be drafted in specially to beat him before the entire school. Throughout the essay, Orwell's youthful perceptions of the bizarre names of his teachers, their outlandish physical forms and their garbled, confusing language have the same warty particularity that was later to be found in the work of Roald Dahl. Both authors tapped into the profound weirdness of the boarding school system when viewed through the uncorrupted eyes of a child.

But it wasn't just the literary radicals who reflected on the absurdities of their schooldays. In his 1930 autobiography, Winston Churchill recalled his deep sadness at being abandoned by his mother at prep school: 'I was . . . miserable at the idea of being left alone among all these strangers in this great, fierce, formidable place. After all, I was only seven, and I had been so happy in my nursery with all my toys.'[44] As soon as his mother leaves, the young Winston is given a Latin grammar by his new teacher and told to learn how to decline 'mensa' before the next lesson. When the time comes, he regurgitates the declensions he has learnt by heart but finds himself in trouble when asked to give the meaning of 'mensa' in the vocative case – 'O table'.

> 'But why "O table?"' I persisted in genuine curiosity.
>
> 'You would use it in speaking to a table.'
>
> 'But I never do', I blurted out in honest amazement.
>
> 'If you are impertinent, you will be punished very severely.'
>
> Such was my introduction to the classics, from which, I have been told, many of our cleverest men have derived so much solace and profit.[45]

For both the young boy and, as the sardonic final sentence suggests, the mature statesman, Latin pedagogy is riddled with absurdity. And yet this nonsensical verbal space is part of the school's wider system of discipline, backed up by stern teacherly injunctions and the ultimate authority of the cane. It is intuitively wrong but also manifestly right, as evidenced by the teacher's threat. In the sequence of Churchill's narrative, the trauma of juvenile abandonment and the absurdities of classical pedagogy are both part of the grim initiation that ushers the young child into the world of men.

In public school memoirs dark surrealism was usually confined to individual passages, isolated eruptions of irrationality within a narrative form that sought to bring order and comprehension to the adult author's childhood memories. But in comic writing and performance edgy nonsense was the dominant mode for depicting public school life and its lasting effects on former pupils. Indeed, twentieth-century British comedy contains a powerful strain of anti-establishment humour that emanates from, and is often directed against, the world of the boarding school. This comic mode made an early appearance in Evelyn Waugh's *Decline and Fall* (1928), which is partially set in the ramshackle Llanabba Castle, a provincial prep school whose staff includes the bumbling ingénue Paul Pennyfeather, the undercover criminal Solomon Philbrick and the serial pederast Captain Grimes ('They might kick you out, but they never let you down').[46] It can be found in J. B. Morton's 'Beachcomber' columns that he wrote for the *Daily Express* in the 1930s, '40s and '50s, which depict the seedy Narkover school and its assortment of criminal teachers and pupils. It crops up regularly in *The Goon Show*'s retinue of upper-class eccentrics, tinpot colonels and deranged subalterns. It is a staple of Ronald Searle's *St Trinian's* cartoons, set in a debauched girls' boarding school inspired by Searle's experiences in a Japanese prisoner of war camp during the Second World War, and his illustrations for Geoffrey Willans's *Molesworth* books, packed with useful information on how to survive at St Custard's, a seedy boys' prep school run by a motley group of sadists and bores. It is also present in the absurdist skits of *Beyond the Fringe* and *Monty Python*, although now mixed with a new vein of abstraction imported from avant-garde writers such as Eugene Ionesco and Samuel Beckett. This comic tradition was both a symptom and a cause of the decline of deference towards both public schools and the ruling establishment over the course of the twentieth century. Dark nonsense was a way to expose, laugh at and also maybe even to forgive the emotional brutality of elite education. Its legacy can be detected to this day – albeit in more polite, moderate ways – in the form of the public school-educated satirists who ply their trade in publications such as *Private Eye* and radio and television panel shows such as *I'm Sorry I Haven't a Clue* and *Have I Got News for You*.

The most acute delineator of public school eccentricity, however, was Peter Cook, one of the founding members of the revue *Beyond the Fringe*, which took the Edinburgh Festival by storm in 1961 and ushered in what has subsequently been called the 'satire boom' of the 1960s. Among the hugely talented cast – the other members were Alan Bennett, Dudley Moore and Jonathan Miller – Cook's speciality was caricatures of ruling class eccentrics and their obsequious subordinates. Many of Cook's most successful characters were drawn from his own boarding school experiences at Radley College, where he was a high-achieving, if somewhat aloof, pupil in the early 1950s. Prefects and masters at Radley dined at 'high table' and were served by an eccentric butler, Mr Boylett, who had the habit of making unintentionally surreal observations to the assembled company. On one occasion Mr Boylett observed to Cook that he thought he saw a stone on the gravel path outside move of its own accord; on another, after serving some food, he gnomically remarked, 'there's plenty more where that came from, if you know what I mean'.[47] These obscure utterances immediately became fodder for Cook's fertile imagination and uncanny knack for mimicry. First in the boarding house, then at the Cambridge University Footlights Dramatic Club and eventually on the West End stage, Cook transformed his old school's butler into Grole, the shabby, mac-wearing, bench-sitting raconteur, who lugubriously relays strings of surrealist factoids in a deadpan tour de force. Grole's most famous routine begins with the immortal line, 'Yes, I would have been a judge, but I never had the Latin.' His subsequent comparison of the 'rigorous' judging exams with the decidedly less challenging mining exams, which consist of a single question, 'who are you?' for which Grole receives 75 per cent, deftly delineate the hidden injustices of meritocratic exam culture.[48] Not only is Grole barred from becoming a judge, but he is also reduced to a mere fraction of his full human potential due to his lack of an expensive classical education.

But it was in the figure of Sir Arthur Streeb-Greebling that Cook directly satirized the old school. In many ways Sir Arthur is a familiar figure, a stiff, upper-class Englishman, whose character has been knocked out of alignment by the rigours of his schooling and the mores of his social class. Yet Cook brings the character to life with such minute attention to gesture and voice, and pursues his flights of surrealism with such unparalleled verve, that Sir Arthur attains a peculiarity all his own. In one famous skit he is interviewed by a glib, feather-light television host played by Dudley Moore, who wishes to discuss Sir Arthur's quixotic attempt to teach ravens to fly underwater. When asked by the host why he has chosen to dedicate his life to this task, Sir Arthur's eyes glaze a little and he becomes ruminative, 'Well it's very difficult to say what prompts anybody to do anything . . . but I think it probably all dates back to a very early age.' It turns out that Sir Arthur's impossible quest, which he pursues with unflagging, even heroic, dedication, was first prompted by a stern injunction from his mother: 'If you don't get underwater and start teaching ravens to fly, I'll smash your stupid face off.' The sketch is not explicitly set in a boarding school, but it nevertheless occupies the same emotional world of parental distance, displaced affections, frustrated desires and warped personalities that was part of the legacy of the total institution. The stern command of Sir Arthur's mother has the same unfathomable brutality that Winston Churchill experienced when his own mother said goodbye to him at prep school. Over time, the emotional wrench of being sent away to school – or, one assumes, being ordered to teach ravens to fly underwater – dissipates. The inmate becomes habituated to the rigours of the institution. School discipline sinks beneath the horizon of everyday awareness, seeps into one's bones, becomes a part of one's habitus. But in the moment of dark nonsense, conjured in the form of a school memoir or a comic skit, the spell is broken and the pain is released in a contorted rictus of laughter.

Indeed, Cook's own childhood was defined by the repeated abandonments that were necessitated by his father's job as an Assistant District Officer in the Colonial Service in Nigeria. Cook shared the experience of Vyvyen Brendon's 'separated children', the sons and daughters of Empire who spent much of their young lives in the care of emotionally distant housemasters and matrons. In interviews in later life, Cook described his lifelong feelings of guilt and absence towards his parents.[49] His sense of humour developed in large part as a response to the experience of parental distance and the rigours of the boarding school. Early in his career at Radley, Cook learned to avoid bullying and gain prestige with his inspired mimicry and subversive nonsense. Both at school and later on the stage, his performances were part of the long tradition of schoolboy nonsense that stretches back to Kipling, Lunn and Carroll, which emerged against the backdrop of school discipline and emotional suppression. The response to this dull, joyless world came in the form of a liberating burst of surrealist humour, a ludic release that mocked but also echoed the alienating logic of the school.

László Moholy-Nagy, 'Pupils watching cricket from the pavilion on Agar's Plough', *c.* 1930.

# FIVE

# Athletes and Aesthetes

One of the most curious inventions of the Victorian public school system was a new kind of secular religion: the cult of athleticism. By the end of the nineteenth century games had ceased to be simply a mechanism for channelling youthful energies and were instead an all-consuming obsession, the living embodiment of the public school ethos of manly character-building. The tightly scheduled school day was packed with house matches, school matches, practice sessions, informal 'punt-abouts' and cross-country runs for weedy boys who were not members of a team. This was the focal point of the school's collective life. Attendance as a spectator at matches was often compulsory, and at some institutions failure to attend could be punished with a beating. Special dinners were served in the boarding houses to celebrate sporting victories; reports of inter-school play were published in the *Public School Magazine* and other boys' journals; the dramatic, last-minute victory was the climactic set piece of many a public school novel.[1]

Importantly, it was team games such as rugby, cricket and football, rather than the more individualistic pursuits of boxing and field sports, that predominated at most schools. Before the Victorian era, football and rugby matches were irregular and frequently disorderly affairs, organized by the boys themselves as part of the culture of pupil self-governance. There were no standardized rules, no common pitch size, and often no limit on the number of players. Beginning around the middle of the nineteenth century, however, team sports were incorporated within the official life of the institution and imbued with the same kinds of systematic organization and symbolic meaning as other school rituals.

The Rugby Football Union was formed by a group of public school old boys in 1871. And while the rules of cricket had been formalized in the eighteenth century, it was only in the nineteenth century that it became a mass spectator sport. The annual Lord's cricket match between Eton and Harrow became a spectacular feature of the sporting season, routinely attracting crowds of 25,000 and more. The ethos of 'fair play', or vigorous competition within a framework of codified rules and mutual respect, was one of the signal ideals of public school sports in the Victorian era, one that was exported around the world by British teachers, engineers, missionaries and civil servants who were posted overseas. Many saw in organized sports an antidote to the political strife and restless change of the modern world.

Beyond the noble ideal of 'fair play', organized sports were also mechanisms for disciplining both the individual and collective bodies of adolescent males. This was the era of *mens sana in corpore sano* (a healthy mind in a healthy body), a Latin tag borrowed from the Roman poet Juvenal and converted into a modern spiritual motto, which proclaimed an almost mystical belief in the connection between moral and physical health. Edward Thring, the headmaster of Uppingham between 1853 and 1887, was one of the first headmasters to embrace athleticism. 'Life is one piece,' he wrote in 1867, 'health of body, health of intellect, health of heart all uniting to form the true man.'[2] Thring's theory drew on a long tradition that stretched back to the ancient Greeks, which saw education as a means of uniting the disparate parts of the individual human being to form a cohesive whole. At Uppingham, Thring fostered a school culture that combined religious devotion, a cooperative relationship between boys and masters, a concerted focus on athleticism and physical conditioning and a reformed curriculum of both classical and modern subjects. The aim of this system was to produce a healthy balance between the different facets of the self: the body, the intellect and the heart. 'Health' in Thring's philosophy was not simply a matter of physical well-being. It was also a matter of identity. To be a healthy adolescent was to find your true self within the framework provided by the school. This was a self-denying selfhood, one that augmented the sense of individuality through the collective identity of team, boarding house, school and nation.

In many cases, however, headmasters did not imbue sports with the same metaphysical ideals as Thring and his followers, but instead saw them as a practical defence against the 'unhealthy' appetites that could all too easily arise in impressionable young men. The headmaster of United Services College, the Devonshire boarding school that Kipling mythologized in his *Stalky and Co.* stories, explained the value of sports thus: 'my prophylactic against certain unclean microbes was to send boys to bed dead tired.'[3] Those 'unclean microbes' were both sufficiently vague and scientific-sounding to suggest a whole range of possible maladies, from masturbation and homosexuality to avant-garde aesthetics and radical politics. This was an extension of the logic developed by William Acton in his 1857 treatise on masturbation, in which he observed that 'it is not the strong athletic boy, fond of healthy exercise, who thus early shows marks of sexual desires, but your puny exotic, whose intellectual education has been fostered at the expense of his physical development.'[4] Acton was ahead of his time not only in attempting to discuss adolescent sexuality in scientific terms, but in his suggestion that strenuous physical exercise could in some way suppress the libido. His remedy for masturbation was soon adopted by headmasters throughout the land: a packed schedule to guard against moments of temptation and frequent exercise to pacify the restless adolescent body.

In spite of the ethic of self-sacrifice that accompanied school sports, the athletic ideal was also a source of enormous personal glamour for those who excelled. Within the hothouse world of the school, the athlete was king. His feats on the cricket and football field won for him prefectorial power, special privileges of dress and bounds and the admiring regard of both pupils and masters. His status was signalled in the arcane semiotic system of the school: coloured ties, tasselled caps and embroidered blazers awarded for sporting distinction; the right to walk arm in arm with his fellow 'bloods' in the middle of the highway. The sporting 'tough' was an archetypal figure within the cultural imagination of late nineteenth- and early twentieth-century Britain, the embodiment of cherished ideals of fair play and enlightened rule.

In his celebratory tome *Our Public Schools: Their Influence on English History* (1901), J. G. Cotton Minchin claimed that, 'if asked what our muscular Christianity has done, we point to the British Empire. Our Empire would never have been built up by a nation of idealists and logicians. Physical vigour is as necessary for the maintenance of our Empire as mental vigour.'[5] This was a new masculine ideal that was based more on physical strength than on the moral and spiritual ideals that had animated Arnold and his disciples half a century earlier. In his later works Thomas Hughes warned against the over-valuation of physical strength and stressed that 'manliness' included qualities of compassion and tenderness, as well as vigour and self-confidence. 'Athleticism is a good thing if kept in its place,' he urged, 'but it has come to be very much over-praised and over-valued amongst us.'[6]

But the archetype of the athlete was also accompanied by its anti-type, the aesthete. In the sports-mad school, a taste for art and beauty was one of the chief means of voicing dissent. Where athleticism valued physical strength, self-discipline and the collective life of the school, aestheticism valued intellect, pleasure and friendship between individuals. In contrast to the idealized physique of the sporting tough, aestheticism valued a different kind of masculine body, one that was more supple and over-ripe than hard and useful. In his account of the total institution, Goffman cast the Victorian boarding school as 'an experiment on what can be done to the self', a vast institutional machinery geared towards producing a particular type of character: the English gentleman.[7] Set against this backdrop, aestheticism was a kind of counter-technology for fashioning alternative ways of being. Artworks, books, private debating clubs and affectations of style, dress and speech were means of creating an alternative world within the closed community of the school. This world within a world provided breathing room for different kinds of character: misfits, eccentrics, dissenters, rebels, queers, intellectuals and refuseniks of all sorts.

Aestheticism refers to the philosophy of 'art for art's sake' that was developed in France by the poets Théophile Gautier and Charles Baudelaire and taken up in England by Swinburne and the Pre-Raphaelites in the 1860s and '70s and later by Oscar Wilde, Aubrey Beardsley and the decadent movement of the *fin de siècle*. In spite of aestheticism's claim to have emptied art of its moral content – Wilde famously stated that 'there is no such thing as a moral or an immoral book. Books are well written, or badly written. That is all.' – the movement nevertheless carried with it an implicit set of political values.[8] In the pure form of the artwork, aestheticism envisioned a free space outside of the constraints of bourgeois society. It is easy to see why this philosophical position had such appeal for disaffected public schoolboys. Aestheticism offered a different model of personal identity than the one that was instilled on the playing fields. Rather than viewing identity as a stable essence that could be imparted from above by prefects and masters, aestheticism treated the self as a work of art, a malleable construct that could be shaped by dressing, talking and thinking in new ways.

The figure of the dandy-aesthete has a long lineage that stretches back to the aristocratic culture of the late eighteenth century, but it was not until the early twentieth century that aestheticism became a fully fledged subculture practised in many different schools and reflected in the popular culture of the day. As with so many later youth sub-cultures, the original desire for individuality would eventually result in its own kind of conformism; the aesthete signifiers of coloured waistcoats, baggy trousers (Oxford bags) and sparkling modernist verse congealed into an off-the-peg style sported by a whole generation of disaffected public school sixth-formers and Oxbridge undergradu-ates. And yet within the airtight world of the school, even the most formulaic gestures of dissent could make big waves. Wearing a daring waistcoat, walking with a pronouncedly mincing gait or carrying a copy of Shelley's verses tucked under one's arm could function as a strategic intervention within the symbolic economy of the school.

Memoirs, diaries and novels from the time describe a constant state of low-level warfare in many public schools, which took the form of periodic 'debaggings' of artistic types by the sporting bloods, fol-lowed by stinging satires on athletic culture in the little magazines run by the school intellectuals. These may seem like trivial, even cartoonish episodes – as though P. G. Wodehouse had rewritten an American frat house comedy – but the conflict expressed wider currents within the culture of the time. In the wake of the First World War, a conflict in which public schoolboys figured prominently among the fallen, the athletes and the aesthetes represented different attitudes towards some of the most fundamental questions of modern life. Was identity a matter of tribal allegiance or personal choice? Was it something handed down from tradition or made anew by individuals? And precisely what forms of loyalty could rightfully be expected from one's school, one's class and one's nation?

WHEN JOHN BETJEMAN took up his place at Magdalen College, Oxford, in 1925 he couldn't help but feel that the 'golden age' of aesthetes had already passed, as its leading lights, Brian Howard and Harold Acton, had recently departed the scene, trailing behind them a glorious perfume of scandal and rumour.[9] Betjeman was something of a hothouse flower himself, who had spent his senior years at Marlborough College publishing the athlete-baiting *Heretick* magazine and discussing avant-garde poetry with his co-conspirators Louis MacNeice and Anthony Blunt. But like so many adherents of cutting-edge subcultures, even the precocious Betjeman felt a melancholy sense of distance from the mythical origins of the cult. Betjeman included among the heroes of the golden age of aesthetes Cecil Beaton, Robert Byron, John Sutro, Christopher Hollis, Evelyn Waugh and Tom Driberg, all glamorous and talented young men, but he reserved the highest accolades for Howard and Acton, the ultra-aesthetes of what came to be known as the 'Bright Young Things'. Waugh would later combine aspects of Howard and Acton's personalities in the character of Anthony Blanche in *Brideshead Revisited*. Like Acton, Blanche proclaims poetry from his rooms with a megaphone and is ducked in the Christ Church fountain by a group of sporting toughs. Like Howard, he has a tendency towards paranoia and shrillness that is born of his queer outsider status.

Unlike many of their peers, who escaped their bourgeois family backgrounds by putting on the aristocratic airs of the dandy-aesthete, Howard and Acton came from highly cultured and cosmopolitan homes. Howard's father was an international art dealer, his mother an American heiress. He grew up in Surrey and London amid a social circle that included Bernard Berenson, James McNeill Whistler,

Henry James and assorted members of the early twentieth-century artistic elite. Harold Acton grew up in his parents' Renaissance Villa La Pietra near Florence, a childhood home that contained not a stick of furniture that dated from later than the eighteenth century. When the two boys met as new bugs at Eton, they formed a close bond that was based on their shared love of art and distaste for the dull conformity of school life. Together they played up their internationalist, high cultural backgrounds, experimented with minute differences of dress and gait, swapped books and art prints and revelled in anecdotes about the exotic personages they met during the holidays. They enabled each other to become their best, most outlandish selves. In his memoir Acton described his astonishment on first meeting Howard: 'His big brown eyes with their long curved lashes were brazen with self-assurance; already his personality seemed chiselled and polished, and his vocabulary was as ornate as his diction ... At the age of thirteen he was definitely a dandy.'[10]

Eton was in many ways more tolerant of eccentricity than most public schools. The school's aristocratic profile and culture of masculine self-display, especially in the form of 'Pop', the sixth-form club who wore brightly coloured waistcoats and ties, meant that it could tolerate one or two rum characters in the senior year groups. But in the early twentieth century Eton was also strongly influenced by the militarism and athleticism of the mainstream public school ethos. Especially for juniors, everyday life was highly regimented and vigorously policed. Howard and Acton were in different boarding houses, and hence were not allowed to visit each other's rooms due to the strict segregation of sleeping quarters. Their friendship was mainly forged out of doors on long rambling walks. Sometimes they would take excursions into Windsor where they could spend time together in Dyson's the jewellers, which rented out gramophones in its back room. The two boys would spend their stolen afternoons pirouetting to Russian ballets while their colleagues were knee deep in the mud of the rugby fields. This was a self-conscious retreat from the environment of the school, an escape to the impregnable fortress of friendship and art.

As they rose through the school hierarchy, however, the two boys grew bolder in their attempts to define themselves in opposition to the orthodoxies of the institution. With a couple of accomplices, they founded the Cremorne Club, whose motto was 'Life is an Art, and to be encountered with a buttonhole of flowers'.[11] While the club's honorary members included Whistler, Beardsley, Swinburne, Mallarmé and Wilde, its actual members never got around to holding any official meetings. In a sense, however, whether the club met or not was beside the point; its true function was not to stage real debates or perform actual intellectual work, but instead to serve as a platform for its members to proclaim their allegiance to an alternative tradition that was inimical to the values of the school. A more practical venture was The Eton Society of Arts, which held actual meetings and contained a number of members who would later become prominent figures in the literary world, including the novelists Henry Yorke (who published under the name Henry Green) and Anthony Powell. The Society of Arts was sponsored by a liberal master, Mr Evans, who supported the boys' initiative as an addition to the formal curriculum. This was how cutting-edge art and philosophy flourished in many schools – as an informal, barely tolerated supplement to the official business of classics, athletics and religion.

In his memoir Yorke describes how the members of the Society of Arts embraced the aesthete identity in defiance of mainstream school culture. Members of the group adopted what he called 'feminine motions'.[12] They dressed in women's sun-bonnets, wore oversized great coats and elongated collars on their shirts and spoke in ornate, mincing tones. In later life Howard and Acton became two of the most renowned dandies of the age, feted both in avant-garde poetry circles and newspaper gossip columns. While they were still at public school, however, they crafted their personae with the limited materials that lay ready to hand. Yorke observed that the aesthetes' sartorial gestures were 'so technical that only boys who had been more than one year at school could appreciate them'.[13]

An early twentieth-century schoolboy's dress was as strictly regulated as every other aspect of his daily life. Most schools had elaborate sumptuary laws that gave sartorial expression to the hierarchical order of the institution. Robert Graves described the 'strict caste system' in place at Charterhouse at the time:

A new boy had no privileges at all; a boy in his second term might wear a knitted tie instead of a plain one; a boy in his second year might wear coloured socks; the third year gave most of the main privileges – turned down collars, coloured handkerchiefs, a coat with a long roll, and so on; fourth year, a few more, such as the right to get up raffles; but peculiar distinctions were reserved for the bloods. These included light grey flannel trousers, butterfly collars, jackets slit up the back, and the right of walking arm-in-arm.[14]

Graves describes a semiotic system as bafflingly arcane and rigorously policed as the tattoos used by Russian criminal gangs to mark their allegiances and histories. Both of these systems are visual expressions of modern tribal societies; they encode the collective memory and social hierarchy of an enclosed, all-male world. Rather than pure expressions of individual identity, aesthete fashions were part of the wider symbolic economy of the school. They were 'technical' interventions that derived much of their meaning and radical charge from the very system they disrupted.

The aim of schoolboy aestheticism, claimed Henry Yorke, was 'to arouse more than disdain, we were out to annoy by being what we called "amusing".'[15] Juvenility and playfulness were deployed as a self-conscious antidote to the school's ethos of maturity and self-discipline. Louis MacNeice called this the 'fashionable child cult' and 'the bacchanalian chorus of youth'.[16] At Marlborough MacNeice teamed up with Betjeman and Blunt to form the Hereticks, an aesthete-intellectual club that published an eponymous magazine with the motto 'Upon Philistia I will Triumph'. On the bright orange cover of the first edition was an image of a bewildered sportsman reeling from the attentions of a group of circling nymphs – a victory for art over athletics. The Hereticks performed a kind of running parody of the school's sporting culture. They threw coloured balls at one another on the sidelines of rugby matches; during chapel services they dangled handkerchiefs from their lapels in parody of the obsession with winning school 'colours'; and on occasion Betjeman would bowl a coloured hoop before him as he danced through the school grounds, a green feather lodged daintily behind his ear. At Lancing a similar revolt was enacted by Evelyn Waugh, Tom Driberg and their fellow members of the 'Corpse Club', who wore black ties, black tassels on their jackets and black buttonholes in their lapels, and corresponded on black-edged notepaper. Dubbed the 'Bolshies' by their more conventional schoolfellows, Waugh and his friends disrupted cadet corps exercises by parading in unclean or disorderly uniforms and contradicting the sergeant's barked orders. The Corpse Club was founded 'for those who are weary of life', a motto which inverted the official school values of athletic prowess and physical health.[17]

The greatest success of Howard and Acton's schoolboy careers was undoubtedly *Eton Candle*, an 'ephemeral', or single-issue, magazine they published in their final year. Both boys were precocious literary talents. By the age of sixteen Howard had published poems in Edith Sitwell's *Wheels* and Charles Orage's *New Age*, two impeccably cutting-edge modernist magazines. And while Acton had to wait until he was at university to have his first book of poetry published, his talents were nevertheless clear to his friends and teachers. *Eton Candle* was a glittering addition to the boys' expanding portfolio of excellences, one that made waves beyond the little world of the school. The magazine garnered positive reviews in *The Times*, the *Morning Post*, the *Daily Express*, *The Observer* and the *Sunday Times*. It also earned the accolade of being nicknamed the 'Eton Scandal', for the consternation it caused among the more aesthetically conservative members of the Etonian community.

Published in 1922, the same year as Joyce's *Ulysses* and T. S. Eliot's *The Waste Land*, *Eton Candle* is a remarkable combination of modernist rigour and aesthete glamour that is all the more astonishing for the fact that it was put together by a couple of schoolboys. Inside its shocking pink covers are large advertisements for the Brooklands model touring motorcycle, 'The All-purpose, Trouble-free, Go-anywhere Mount', as well as for Chapman Brothers fine art dealers, Adamson's tailors and Murray's booksellers, all of which attest to the well-heeled audience at which *Eton Candle* was aimed. But the contents of the magazine had a strong bent in favour of literary modernism, including original contributions from Aldous Huxley and Osbert Sitwell. When the Poet

Laureate Robert Bridges declined to contribute, Howard didn't miss a beat in dismissing him as a naive upstart: 'Amazing how some people will throw away their opportunities, isn't it?'[18] Cyril Connolly recalled that the whole affair was a 'weapon' of 'aggressive aestheticism'.[19]

Many historians have described how the hedonism of the 'roaring twenties', with its new styles of music, fashion, art and nightlife, constituted a semi-conscious response to the traumatic memory of war.[20] The Great War saw the slaughter of young men on an almost unimaginable scale. A large proportion of those fatalities were recent graduates from public schools: Eton lost 1,157 and Harrow 516 old boys during the four years of fighting.[21] Trained in the public school virtues of athleticism, discipline, respect for authority and veneration of tradition, these young men were bred for chivalric self-sacrifice and martial valour. But in the wake of the bloody attrition of Ypres and the Somme, the chivalric ideal rang hollow. A jarring disconnect had opened up between the grim reality of modern, mechanized warfare and the antique postures of the gentleman soldier. Dandy-aestheticism was more than just a way of acting out against hearties and headmasters; it was also a way to repudiate the values of martial honour and group loyalty that had fuelled the war.

One of the standout contributions to *Eton Candle* was from Howard himself, a short poem entitled 'To the Young Writers and Artists Killed in the War, 1914–18'. The poem captures the mood of generational animus that underpinned schoolboy aestheticism.

> We haven't forgotten you! We haven't forgotten!
> You were the first generation of the world's greatest century,
> And you were doing, and were going to do, fine things . . .
> You were a great Young Generation . . .
>
> And then you went out and got murdered – magnificently –
> Went out and got murdered . . . because a parcel
>     of damned old men
> Wanted some fun, or some power, or something.
> Something so despicable in comparison to your young lives.[22]

Schoolboy aestheticism could easily become a self-absorbed and brittle affair, a subculture that failed to break free from the institution it kicked against, but 'To the Young Writers and Artists Killed in the War, 1914–18' captures the authentic moral outrage that underpinned its best moments.

The origins of dandyism lay in the late eighteenth century, when a new culture of masculine fashion and self-display emerged in London's fashionable West End. The prince of this new scene was Beau Brummell, who first acquired his taste for fine clothing and classical poise at Eton in the 1790s.[23] Brummell adopted the elements of his look first from his costume as a 'Pole man' at Eton's carnivalesque 'Montem' festival, and later from his elaborate uniform as an officer in the 10th (Prince of Wales's Own) Regiment of (Light) Dragoons. These influences were then combined with the craftsmanship of the highly skilled tailors clustered around Savile Row in London. The result – fine fabrics, clean lines and muted colours, all designed to accentuate the natural contours of the male body – was a thoroughly modern makeover of the traditional signifiers of aristocratic masculine glamour. But dandyism is best understood not as a coherent style but more as a general attitude towards the expression of self through sartorial display. Indeed, dandyism can take many different forms; it can be played straight or queer, hard or soft. In his study of 1920s aestheticism, the literary scholar Martin Green described a continuum of dandy types – from the hyper-masculine tory 'rogue' to the effeminate liberal 'naïf' – who might have differed in politics but were united in their rejection of the bourgeois values of gentlemanliness and good character that defined the Victorian public school ethos.[24] Historically, many public school dandies had embraced the roguish, libertine aspects of the style. This is the style of dandyism that Harry Flashman exhibits in Fraser's novels: hyper-masculine, aligned with the more fashionable parts of the military, impatient of institutional restraint and with a tendency towards debauchery and violence. But in the hands of Howard and Acton, who were influenced by the *fin de siècle* decadence of Wilde and Beardsley, the ambiguities inherent in Brummell's style of masculinity were accentuated. This was the masculine self-display not of the dashing cavalry officer but of the wilting hothouse flower, a strange bloom who flourished in the artificial environments of art galleries and salons, rather than the rugged outdoors world of the dandy-rogue.

For the dissident schoolboys of the 1920s, aesthete posturing was a new way of expressing adolescent sexuality. Homosexuality had been a feature of public school life for centuries, but in almost all cases it was either sanitized in the form of semi-official romantic friendships or confined to the darker corners of the institution, away from the gaze of officialdom. The historian A.J.P. Taylor observed that

> The strange one-sexed system of education at public schools and universities had always run to homosexuality. In Victorian times this, though gross, had been sentimental and ostensibly innocent. At the *fin de siècle* it had been consciously wicked. Now [in the 1920s] it was neither innocent nor wicked. It was merely, for a brief period, normal.[25]

Taylor overstates the degree to which homosexuality was 'normalized' within the upper-class culture of the 1920s. In his senior year at Lancing, Tom Driberg was almost expelled for propositioning another boy, but his execution was stayed due to the recent death of his father. In part in reaction against the loosening of moral codes, the authoritarian Home Secretary Sir William Joynson-Hicks used the Defence of the Realm Act, an emergency measure introduced during the First World War, to wage a public campaign against 'vice', especially in the form of nightclubs, obscene publications and homosexuality. With their 'effeminate motions' and playful embellishments of their uniforms, public school aesthetes were engaging in a wider culture war that raged throughout British society in the 1920s. Howard and Acton in particular embraced queerness as an explicit identity, one that was telegraphed, albeit in coded forms, to the school at large. The heterosexual Yorke might have claimed in his memoir that 'we were feminine not from perversion . . . but from a lack of any other kind of self-expression', but for Howard and Acton, sartorial experiment was directly linked to a burgeoning queer identity.[26]

IN HIS ANALYSIS of post-Second World War youth subcultures, the cultural critic Dick Hebdige defined street fashions such as the punk's safety pin or the Teddy boy's pointed shoes as 'tokens of self-imposed exile', minute semiotic gestures that communicated the individual's dissatisfaction with the dominant culture of the day.[27] Hebdige and his followers were instrumental in the formation of the new academic field of cultural studies, which brought the intellectual tools of literary analysis and social critique to bear upon cultural forms that had previously been deemed beneath the concern of serious scholarship, things like popular musical genres and the social practices of marginalized groups. The gay antics of hyperprivileged schoolboys in the elegant purlieus of Eton and Marlborough were emphatically not among Hebdige's interests. And yet, ironically, Hebdige's analysis can also be used to explain the public school subculture of aestheticism. The dandy-aesthete's sartorial style and literary tastes were precisely what Hebdige calls 'tokens of self-imposed exile', subtle gestures of dissent that had meaning only against the backdrop of public school discipline and the social norms of the ruling elite.

Hebdige was also acutely aware of the limitations of subcultural self-fashioning. When faced with the deeply entrenched power structures of a class-bound society, the iconography of punk, mod, ska and goth amounted to little more than 'graffiti on a prison wall'.[28] Youth subcultures were radical postures that rarely disturbed the smooth functioning of the systems they opposed. Throughout the second half of the twentieth century bleeding-edge subcultures have repeatedly been co-opted by large corporations eager to sell the latest styles and sounds straight back to the very groups who invented them in the first place. Yesterday's radical gestures are today's mainstream style.

Public school aestheticism was subject to the same logic of rebellion and containment as other subcultural styles. What began as radical acts of dissent were quickly reabsorbed into the school's wider system of authority. After the initial furore caused by the little magazines and the dandyish provocations died down, many schools found a semi-official home for aesthete-intellectual culture in sixth-form literature classes, informal art tutorials and extracurricular clubs. Over time these informal practices were incorporated within the official curriculum. One could even argue that aestheticism's biggest impact was not its successful disruption of authority, but instead the role it played in modernizing public school life by prompting it to become more flexible and less dogmatic. This was certainly the aim of Alec Waugh, whose novel *The Loom of Youth* (1917) depicted the clash of cultures between the loyalist hearties and the individualistic aesthetes.[29] Waugh's novel was written in the early mornings before he had to report for duty at his officer training camp, as he and his fellow recruits prepared to depart for the Western Front. The novel's *succès de scandale* was fuelled by its author's status as a schoolboy soldier (he was nineteen when he wrote it), the living embodiment of the national ideal celebrated in the popular novels and magazines that were satirized in its pages. *Loom* was widely reviled for its open critique of the public school code that helped to fuel British militarism. It also courted scandal with its representation of romantic relationships between boys, a crime for which Waugh himself had been expelled from Sherborne in his final year. This disgrace meant that Alec's younger – and now significantly more famous – brother, Evelyn, was barred from entering the school and had to make do with the less prestigious Lancing. In his autobiography, however, Waugh described the novel as 'a love letter to Sherborne'.[30] In the figure of Gordon Carruthers, the novel's main protagonist, Waugh envisioned the synthesis of the school's two opposing factions: the athletic hearties and the aesthete intellectuals. His intentions, in short, were reformist rather than revolutionary. His aim was to spur the system he loved to heal the rift within its divided self, and thus to produce fully rounded pupils, cultivated in the arts but also hardened on the playing fields. His ideal was not so very far from Thring's belief that 'life is of one piece'.

For all of their scrapes and skirmishes, the warring tribes of the athletes and the aesthetes were products of the same environment, shaped by the same institutional pressures. Looked at from the perspective of posterity, it is easy to see how these distinct types in fact shared many characteristics. The sporting blood's excessive attention to details of dress and deportment shades over into a kind of prissy self-regard that ceases to be entirely 'manly'. Conversely, there is also a kind of athletic vigour in the figure of the English dandy-aesthete that is born of the culture of the school. In his memoir, Louis MacNeice acknowledged that the school was itself a 'forcing frame' that shaped the personae of the dandy-aesthetes: 'Marlborough in our time was fairly tough soil but grew a useful crop of, in their way, equally tough aesthetes.'[31] Harold Nicolson also welcomed the indirect benefits of the marginalization suffered by aesthete-intellectuals within the philistine culture of the school: 'true originality will by such measures merely be pruned to greater florescence; and sham originality will, thank God, be suppressed.'[32]

Many schoolboy aesthetes used the language of political struggle to describe their experiences. Walter Le Strange, who was at Eton in the 1920s, confided his political hopes to his diary: 'May everyone be free! Let not the wretched new boy be oppressed and mishandled just for the convenience of the idle Capitalists, that is to say, the self-made priests of Athleticism, of the Public School Spirit of Imperialism.'[33] This is not just overheated fantasy – although it does have a strongly hormonal reek to it – but also a self-conscious use of the trope of the public school as a microcosm of the nation state. When they looked back on their younger selves from the perspective of posterity, however, many former aesthetes sought to downplay the significance of their rebellion. In his 1973 article 'From Bloomsbury to Marxism', Anthony Blunt explained the motivations behind the formation of the Hereticks:

> to express our disapproval of the Establishment generally, of the more out-of-date and pedantic masters, of all the forms of organized sport, of the Officers' Training Corps and all of the other features that we hated in school life, not so much the physical discomforts – they were almost taken for granted – but you might say the intellectual discomforts of the school.[34]

In Blunt's telling, the chief purpose of the magazine was to voice dissatisfaction with the school itself, rather than to mount an attack on social injustice. At its core aestheticism was a philosophy of individual freedom and self-fulfilment that was pitched against the peculiar institutional culture of the ruling elite. Perhaps it is best understood as a new kind of identity politics that was confined to the rarefied world of the upper classes. It was a way of wearing one's privilege – with flair and irony, instead of entitlement and duty – rather than a fundamental challenge to the social system that reproduced that privilege.

Ultimately, the most significant legacy of aesthete subculture was its redefinition of how to achieve success in the world beyond the school. Acton recalled that in his senior year at Eton, when the time came for him to discuss his career plans with his parents, 'my sole ambition was to write poetry and more poetry . . . I would not compromise. My parents would have liked me to enter the diplomatic service, but in spite of the argument that some diplomats had found leisure for writing – I was too obstinate to be persuaded.'[35] This is a common thread that runs through aesthete memoirs: the desire to avoid respectable careers in favour of a life devoted to artistic creation. The pathways that they took to reach that goal were myriad. Some, including Betjeman, Evelyn Waugh and MacNeice, taught at schools or universities to buy themselves time to write. A few dropped out of upper-class society altogether in order to experience 'ordinary' life and gather material for novels or memoirs: Henry Yorke worked anonymously in his father's Birmingham factory; George Orwell went down and out in Paris and London. Some floundered in the wider world beyond the institution. One of the best scholarly studies of Howard bears the subtitle 'portrait of a failure'. Freed from the demands of regular work by his inherited income, Howard flitted back and forth between London and the Continent, always seeking out new intensities of pleasure and feeling, but all the while failing to make good on his youthful promise by producing the magnum opus that everyone expected. Howard's later years were haunted by a sense of unfulfilled potential, the creeping realization that he would never live up to the stunning precocity he displayed as a thirteen-year-old dandy at Eton.

The most common career path for the former schoolboy aesthete, however, led into the upper reaches of the cultural establishment. Connolly famously observed in *Enemies of Promise* that the two greatest obstacles to literary success were 'the pram in the hall' and periodical journalism.[36] The latter of these distractions was especially pronounced for Connolly and his peers, who enjoyed easy access to a network of cultural institutions that were dominated by men who shared the same class and educational backgrounds. Not only the quality Sunday broadsheets – Connolly was joint chief book reviewer of the *Sunday Times* from 1952 – but also niche literary and artistic magazines, political weeklies, such as *The Spectator* and *New Statesman*, the new BBC radio service, especially the high-brow Third Programme, which began life in 1946, the booming publishing industry and government bodies such as the Arts Council and the British Council were the preserve of a new cultural elite that was predominantly upper middle-class and public school-educated. In *Our Age*, his insider's portrait of mid-twentieth-century intellectual life, Noel Annan characterizes this elite as 'protean', defined by achievement and skill, as well as by family background, personal connections and social class.[37] Broadly speaking, members of the mid-century cultural elite were more cosmopolitan, pluralistic and permissive than their predecessors in the pre-war era. They were also defined in large part by their ironic or ambivalent relationship to their own educational privilege. A lifelong resentment of the school's phoney *esprit de corps* and hidebound conservatism went hand in hand with the polished manners and cultural range that were a product of the very same educational background. As Annan puts it, his generation both rejected the old school tie and enjoyed its continuing resonance as a powerful 'cultural bond'.[38]

Many former schoolboy aesthetes found themselves ideally placed to thrive in this new cultural landscape, which now encompassed film and radio as well as newspapers and novels. A few standout examples demonstrate the new career trajectory. Betjeman, who we last encountered prancing like a nymph on the sidelines of a Marlborough rugby match, went on to become Poet Laureate and a regular fixture on BBC radio and television. In addition to serving as a Labour MP, Tom Driberg, one of the Lancing 'Bolshies', wrote an enormously popular gossip column in the *Daily Express* under the nom de plume 'William Hickey', in which he combined reports of stodgy society gatherings with glancing references to avant-garde culture and radical politics. John Sutro, a member of the Eton Society of Arts and part of what Betjeman dubbed the 'Golden Age of Aesthetes', became a successful film producer and served as a judge at the 7th Berlin International Film Festival in 1957.

The dandy-aesthetes of the early twentieth century helped to forge what would later become one of the established career paths for the sons and daughters of privilege: from public school art rebel to establishment taste-maker. Their legacy is registered in today's employment statistics, which show how the cultural industries – journalism, museums, the theatre and so on – are still dominated by public school graduates.[39] Indeed, the very use of the term 'the establishment' to refer to the informal networks of power and privilege that exist alongside the official channels of government was popularized in the 1950s to refer to a prominent group of former schoolboy aesthetes. The journalist Henry Fairlie used the term in an article for *The Spectator* in September 1955 to describe what he called 'the meteorology of power' that emanated from the opinion-forming professions of journalism, the arts and academia. This 'climate of opinion' set the parameters within which actual governmental power could be wielded. Broadly liberal in its politics, the establishment, as Fairlie saw it, dampened the radical edges of British political life: 'quite as resistant to true Conservatism as to true Socialism, the voice of the status quo'. The tone of this voice was 'moderate, civilised, insinuating, as irresistible as the cadences of Sir Harold Nicolson'.[40] Nicolson was a former schoolboy aesthete who had escaped the dull grind of life at Wellington College in the Edwardian period by fleeing to the aesthetic elsewheres of Lucretius, Shelley, Max Beerbohm and Walter Pater. His series of biographical sketches, *Some People* (1927), includes perhaps the most perfect encapsulation of the antithetical figures of the athlete and the aesthete. In the forms of J. D. Marstock, school cricket captain, loyal perfect, paragon of 'good form' and entirely empty-headed drone, and Lambert Orme, the louche, undulating dandy-aesthete, Nicolson defined the outer reaches of upper-class English masculinity.

Nicolson's own character was an urbane synthesis of these two impossible extremes, the ultimate establishment insider on the one hand and a paragon of bohemianism on the other (he and his wife, Vita Sackville-West, conducted one of the most famous bisexual open marriages in English history). After school and university, Nicolson worked his way through most of Britain's elite institutions, including the Diplomatic Service, the Foreign Office, parliament (as both a Mosleyite and a Labour MP) and the BBC. He produced journalism for the *Evening Standard* and *The Times*, wrote biographies of Swinburne, Tennyson and Byron and published his own diaries to considerable acclaim. This is the ultimate fate of a certain kind of schoolboy dissident in the age of aestheticism: a comfortable position at the heart of the liberal establishment. It was partly this sense of clannish solidarity among a small coterie of privileged radicals that led to the intellectual counter-revolution that was waged in the 1950s by F. R. and Q. D. Leavis, the husband and wife critics who skewered the aesthetes of the 1920s as the products of unearned privilege. In reviewing Connolly's *Enemies of Promise* in the magazine *Scrutiny*, Q. D. Leavis complained that the literary elite was a closed shop run by a cabal of old school chums: 'Those who get the jobs are the most fashionable boys in the school, or those with feline charm, or a sensual mouth and long eyelashes.'[41]

THROUGHOUT THE TWENTIETH century, long after the golden age of the Bright Young Things was left behind, the struggles between the schoolboy tribes of athletes and aesthetes continued to resonate in the unlikely realm of popular adventure fiction. Cultural and political tensions that began in the boarding house were replayed in the pages of spy thrillers by such luminaries as John Buchan, H. C. McNeile (otherwise known as 'Sapper'), Ian Fleming and John le Carré. In the iconic forms of Richard Hannay, Bulldog Drummond and James Bond, the schoolboy athlete matured into the figure of the gentleman spy, who triumphs over the nation's foes by virtue of his physical strength and worldly *savoir faire*. But while the gentleman spy always comes out on top, his life is made difficult by a motley crew of perverse criminal masterminds, treacherous double agents and deracinated political radicals, all of whom confirm the philistine schoolmaster's distrust of art and intellectualism as a potential gateway to treason. This is another unexpected way in which the British public school has left its mark on the wider reaches of popular culture. Next time you find yourself at the multiplex with the latest multi-million-dollar instalment of the James Bond franchise booming away in widescreen, pinch yourself and remember that this global icon of British masculinity was created by an author who was a contemporary of Howard and Acton at Eton in the 1920s.

The writer and critic Richard Usborne famously dubbed the leading men of British adventure fiction's golden age 'clubland heroes'.[42] Perhaps the clubland hero most familiar to readers today is Buchan's Richard Hannay, a South African mining engineer who leaves his beloved veldt for the fleshpots of London, only to become embroiled in a global conspiracy that leads him into the very highest echelons of the British secret state. In spite of his self-educated colonial background, Hannay's character is Edwardian public school through and through. He is self-reliant, physically strong, feels cramped and 'slack' in the urban scene, respects intelligence but distrusts intellectualism, travels the world but feels most at home wherever the Union Jack is flown. More than anything, however, it is Hannay's capacity for physical exertion that makes him a paragon of the early twentieth-century public school spirit. As Usborne notes, for Hannay, 'exhaustion is an end in itself'.[43] His tireless tramps across the moors, as well as his resistance to bad weather and physical discomfort, bespeak the same need to pacify the wayward male body that was expressed in the public school in the form of organized games, cold showers and prefect surveillance. The archetype is still with us today in the form of public school explorers such as Sir Ranulph Fiennes, Pen Hadow and Bear Grylls, all of whom sound like they should be fictional characters in an adventure novel, and all of whom share the same delight in subjecting themselves to extremes of physical endurance in the service of some obscure ethical ideal.

If Hannay's natural habitat is the Highland moor, then Bulldog Drummond's is the bar at his club, or the dining room at the Ritz, or at the wheel of a Rolls-Royce Silver Phantom. Indeed, Bulldog Drummond is the clubland hero par excellence, many of whose adventures unfold in and around the eminently clubbable purlieus of Mayfair and the Home Counties. Bulldog lodges at Half Moon Street, is a member of the Junior Sports Club on St James's Square, is frequently clad in the very best English tailoring, often with a fetching carnation in his buttonhole, and is forever dumping heaps of well-used sports equipment in the hallway for his sharp-tongued housemaid to clear away. He is also a First World War veteran, who is bored stiff by the return to civilian life. In order to relieve his lassitude, he places an advertisement in *The Times*: 'Demobilised officer, finding peace incredibly tedious, would welcome diversion. Legitimate if possible; but crime, if of a comparatively humorous description, no objection.'[44] Not for Bulldog Drummond the post-war revolt against the generation who sent its sons to die for an empty ideal. Instead he seeks out further adventures that will confirm his loyalty and satisfy his appetite for violence. When a case becomes particularly hot, he calls upon a group of old schoolfriends to form a team of elite crime fighters, all of whom acknowledge Bulldog's natural superiority and fitness to lead. This is often the moral of a Bulldog Drummond tale: it is the absence of leadership, forcefully exercised from above by a natural ruling class of aristocrats and gentlemen, that has led to the creeping influence of socialists, liberals, intellectuals, Jews, financiers and trade unionists that threatens to destroy civilization. When Bulldog and his friends capture these assorted rotters, they administer their own brand of freelance justice, which seems suspiciously similar to the treatment meted out to aesthete poseurs after a good bump supper. Bulldog and co. drag their foes behind a moving car, partially shave their heads, duck them in moats and round them up and incarcerate them in what looks to all intents and purposes like a concentration camp. This is prefect justice administered on the global stage.

But even in the works of Buchan and Sapper there are little shivers of doubt that trouble the granite self-confidence of the gentleman hero. Both Hannay and Bulldog fear the enemy within. Over the course of their many adventures, Hannay and his friends adopt a variety of disguises in order to outwit their enemies. This is a common thread within British adventure fiction that runs through the works of Kipling, Rider Haggard and Robert Louis Stevenson. The hero's breadth of ethnographic knowledge and cunning spycraft enable him to adopt the dress and customs of different ethnicities almost at will, all the while retaining his core identity as a British gentleman. But in *The Thirty-nine Steps* Hannay is confronted with the inverse scenario:

the fanatical German spies plotting to smuggle military secrets out of Britain who disguise themselves as pukka, sports-loving Englishmen. These spies don the garb of the English gentleman with such incomparable skill that Hannay experiences a kind of vertigo that threatens to undo the very fabric of his identity. The scene takes a horrifying twist when Hannay confronts the spies in their cottage, which is decked out with sports trophies and invitations to clubland dinners. Hannay looks directly into the eyes that peer out from beneath the gentlemanly exterior and perceives that 'a white fanatic heat burned in them'.[45] This is a chilling moment that reveals the fundamental instability of the gentlemanly identity that Hannay so cherishes: it too can be converted into a theatrical performance and deployed for inimical ends.

Bulldog Drummond experiences a similar moment of existential crisis during his first adventure, which sees him foil a dastardly plot by a group of international capitalists, trade unionists and university lecturers that is organized by Carl Peterson, who is to Drummond what Ernst Blofeld would later be to James Bond. Peterson's aide, Henry Lakington, is an Oxford-trained scientist with the 'artistic touch', whose sadistic excesses include dipping his live victims in a bath of acid.[46] Lakington is the perfect embodiment of the dangers of intellectualism, a brilliant Englishman who has been led astray because he trusted the values of intelligence and creativity over those of character and self-discipline. When Bulldog reflects on what caused Lakington's swerve from brilliant Oxonian to demonic criminal genius, he concludes that 'some kink in the brain, some little cog wrong in the wonderful mechanism', has led to his perverse hatred for English values.[47] The horror of the scene lies in the fact that Bulldog Drummond is seeing an alternative side of his own personality. Bulldog and Lakington are the divided halves of a whole man: hero and villain, loyalist and traitor, athlete and aesthete.

Fleming's Bond was a post-war remodel of the gentleman spy hero inherited from Buchan and Sapper. This was the Edwardian public school ideal refashioned for the new world of the welfare state, angry young men and the glossy lifestyle journalism of the kind Fleming himself wrote for the *Sunday Times*. Bond is more individualistic, less of a team player and much more sexually predatory, but he is still an iteration of the old clubland archetype. He has the same fetish for 1930s Rolls-Royces, feels most at home in the same wood-panelled rooms, amid the same thick curls of cigar smoke, and embodies the same strenuous capacity for dishing out and withstanding extreme violence. In his first novel, *Casino Royale* (1953), Fleming accentuated the moral ambiguity of the genre and played up the two-sidedness of his gentleman hero. In a pivotal scene, the global terrorist network SMERSH uses a suitcase bomb to blow up both enemy agents and innocent bystanders on a Monte Carlo high street. Reeling from the shock, Bond confides to Mathis, his counterpart in the French secret service, that 'when one's young, it seems very easy to distinguish between right and wrong, but as one gets older it becomes more difficult. At school it's easy to pick out one's own villains and heroes and one grows up wanting to be a hero and kill the villains.'[48] Bond's traumatized response exposes the paper-thin line between his identity as a renegade but loyal servant of the Crown and his alternative life as an enemy of the state. In many ways *Casino Royale* is the most thoughtful of Fleming's Bond books. Not only is the spare narrative voice and tight focus on Bond's inner consciousness an echo of the existentialist fiction of Sartre and Camus, but the canny identification of the school as a potentially fallible mechanism for inculcating lifelong loyalties in its pupils would also prove insightful as details of the Cambridge spy ring emerged over the subsequent decades.

*Casino Royale* was written in the wake of the 'missing diplomats' scandal, in which Guy Burgess and Donald Maclean fled to the Soviet Union fearing their cover had been blown. This was the first instalment of what would become a long-running saga, during which it was revealed that a group of five double agents within the British intelligence services had been passing state secrets to the Soviets. Apart from the 'fifth man', John Cairncross, who was the son of a Scottish ironmonger, the Cambridge spies were all products of the late-imperial public school world. They were schoolboy dissidents who had crafted their identities in opposition to the mindless conformity of the institution: Guy Burgess, the debauched, high-living history scholar; Donald Maclean, the superstar linguist; and Kim Philby, the suave well-rounded man. The last of the Cambridge Spies to be publicly identified was Anthony Blunt, Director of the Courtauld Institute, the prestigious art-historical research centre, Surveyor of the Queen's Pictures and former Marlborough Heretick. Blunt described how 'the intellectual influences I underwent [at school] coloured the whole of my later development'.[49] This is the inverse image of Bond's claim that 'at school it's easy to pick out one's own villains'. In spite of their subtly staged conversions to respectability in the later 1930s, the Cambridge spies harboured a secret core of resentment against the institutions that had nurtured them, educated them and prepared them for positions of authority and command. In his article on the soft power of the liberal establishment, Fairlie even suggested that Burgess and Maclean's friends in high places had actively colluded in covering up their defection when they fled to Moscow in 1951.

After Bond's moment of doubt in Monte Carlo, Fleming ensured that his hero remained on the straight and narrow for the rest of his career. Despite often falling foul of his bureaucratic handlers, 007's renegade impulses never again tended towards outright defection. In *You Only Live Twice* (1964), the last of Fleming's Bond books, the author included an obituary that sketched out his dead hero's early life. Like Kipling's Stalky, Bond is a licensed rebel, whose maverick style enables him to operate at the very edges of legality but always in the service of authority. We learn that Bond is the son of a Scottish father and a Swiss mother, both of whom were killed in a plane crash when he was a boy. Taken in after his parents' death by a maiden aunt, Bond grows up first in the downy folds of a Kentish village called 'Pett Bottom', then in the harsher environment of Eton College, from which he is expelled for an indiscretion with a chambermaid. After Eton, he is transferred to Fettes, his father's old boarding school in Edinburgh, which seems better suited to the prickly, Scottish side of his character. At Fettes he makes some lifelong friendships 'among the traditionally famous athletic circles at the school', represents the school as a lightweight boxer and starts the first ever public school judo club.[50] This is an ideal start for a young boy who is to become a 'blunt instrument' of covert state violence – just the right combination of orphaned outsider and establishment insider.

But in spite of his 24-carat credentials, there is always something not quite right about Bond's gentlemanly persona, something a little *de trop* in his keen eye for the outward appurtenances of upper-class masculinity. Fleming equipped Bond with a fetishist's eye for the finer things in life, including classic automobiles, vintage brandy, fine tailoring, expensive watches, haute cuisine and women's bodies. Bond is the living embodiment of the adman's promise that you too can be a pukka English gentleman if only you purchase the right consumer goods. A number of contemporary critics noted the hint of vulgarity in Bond's delight in the externalities of gentlemanly taste to the exclusion of the previous generation of clubland heroes' moral code of chivalry and reserve. In his 1958 essay on 'The Case of Mr Fleming', Bernard Bergonzi dismissed Fleming's depiction of upper-class gentility as a fiasco of 'vulgarity and display'.[51] Paul Johnson pursued a similar line of attack when he observed that Bond combines 'the sadism of a schoolboy bully, the mechanical, two-dimensional sex-longings of a frustrated adolescent, and the crude snob-cravings of a suburban adult'.[52] Fleming himself might have come from the right background – Eton, Sandhurst, naval intelligence, broadsheet journalism – but the suspicion was that in selling the gentlemanly ideal to the masses, he had turned it into a rather vulgar mixture of sex, violence and brand name consumer goods.

Fleming's close friend Cyril Connolly went a step further in his deconstruction of the Bond myth with his delicious parody 'Bond Strikes Camp'. At the beginning of Connolly's story, M asks Bond to go undercover as a drag queen to entrap a visiting Russian spy with a taste for cross-dressing. In Connolly's parody, Bond is literally rebuilt from the ground up for his undercover mission, like some kind of action figure mannequin. He is shaved, waxed, bewigged and clothed in preparation for deep cover in the shadowy world of the 'Homintern', the queer cabal at the heart of the Russian security establishment. He is even equipped with 'the very latest in falsies – foam-rubber, with electronically self-erecting nipples', in order to pull off the complete Femme-Bot makeover.[53] Connolly plays on Bond's queer eye for an object, his aesthete's taste for the finer things, his prissy concern for couture. He suggests that Bond's hyper-masculine excess of sex and violence is a smokescreen that conceals a more tender inner-life. Bond also is a two-sided man.

Fleming was himself a product of the very same 1920s world of athletes and aesthetes that was the seedbed for the spy scandals of the Cold War era. And while he was, like his fictional creation, a somewhat maverick member of the athletic set, who represented his school at steeplechase and hurdles, he also had a touch of the schoolboy artist about him. In his senior year at Eton he put on Byronic airs and published his own 'ephemeral', *The Wyvern*. This little magazine may not have had the same pink-covered cachet as the *Eton Candle*, but Fleming drew on his socialite mother's connections with the Chelsea arts set to solicit contributions from Augustus John, Sir Edward Lutyens and Vita Sackville-West. In later life Fleming hardened into a more conventional kind of golf club bigot, but he always retained the impression of his formative youth in the aesthetic twenties.

Taking a cue from Connolly's parodic vamping, we might indulge in a little pop psychology of our own and point out the way in which Bond's nemeses function as disavowed projections of his own deeper self. Fleming was famously dismissive of attempts to psychoanalyse either himself or his creation, but then he would be, wouldn't he, especially if Bond gives subconscious expression to the central fault line within his class's dominant construction of masculinity? Many of Bond's enemies inherit their aesthete-intellectual tendencies from the moral universe of Buchan and Sapper. Mr Big revels in the 'artistry' of his crimes.[54] Auric Goldfinger is a 'poet in deeds'.[55] Ernst Blofeld is inspired by decadent literary heroes like Poe, Lautréamont and de Sade.[56] Hugo Drax worms his way into the heart of the British establishment by adopting 'the façade of a gentleman'.[57] This is a rogue's gallery of aesthete-intellectual enemies within. The whole thing reeks of the Eton prefects' common room, circa 1922.

For all of the moral ambiguity of *Casino Royale*, the most nuanced portrait of the two-sided gentleman spy is surely John le Carré's classic 1974 novel *Tinker, Tailor, Soldier, Spy*. If Buchan, Sapper and Fleming helped to create the myth, then le Carré sought to cut through to the historical reality that lay behind it. By the time he came to write *Tinker, Tailor*, le Carré had already had ample opportunity to observe the ruling elite at close quarters, first as a junior master at Eton and later as an intelligence officer for the British Foreign Service in Germany. In the narrative of George Smiley's return from retirement to hunt a Soviet mole in the highest echelons of the British Secret Service, le Carré found a fictional form in which to explore the social and psychological pressures that shaped the Cambridge spy scandal. With its intricate web of suspicion and paranoia, cross and double-cross, as well as its setting in the ancestral spaces of the prep school, the gentlemen's club, the country house and the *sub rosa* government agency, *Tinker, Tailor* describes nothing less than the slow death of an empire in the form of a series of personal betrayals.

The two sides of the gentlemanly ideal are expressed in the forms of Jim Prideaux and Bill Haydon, old university chums and one-time lovers, who find themselves on opposing sides in a covert war. Prideaux is the athlete-warrior to Haydon's aesthete-intellectual. Prideaux is terse and watchful, enjoys long tramps over the misty Quantocks, distrusts 'ju ju men' or any kind of obtuse intellectual type, reads Buchan novels to his boys in the dormitory at night and thinks Britain 'the best place in the whole damn world'.[58] Haydon is charming, ironic, priapic, a gifted painter who once exhibited in the finest Oxford galleries, a hatcher of daring plots and cunning ruses, a ruling class golden boy who shines with a special kind of English glamour. In their binary characters, Prideaux and Haydon stand for the two halves of a divided self that finds its expression first in the form of schoolboy and undergraduate factions and later as ideological opponents. In a report to his university tutor and secret service handler, Haydon describes Prideaux as 'my other half'.[59]

Le Carré often uses the language of the boarding school to describe secret intelligence work. The ministerial aide, Lacon, acts like 'Whitehall's head prefect'.[60] After a late night at work, the officers and secretaries relax in the atmosphere of a 'dormitory feast'.[61] Even the Circus jargon that dubs the female secretaries 'mothers' reinforces the profoundly male character of the institution. This is yet another masculine culture that emanates from the boarding school and then seeps throughout the wider reaches of the establishment, from the Oxford college to the gentlemen's club to the officers' mess. But *Tinker,*

*Tailor* exposes the rot that has eaten its way into this wood-panelled world. Connie Sachs, one of the few women to forge a meaningful role for herself in the wartime Circus as head archivist, weeps tears of nostalgic reverie for the lost days of Imperial purpose. 'Poor loves,' she says of her darling boys, Prideaux and Haydon, 'trained to Empire, trained to rule the waves. All gone. All taken away. Bye-bye, world.'[62] Although written later, *Tinker, Tailor* deals with the same moment of post-Imperial soul-searching that Fleming dramatized in *Casino Royale*. While Fleming pulls Bond back from the abyss and reinforces his identity as a machine-tooled gentleman hero, Le Carré amplifies the mood of ambiguity and confusion.

At the conclusion of the novel, through a thick fog of sedatives and false consciousness, Bill Haydon reveals the motives for his treachery. After what Smiley dismisses as boilerplate denunciations of Western capitalism, Haydon achieves a modicum of moral clarity when he describes his hatred of American materialism and laments the decline of the civilized ideals of the nineteenth century. He concludes with the vague but revealing assertion that 'it's an aesthetic judgement as much as anything.'[63] Le Carré may depart from the mainline of espionage adventure fiction in almost all respects, but when he cites Bill Haydon's aesthetic sensibility as the source of his treachery, he is firmly in line with his predecessors. Earlier in the narrative, when the identity of the mole remains a matter of page-turning mystery, le Carré drops numerous hints about Haydon's guilt. Discussing Haydon's artistic endeavours, Roy Bland misquotes F. Scott Fitzgerald's famous statement that 'an artist is a bloke who can hold two fundamentally opposed views and still function.'[64] And when Haydon sweeps past the star-struck Peter Guillam in the Circus corridor, he is compared to Dorian Gray, a hint not only at his split personality but to the fluid political ideals of the aestheticist movement. Even at the height of the Cold War, many decades after the heady days of the 1920s, the aesthete factions are at war with the hearty loyalists.

Giles and Esmond Romilly at Wellington College, 1934.

# SIX

# Red Menace

In the small hours of 8 February 1934 Esmond Romilly sneaked out of his boarding house at Wellington College and made his way to the local train station. His escape had been carefully planned. He went to sleep that evening fully clothed, with a packed suitcase stowed beneath his bed. All he had to do was push the covers back, grab his belongings and don his anarchist's Homburg hat, before stealing down the corridor. In a downstairs classroom Esmond waited for his brother Giles, who had agreed to carry his suitcase and help him sneak past the porter's lodge. But Giles couldn't get out of his boarding house that night, so after a short wait, Esmond decided to go it alone. Undeterred, he walked into town only to find the station locked for the night. After a fearful wait in the cold February morning, Esmond was glad to see the stationmaster arrive and open the gates without asking why a fifteen-year-old boy with a public school accent was so eagerly awaiting the first train to London.

Esmond Romilly was bound for 4 Parton Street, WC1. This was the address of Parton Books, a radical bookstore that served both as a supplier of left-wing literature and an informal community centre for the radicals and bohemians of 1930s Bloomsbury. In the poorly lit store, tables groaned under the weight of back issues of the journal of the Marx-Engels-Lenin Institute; the floor was covered with disorderly piles of *Communist International* and the *Daily Worker*; and the walls were adorned with the bold and angular forms of Soviet propaganda posters. The place resonated with what another schoolboy runaway, Philip Toynbee, would later call 'a marvellous atmosphere of conspiracy and purpose'.[1] For Esmond, Parton Street was a shabby heterotopia, a disorderly space of possibility and adventure that seemed a million miles away from Wellington College – except that when he first discovered the shop, he found that its owner, David Archer, was an old Wellingtonian. At their first meeting, Archer and Romilly salted their talk of international socialism with reminiscences about their old school.

Over the next few months Parton Street became the nerve centre for *Out of Bounds*, the underground newspaper that Esmond and his brother had started to publish in January of that year. The fallout from the publication of the first issue was one of the reasons for Esmond's flight from Wellington. *Out of Bounds* included on its first page a manifesto, which outlined the core principles of the newspaper:

> *Out of Bounds* is against Reaction, Militarism and Fascism in the Public Schools. We attack not only the vast machinery of propaganda which forms the basis of the public school system, and makes them so useful in a vicious and obsolete form of society; we oppose not only the semi-compulsory nature of the OTC [Officer Training Corps] and the hypocritical bluff about 'character-building'. We oppose every one of the absurd restrictions and petty rules and regulations which would be more applicable to a kindergarten than to boys between the ages of fourteen and nineteen.[2]

The newspaper wore its outlaw credentials with pride. In his editorial in the first edition, Esmond stated that, 'we shall be deliberately corrupting youth'. 'Banned in Uppingham – banned in Cheltenham', boasted the masthead for the second edition. This was an all-out attack on the public schools, delivered in the mixed tones of juvenile delinquency and doctrinaire Marxism.

When the press got wind of this extraordinary publication, the reading public was treated to a variety of alarmed headlines. The scandal was rendered all the spicier by Esmond's family pedigree. His father, Bertram, was a high-ranking officer in the Army, and his mother, Nellie, was the daughter of the 10th Earl of Airlie and the sister of Winston Churchill's wife, Clementine. While the *Daily Telegraph* and *Daily Express* both published short, disparaging pieces about *Out of Bounds*, it was the *Daily Mail* that proved the most reliable source of tabloid outrage. Its multiple headlines over a two-column story thundered 'Red Menace in Public Schools! Moscow Attempts to Corrupt Boys. Officer's Son Sponsors Extreme Journal. Scotland Yard Enquiry'.[3] Esmond conducted interviews with reporters from his boarding house's public telephone and the press coverage continued for days. When it heard of Esmond's flight from the school, the *Daily Mail* once again made hay with the story, highlighting his well-connected, upper-crust family: 'Mr Churchill's Nephew Vanishes from Public School'; '"Under Influence of London Communists" Says Mother'.

Esmond refused all entreaties from his parents to return to school or move back into the family home in Pimlico. Instead he lodged above the bookshop, worked on the next issue of *Out of Bounds* and enjoyed the delights of youth and freedom in bohemian London. Parton Street became the nerve centre for the campaign to radicalize the nation's youth and counteract the baleful influence of the public schools. Esmond received runaways from other boarding schools who fled to join the cause, and he made connections with sympathizers who remained immured within their institutions. In a similar scene to Esmond's escape from Wellington, Philip Toynbee sneaked out of Rugby College and boarded the first train for London. 'This was a period of noble schoolboy passion,' he recalled in his memoir, 'I was dry tinder to this spark.'[4] Gavin Ewart joined from Wellington, John Peet from Bootham, H. W. Stubbs from Charterhouse and Phyllis Baker from Ashford Girls' School. These contributors wrote articles about Fascist youth organizations, the Officers' Training Corps (OTC), Marxist theory, world politics, school discipline and how, contrary to the threats of spurious medical authorities, masturbation had no ill effects upon the health.

Esmond quickly learned how to manipulate the press, using his upper-crust background and bombastic rhetoric to lure journalists into disseminating his ideas. He did, however, have to adapt to life in the tabloid spotlight. When the papers first picked up on *Out of Bounds*, he found his startled features plastered over the front pages and his ideas traduced. He learned to fight back with his own attempts to craft the narrative of his escape and curate his public image. On 14 April 1934 Esmond convened the *Out of Bounds* conference at Meg's Café, a local haunt of the Parton Street crew. Delegates from Wellington, St Paul's, University College School and North London Collegiate School for Girls discussed the reactionary influence of the public schools in modern society and radical strategies for change. Esmond arranged for the conference to be covered by the *Sunday Graphic*, which obliged in spectacular style by running a photograph of the delegates on its front page under the headline, 'War on "Play the Game You Cads!" Schoolboys' Plan to Put the World to Right'.[5] Esmond succeeded in presenting himself as a radical young man in a hurry. His youthful precociousness became a national media phenomenon. At Parton Street he received fan mail written by besotted girls after lights out in their dormitories. One girl wrote from Auckland Girls' Grammar School: 'I am writing to you because . . . well; I don't exactly know why. But it's *you* I want to write to; if you understand, Old Chap!'[6] This was upper-class delinquency for the mass-media age, a teenage escapade carefully designed to provoke outrage from parents and desire from their children.

The four issues of *Out of Bounds* that appeared between January 1934 and June 1935 mounted a consistent, if somewhat rhetorically rigid, attack on the public school system. According to the magazine, the public school was the very cornerstone of the corrupt system of privilege and inequality that prevailed in Great Britain. The ethos of gentlemanly 'character' was a recipe for narrow-mindedness and conformity. Muscular Christianity, militarism and prefect-fagging were part of an institutional machinery that protected the interests of the ruling class and helped to thwart the socialist brotherhood of man. Rigid discipline, lack of privacy and the enduring bugbears about sexuality bred neurosis and repression. If it wasn't already explicitly fascist, then the public school system was vulnerable to reactionary elements that were plotting to make it so. The modernist cover design of the first issue depicted a densely packed urban scene, the gleaming white forms of which cut sharply against a smaller image in the bottom right corner of a dark clump of ancient school buildings. This was aesthetic as well as ideological warfare, in which the bold new forms of modernity were pitted against the reactionary Gothicism of the public school ideal. The critique was continued inside with a dramatic parody of public school fiction, 'Derek: Or Tittle by Tattle, a Contemporary Mime', a broad comedy in which communist agents in black silk pyjamas shoot Plainbottom, the cricket captain, in the eye just as he is about to score the winning boundary in the big cricket match. This is a long way from the aesthete polish and intellectual ambition of Howard and Acton's *Eton Candle* of just over a decade earlier. *Out of Bounds* was a rough-and-ready mixture of fiercely ideological critique, cartoonish satire and knockabout wit.

Indeed, as the 1920s became the 1930s, the language and symbols of schoolboy rebellion shifted. In place of the aesthete hedonism of the 1920s, the youth culture of the 1930s took on a much harder political edge. Where the previous generation had signalled its dissent by enveloping itself in what Louis MacNeice called a 'private world of sense impressions', the radical schoolboys of the 1930s turned to national and global politics for the terms of their revolt. Many of the articles in *Out of Bounds* also express a desire to undo the false boundaries between genders and classes that were maintained by the elite education system. Alongside Marxist critiques of Imperialism and the OTC, *Out of Bounds* published articles on co-education, progressive schools and the psychosocial effects of gender segregation in the boarding school system. One contributor denounced the 'warped attitude to women' fostered by the boys' public school system, while another lamented that public schoolboys were 'incapable of sensible personal relationship' with the opposite sex.[7] Parton Books was a predominantly masculine zone, but it was not exclusively so. Esmond and Giles made a point of including female contributors in the magazine and inviting girls' schools to send delegates to their conferences. The aim of the magazine was not just to launch barbs against a hated institution, but also to build new alliances that crossed the old divisions of class and gender.

In addition to the essays and poems contained in each issue, *Out of Bounds* also carried regular dispatches from the frontlines of the anti-Fascist struggle within the public schools. A network of activists sent in dispatches that Esmond and his editors then collated and published in a regular column. In effect, Parton Street served as the sorting office and *Out of Bounds* as the delivery mechanism for an underground postal service that joined up the radical elements within the nation's boarding schools. Esmond saw this is an invaluable service, especially in view of the isolation and persecution often suffered by left-wing students within the hostile environment of the total institution. The first two issues of the paper included bulletins on the suppression of left-wing literature at Aldenham, protests at Charterhouse over a new inscription in the chapel that read 'Who Dies for England Lives', sales figures for *Out of Bounds* at Eton and Wellington, the success of a motion at the Gresham's debating society in favour of Fascism over Socialism, and a group of officers at Wellington who wore swastikas at an OTC field day.

In the memoir he co-authored with Giles in 1935, Esmond explained the rationale for his strategy of resistance: 'I found in the public school system an elaborate organisation for propaganda which was to produce in the minds of the boys a ruling class ideology. All right, I thought, I will fight against that propaganda with my propaganda.'[8] This explains a lot about Esmond's well-publicized antics, both during the runaway spring of 1934 and throughout his later life. Esmond crafted for himself a public image as a glamorous schoolboy runaway. With his rhetorical bombast, frequent scrapes with authority and scrappy, street urchin style, he became the radical alter ego of the traditional public school man. Even the elaborate Marxist jargon that he spouted was a kind of linguistic weapon, intended as much to offend the sensibilities of the upper classes as to diagnose the structural contradictions of global capitalism. In his editorial to the first edition of *Out of Bounds*, Esmond observed that, 'the public schools are sly creatures. They have a horror of publicity, of being in "the news". They like to remain powerfully behind the scenes, accepting their tremendous responsibilities, fulfilling their functions, but never discussing them.'[9] Running away from school and publishing an underground magazine wasn't simply a hare-brained adventure – although it was no doubt enormously good fun – but was also a strategic decision designed to puncture the public schools' culture of secrecy and air of unflappable permanence.

Between organizing the *Out of Bounds* campaign and writing articles for the national press, Esmond spent his time in London campaigning against Oswald Mosley and his British Union of Fascists (BUF). In the 1920s and '30s both Communist and Fascist groups sought in particular to enlist the young to their causes. The membership of the BUF was predominantly under the age of thirty and drawn from working-class areas with high levels of unemployment. Mosley peddled a message of national purity, youthful vigour and state-funded employment schemes. On the other side, organizations such as the British Federation of Youth, the National Union of Students, the University Socialist Federation and the Young Communist League enlisted progressive-minded youths in the cause of international socialism.[10] These political groups were part of a much longer history that stretches back to the French Revolution, in which youth has been cast as a political vanguard and an emblem of futurity. The same symbolic resonance – as well as the same impetus to organization and discipline – underpinned the formation of the Scouts, the Boys' Brigade and the public school reform movement of the Victorian era.

*Out of Bounds* had originally grown out of a meeting of the Federation of Student Societies, a Marxist organization that sought to coordinate the efforts of different left-wing student groups around the country. At that meeting Esmond had proposed a newspaper as an ideal way to gauge support within the public schools and coordinate any subsequent campaign. But *Out of Bounds* quickly became an autonomous entity, driven by Esmond's enormous personal charisma and subject to his distrust of well-meaning but ineffective organizations. Nevertheless, Esmond, Giles, Philip Toynbee, John Peet and the rest of the *Out of Bounds* team saw themselves as part of a youthful vanguard whose duty it was to define the political future.

But Communist austerity also went hand in hand with youthful hedonism. Before they joined the violent protests against Mosley's BUF at the infamous Olympia rally in April 1934, the gang sneaked into the Romilly family home while Nellie and the Colonel were out. With a Marlene Dietrich record playing in the background, they handed round a volume of John Betjeman's poems and tucked into the Colonel's port while they painted their anti-fascist banners in preparation for the rally. Communism was a serious political commitment, but it was also part of a larger romance that encompassed art, books, music and the thrill of living free from parents and teachers in the capital. When Toynbee first arrived on the train from Rugby, he found himself plunged into a different London than the one he had experienced on visits with his family. This new, underground city was the London of 'station hotels, of snack bars, one-room lodgings and Indian students'.[11] Both he and Esmond were thrilled by the new cast of characters they encountered at Parton Street, Meg's Café and anti-fascist rallies: Bloomsbury bohemians with their stories of 'Jinny' Woolf and 'Jimmy' Joyce, Jewish communists, East End toughs, surrealist poets, radical booksellers, raffish nightclub singers and a young Dylan Thomas, whose first volume of poetry was published by David Archer from the Parton Street store.

Through the various left-wing youth organizations that operated in the capital, Esmond also came into contact with young people from beyond the narrow confines of his school and class. The Stanley brothers, Ruddy and Sidney, were two East End wide boys, who were intermittently engaged in left-wing campaigning. They were also the proud owners of a battered old motorcar, which they decorated with anti-fascist slogans and used to transport Esmond and his gang around the public schools to sell *Out of Bounds*. This occasioned several run-ins with the resident 'bloods', who turned out to repel the communist agitators. When they showed up at Wellington, the *Out of Bounds* crew were forced to retreat by a gang of toughs and a grisly old porter, who marched towards them and gave a fascist salute. When they showed up at Eton, they were saved from being dumped in Barnes Pond by the arrival of the police.

The tension between political commitment and youthful hedonism was a recurrent feature of Esmond's life. Even during his runaway months in London, he would spend weekends at country house parties with his old family connections. He enjoyed the contradictions between these two separate worlds: the grandeur and ease of a weekend at Chartwell with uncle Winston and family gained a special piquancy when set against the weekday world of anti-fascist rallies and conspiratorial meetings. Sometimes Esmond tried to convince himself that his communist principles were exclusively the product of 'intellectual understanding', but at other times he acknowledged that they stemmed from 'a wish for change and excitement'.[12] As a mercurial fifteen-year-old, still in the throes of puberty and free from the discipline of school, Esmond's character remained unformed. This made it all the easier – and all the more satisfying – to flit back and forth between two worlds and two identities.

The final issue of *Out of Bounds* was published in July 1935, shortly after Esmond and Giles's book-length memoir was released under the same title. By this point the newspaper had run its course. The articles had become repetitious and Esmond was having to write more and more of the content himself under a variety of pseudonyms. At its peak *Out of Bounds* sold 3,000 copies per issue, a more than respectable figure for a radical newspaper published by runaway schoolchildren. The paper had also helped to make Esmond a regular fixture in the national press, his scruffy appearance and strident rhetoric forming a powerful counterimage to the athlete hero of the mainstream public school imagination. The *Out of Bounds* campaign was an offshoot of the crop of Marxist youth organizations that sprouted in the late 1920s and '30s, but with its radical panache and media buzz it stood sharply out from the crowd. It had done more than most to disrupt the 'sly' secrecy of the public school world.

T. C. WORSLEY, an assistant master at Wellington during Esmond's brief time there, estimated that the school lagged around forty or fifty years behind the public school system as a whole. Wellington was a dour and disciplinarian institution, which held fast to its historic links with the military. While not absolutely compulsory, the OTC was a central part of school life and all boys joined up as a matter of course. Worsley complained that, unlike other more up-to-date institutions, Wellington had no arts society, no literary society and no political club – in fact, no provision for its pupil's interests beyond the playing fields and the parade ground. The school day was rigorously scheduled and crammed with commitments. In his memoir Giles describes the clockwork discipline of a typical day: 'I hurried from work to call-over, from call-over to games, from games to work again, inky, harassed, and perplexed, and had never a moment of the day to myself."[13] Wellington was the very acme of Goffman's total institution, a hermetic world that accounted for every aspect of the individual's daily life.

Yet Worsley was not entirely accurate when he described Wellington as forty or fifty years out of date. His statement implies that there was a uniform rate of progress within the public school system as a whole, behind which Wellington lagged. But this is a distorted picture of how historical change happens within any complex social system, let alone one that was so deeply attached to its own traditions and sense of separateness from the world at large. Historical change is more often gradual, piecemeal, halting and local, than wholesale, uniform, coordinated and complete. Wellington was renowned as a tough institution, but it was not unique in its rigour and philistinism.

Like many schools at the time, Wellington was divided into conservative and progressive factions, which struggled over the petty details of everyday life and thus sought to define the character of the institution as a whole. Worsley describes a protracted battle between factions of masters over the official protocols for the wearing of caps on school grounds.[14] Conservatives insisted that it should remain an offence punishable by beating for a boy to be found without his cap, while progressives pushed for a modest relaxation of the rule. This local dispute over what seems a ridiculously mundane piece of discipline was a flashpoint for a wider struggle to define the very nature of the school. Was Wellington a total institution in the Victorian mould, one that saw the proper wearing of caps as an index of moral health and good character, or was it a liberal, modern institution that concerned itself with the cultivation of intellectual excellence instead of the minutiae of its pupils' dress?

In this respect, Wellington reflected the wider tensions that shaped the public school system in the interwar period. In the 1920s and '30s the monumental certainties of the Victorian public school ethos – the almost religious faith in the virtues of classics, athletics and robust gentlemanly character – came under concerted pressure from a range of modern creeds, including progressive liberalism, Marxism and Freudianism. This was also the era of the General Strike, the Wall

Street Crash, the Great Depression, mass unemployment, hyper-inflation, hunger marches, Britain's first Labour government and the rise of Communism and Fascism at home and abroad. Set against the wider political context of the times, the public schools began to look like relics from a different age. In terms of their customs and routines, this is precisely what they were: Victorian institutions in a twentieth-century world of economic strife and political extremism. During the prolonged economic slump of the early 1930s, a number of public schools suffered from steep declines in enrolments.[15] Many middle-class parents found that they couldn't afford, or no longer valued, the traditional benefits of a classical education. In 1938 a delegation from the Headmasters' Conference held a series of confidential meetings with the Board of Education to discuss potential emergency measures to keep the public school system afloat. In 1939 no less an institution than Harrow had to lay off staff and close one of its boarding houses due to lack of demand.[16]

In a 1939 essay Harold Laski, professor at LSE (the London School of Economics) and one of the leading Fabian socialists, skewered what he saw as the out-of-date figure of the public school gentleman. After identifying the key features of the species – the bluff amateurism, the emotional detachment, the membership of the right London clubs – he set out what he saw as the chief dangers of gentlemanliness in the modern world: 'The gentleman's characteristics are a public danger in all matters where quantitative knowledge, unremitting effort, vivid imagination, organized planning are concerned. How can the English gentleman govern India when he starts with the assumption that the Indian is permanently his inferior?'[17] From Laski's technocratic-socialist perspective, not only was a public school education anti-democratic, and hence morally wrong, it was also dangerously ineffective when confronted with the challenges of the modern world. To survive in straightened times, argued Laski, Britain would require a new form of forward-looking, scientifically minded and meritocratic leadership. The public school ideal singularly failed to fulfil these requirements. Laski offered a surprisingly fond assessment of gentlemanly government in the nineteenth century and praised the fair-minded attitudes of the Victorian ruling class.

But, he argued, if these attitudes were not updated to suit modern realities, the charming but limited figure of the gentleman amateur would be shouldered aside by the altogether more sinister figure of the modern dictator.

Esmond made a similar connection between the weakness of the public school system and political radicalism during his press campaign in 1934. In an interview with the *Sunday Referee*, he observed that:

> Ten years ago those in the public schools were not affected by economic crises. Their parents or their relations probably held the strings to 'cushy' jobs. But there is a different situation today. Anybody is glad to be offered a job; and this no doubt accounts in no small part for the changed outlook of modern youth.[18]

Esmond points to the severe economic conditions of the 1930s as an underlying cause of student radicalism. Without the old assurances of easy privilege and cushy jobs, public school graduates could no longer take their own social status for granted. During the economic slump of the 1930s, Britain lost between 300,000 and 400,000 of a total of roughly 2 million white-collar jobs.[19] For a certain kind of public schoolboy, economic instability was not simply a source of anxiety but instead an impetus to critical thinking and political engagement. Esmond describes an earlier version of a figure that has risen to prominence once more in the wake of the global financial crisis of 2008: the 'graduate with no future'.[20] Esmond and his comrades were the beneficiaries of high levels of education without the assurance of – or desire for – commensurate levels of employment and wealth. As many contemporary writers have pointed out, this is a sure-fire recipe for political radicalism.

From the perspective of many left-wing intellectuals, the final demise of the public school system seemed to be close at hand. In 1934, the year of the final issue of *Out of Bounds*, Graham Greene edited a volume of essays about school life. In his preface, Greene gave voice to a feeling that was shared by many of his contributors:

Like the family album, this book will, I hope, be superficially more funny than tragic, for so odd a system of education does not demand a pompous memorial ... Whatever the political changes in this country during the next few years one thing is almost certain: the class distinctions will not remain unaltered and the public school, as it exists today, will disappear.[21]

Greene's sentiment was echoed by Louis MacNeice when he said that 'the public schools will die like the dinosaurs – from over-specialisation and a mortal invulnerability', and Worsley, who speculated that 'in the ordinary course of things they would probably be finished in twenty years'.[22] Enchanted with the Marxist theory of historical necessity, many saw the public school system as fatally incompatible with the spirit of modernity that was so tumultuously at work in the world. Maybe not next year, and maybe not the year after, but certainly in a decade or two, the Victorian-style public school would be crushed under the wheels of historical progress.

ONE SIGNIFICANT NEW feature of the public school landscape in the 1920s and '30s was a small crop of private, fee-paying institutions that were founded on a variety of liberal and socialist principles. The progressive school movement sought to provide alternatives to the monolithic system of elite education that had grown up in the second half of the nineteenth century. In place of the traditional public school apparatus of classics, exam preparation, competitive athletics, prefect-fagging and the OTC, progressive schools adopted various forms of student democracy, manual labour and relaxed discipline. The aim in most cases, however, was not to abolish, but rather to purify the original public school ethos of character formation and community spirit. The pioneers of the progressive school movement sought to outflank the public school system, appropriate its best features and start a vigorous new pedagogical growth that would eventually replace the withered stem from which it had sprouted.

The movement began in the late Victorian period with Cecil Reddie's Abbotsholme, a private school based on socialist principles. Reddie was a highly strung Christian Socialist who had been educated at Rugby in the high Arnoldian manner. The school that he founded represented an act of rebellion against the ideals of his own education, eschewing classics and conformity in favour of modern academic subjects, manual labour and non-sectarian religion. Like his former headmaster, Thomas Arnold, Reddie cultivated a loyal corps of disciples, some of whom, like J. H. Badley, who went on to found Bedales in 1893, devoted their careers to spreading the founder's ideals. Just as the progressive school movement sought to purify the public school ethos, to raise it to a higher pitch of moral and spiritual intensity, it also put a new spin on the figure of the English gentleman. In place of the old school tie and athletic toughness, men like Reddie and Badley were passionate eccentrics who preached the values of free thought, community spirit and practical good sense as the true markers of gentility.

But while it had its roots in late Victorian socialism, the progressive school movement really came into its own in the 1920s and '30s with the founding of schools such as Dartington Hall in Devonshire, Gordonstoun in Morayshire in the highlands of Scotland and Summerhill in Suffolk. These schools differed widely in terms of ethos and ideology, but all were slanted at oblique angles to the mainstream public school system. Dorothy and Leonard Elmhirst's Dartington Hall preached a form of agrarian socialism inspired by the Bengali writer Rabindranath Tagore; Kurt Hahn's Gordonstoun sought to cultivate an elite Platonic leadership class through outward bounds activities and a rounded modern curriculum; A. S. Neill's Summerhill did away with all formal rules, had no specific curriculum and focused on psychoanalytic therapy in order to heal the wounds of an alienated society. To varying degrees, they all tended to confirm the judgement of the writer Patrick Leigh-Fermor, who was himself expelled from a variety of both public and progressive schools, that 'English schools, the moment they depart from the conventional track, are oases of strangeness and comedy.'[23]

Progressive schools educated a tiny proportion of British schoolchildren. Summerhill had between twenty and thirty pupils in residence at any one time. Dartington began with a handful and grew modestly over the course of its first couple of decades.

Bedales's numbers fluctuated, but averaged about twenty for most of the early years. These were small-scale, often very intimate organizations, moulded in the image of their idiosyncratic leaders. Over time, many progressive schools reformed their curricula and added a more rigorous academic focus. The more visionary fringes of the movement were tamed, but the liberal ideals and progressive curricula of many such institutions survive to this day, often serving as a useful means of differentiation in a crowded educational marketplace. But the significance of the progressive school movement has less to do with raw numbers and more to do with its relationship to the mainstream public school system to which it provided an alternative. On the most obvious level, progressive schools were the expression of a long-simmering dissatisfaction with the rigidity and conformity of the traditional public school. But on a less obvious level, the progressive schools were also attempts to unlock the utopian ideal that lay imprisoned within the institutional framework of the Victorian public school, to restore the ideals of 'character' and 'community' to a system that had calcified.

When Esmond agreed to return to school in the summer of 1934, he was sent to co-educational Bedales, where lessons were optional, rules were negotiated in a student parliament and the extra-curricular focus was on manual labour rather than competitive athletics. In addition to learning Greek and Latin, students churned their own butter and took turns to empty the compost toilets. Esmond lasted a mere eight weeks in what he later described as Bedales's atmosphere of 'amateur psychology' and 'social sex of a lemonadish variety'.[24] In his 1935 memoir, written at the tender age of sixteen, he presented a cutting analysis of the relationship between progressive schools like Bedales and the mainstream of the public school system. Bedales was a sop to the liberal conscience and nothing more. It preserved the same system of social inequality by adding a delicate garnish of compost and Freudianism. Giles echoed these sentiments in his memoir:

> The enemy in public schools, the reactionary element against which this book is directed, is no longer a 'stolid' conservatism,

but a 'progressive' liberalism. Everywhere in England opinion has shifted to the left, and the public schools can point out reforms as much as anyone else. But it is reform within a framework in which no real improvement is possible.[25]

The nineteen-year-old Giles was offering an incisive analysis of how the public schools would maintain their social status throughout the twentieth century – not by remaining intractably attached to the past, but by outwardly adapting to modern trends so as to preserve their elite status and cultural cachet. This is the same form of cultural ju-jitsu that the public schools practise today: using the apparent momentum of reform to wrong-foot opponents and retain a core identity as enclaves of the rich and powerful. The Romillys' strategy was to eschew reform in favour of spectacular gestures of adolescent rebellion. The aim was to provoke outright confrontation, rather than settle for minor concessions and gradual reforms.

LINSEED OIL, VARNISHED wood, unwashed urinals, leaking gas, mutton stew, sizzling sausages, mildewed towels, mown grass, sweaty socks, illicit tobacco: these are just some of the odours that waft their way through memoirs of public school life in the early twentieth century. Again and again, it is the sense of smell that triggers the deepest, most ineradicable school memories. Of course, the olfactory is tangled up with the visual, sonic and tactile senses, but smell comes first, transporting the subject back into the deep fabric of the past, the very marrow of memory. Cyril Connolly describes his first days at St Cyprian's prep school in exactly these terms: 'I came to know the smell of the classrooms, of slates, chalk and escaping gas, and to fear the green baize doors which separated the headmaster's part of the house from the boys. On the one side, silence, authority, the smell of savouries; on the other noise and freedom.'[26] For Connolly, smell is primary. The past is present first as a subtle whiff, and only then is it fleshed out in the more enduring registers of sight and sound. And with smell comes the equally primordial sense of fear, his earliest awareness of the school's authority and his terror of what lies on the other side of the green baize door.

The human sense of smell is generated in two of the oldest parts of the brain, the amygdala and the ventral insula, both of which evolved earlier in the life of humankind than the neocortex, which is the seat of our more refined linguistic and rational faculties.[27] In evolutionary terms, smell is the most atavistic of senses, which stems from the least rational parts of the brain. It triggers deep-seated associations of fear and lust, repulsion and desire, and is the source of some of our most ancient taboos, which stem from the visceral, involuntary recoil from shit and rotting meat. With its deep evolutionary history, smell transports us not only back into childhood, but into the early life of the tribe. It reactivates the primal fears and desires that would otherwise remain buried by civilized society and adult behaviour. No wonder, then, that smell is so central to boarding school memoirs.

In the mid-twentieth century the critical public school memoir became an important subgenre of English literature. Seemingly all of the major (male) authors who came of age between 1910 and 1940 wrote some form of wounded school memoir, including Robert Graves, Henry Green, Harold Nicolson, Anthony Powell, George Orwell, Cyril Connolly, W. H. Auden, Christopher Isherwood, Louis MacNeice, John Betjeman, Cecil Day-Lewis, C. S. Lewis and many more. It was to this genre that Giles and Esmond turned for their first book-length publication in 1935, hoping to ride the wave of publicity that had been generated by Esmond's flight from Wellington and the publication of *Out of Bounds*. For the Romilly boys, this was part of the extended propaganda war against the public school system and the repressive society it helped to sustain. Esmond even chose to spend his publisher's advance on setting up an alternative news agency that would gather and sell critical stories about the public schools to the mainstream press. The news agency didn't last long, but the memoir was favourably reviewed and sold well, running to a second edition only two months after it was published.

The genre emerged in large part as a corrective to the romantic myth of school life that was conjured again and again in public school fiction. These were antithetical genres, in terms of both political outlook and literary form. The school story tended to be conservative in politics, venerated the collective life of the institution and worked towards a narrative climax in which the wayward individual fully committed to the ideals of his school, class and nation. The school memoir, by contrast, tended to be liberal or socialist in politics, valorized the inner life of the individual and described the gradual formation of the author's mature identity in opposition to the meaningless discipline of the institution and the inauthentic 'character' of the typical public schoolboy. This process of dissident self-formation usually involved the author's embrace of the twin gods of the age – art and communism, or some conflicted mixture of the two.

A telling exception to this rule is C. S. Lewis's *Surprised by Joy* (1955), which mixes boarding school misery memoir with Christian apologetics. Lewis's memoir describes the common experience of his class: early separation from the home (exacerbated in Lewis's case by the death of his mother when he was ten), emotional deprivation, feelings of abandonment and futility, the oppressive conformism of institutional life and the flight to art and books as a refuge from his immediate environment. But unlike the majority of his peers, for Lewis the final escape from the values of the old school came through religious faith, rather than political commitment. 'Looking back on my life now,' he recalls,

> I am astonished that I did not progress into the opposite orthodoxy – did not become a Leftist, Atheist, satiric Intellectual of the type we all know so well. All the conditions seem to be present. I had hated my school. I hated whatever I knew or imagined of the British Empire.[28]

Art, Communism and God: these were the only forces grand enough and glamorous enough to furnish a viable alternative to the all-encompassing public school ideal.

But while they were bitter critiques of the system, public school misery memoirs were also examples of the privilege that elite education conferred. Indeed, the narrative arc of the school memoir leads ultimately to the formation of the narrator's adult self – urbane, cultured, ironic – from which perspective he looks back upon his schooldays with a mixture of resentment and nostalgia. From the safety of adulthood, the author is able to review his schooldays with magnanimity, examine the case from all sides and capture both the light and shade that fall upon the scene. Public school memoirs bristle with tales of bullying, abuse, corporal punishment, casual sadism, arcane customs, unfathomable rules, grinding boredom and emotional despair. But they also register the joy of intimate friendships, intellectual and aesthetic awakenings, dissident camaraderie and the slow ascent after graduation to prestigious positions within the cultural and political establishment.

The danger, however, was that the public school misery memoir would become an opportunity not only to diagnose the ills of the institution, but to wallow in the obscure details of one's own bewitchment by a perverse system. The literary critic Regenia Gagnier has argued that the nostalgia that many left-wing intellectuals felt towards their schooldays had a dampening effect on the spread of socialism in twentieth-century Britain. In rejecting their privileged education, she observes, critical memoirists also 'rejected totalitarianism . . . But they had always fought totalitarianism with art, creativity, and individualism in isolation; therefore, they could not quite trust socialism, either.'[29] Instead of putting their shoulders to the wheel of practical reform, as their political beliefs dictated they should, public school radicals more frequently pored over the details of their own personal sense of alienation, replayed in their memories their individual resistance through art, friendship and radical politics. While popular spy novelists like John Buchan and Sapper suggested that schoolboy aestheticism went hand in hand with political extremism and treason, the opposite was in fact true. More often than not, the secular religion of art, as expressed in the form of the public school memoir, tempered the radicalism of upper-class dissidents by maintaining their nostalgic attachment to the old school.

Recalling his days at Harrow in the 1910s, L. P. Hartley refers to the 'Freudian bruise' of his school memories.[30] Hartley begins his essay with a description of his irrational fear in later life of falling asleep on a train from Rome to Venice. This fear stems not from any serious concern about missing his stop, he realizes, but instead from the persistent memory of his schooldays and the constant dread of being late for morning call-over. Decades after leaving the school, Hartley bears the residue of institutional discipline in his subconscious. His fear of teachers and prefects, rules and conventions, remains with him in adulthood in the form of a 'dent on my consciousness'.[31] In fact, Hartley's phrase 'The Freudian Bruise' would make a good title for an anthology of autobiographical writing about public schooling in the first half of the twentieth century, certainly a better one than Greene's rather unimaginative *The Old School*. These narratives are often organized around key moments of desire, taboo, repression and transgression. They deal with memory as a kind of wound that will not heal, and they stage a return, in the aestheticized form of the memoir itself, to the source of these deep-rooted aspects of the self.

Cecil Day-Lewis echoes Hartley's phrase in his own autobiography, *The Buried Day* (1960), in which he describes his experiences at Sherborne as 'an invisible compost' from which his adult identity grew.[32] Like the 'Freudian bruise', the image of the 'invisible compost' conveys the subject's ambivalent feelings of attraction and repulsion towards his adolescent memories. Day-Lewis casts his schooldays as a thick, oozing mulch, rank smelling but also endlessly appealing, something to be churned under but also lingered over and enjoyed. In later life, in spite of his rejection of the 'false heroics' and 'distorted values' of the public school ideal, Day-Lewis finds himself returning to Sherborne and immediately 'falling under its spell'.[33] By mixing the language of shit and magic, realism and romance, he captures the perversity of the boarding school experience.

Christopher Isherwood used a more antiseptic, medical register to convey the spell cast by the school over his developing character. Isherwood's memoir takes its name, *Lions and Shadows*, from the novel that he worked on throughout his schooldays, a juvenile hybrid of public school fiction and experimental *Bildungsroman* that depicted a series of 'tests' undergone by the protagonist in order to prove his masculinity in the eyes of the school. Looking back from the perspective of maturity, Isherwood describes this text as 'less a work of art than a symptom – of a certain stage of pubic development in a member of a certain class, living in a certain country, and subjected to a certain system of education'.[34] The effect of this perverse system is to turn the child into a 'spurious adult', so that in later life the old boy feels 'bound to try to regain his childhood – by means which, to the outside world, appear ever more and more unreasonable'.[35] Isherwood describes the same sense of stalled development that Connolly captured with his theory of 'permanent adolescence', the stunted, backwards-looking, indelibly nostalgic mentality that ensured that members of the ruling elite remained in thrall to the memory of their schooldays. The word 'nostalgia' is derived from the Greek roots *nostos*, to return home, and *algos*, pain. Rather than a longing for the past, which is the predominant meaning of the word today, the roots of nostalgia lie in a desire to return to one's true home, to cease wandering and to re-engage with the source of one's identity in a familiar, cherished place. The deep vein of nostalgia that runs through even the most critical of public school memoirs confirms that, in spite of its inhumanity, the boarding school was the author's home for the majority of his childhood, the site of his most formative experiences and the foundation of his mature identity.

The defining feature of Giles and Esmond Romilly's co-authored school memoir, by contrast, is its lack of nostalgia. Published in June 1935, when the brothers were nineteen and seventeen years old, *Out of Bounds: The Education of Giles Romilly and Esmond Romilly* is divided into two sections, the first written by Giles and the second by Esmond. Like other school memoirs, it describes in forensic detail the alienating apparatus of the total institution and the authors' embrace of communism as an alternative source of both moral value and personal identity. Unlike better-known memoirs by the likes of Graves and Orwell, however, the Romilly brothers wrote from the perspective of youth. They drew on experiences that hadn't yet been converted into the 'invisible compost' of childhood memory, and weren't yet registered in the psyche as a 'Freudian bruise'. The defining mood of the book is not one of wistful nostalgia for lost youth – how could it be? – but instead of boredom and rage.

The boys' anger builds as they progress through the stages of a typical upper middle-class English education. When he first enters prep school, Giles's mood is one of numbed dislocation rather than active hatred. 'The first days of going to school are always memorable,'

he explains, but 'above all, I remember the hallucinated sense of un-
reality, which prevented me from being entirely depressed.'[36] Soon,
however, the sense of stunned surrealism gives way to a profound state
of boredom, which 'settled over me like a fog'.[37] When Giles makes
the transition from prep school to public school, however, boredom
modulates into depression. It is only once he has begun to master the
complex rituals of school life that he has the time to register his own
deep unhappiness: 'depression came when I began to know my way
about, and could take my time over things, when the tempo of my
activity was slowed up'.[38] As with other memoirists, Giles describes
an almost metaphysical sense of desolation, a feeling that the school
is a self-contained universe that obeys unfathomable laws that are
inimical to human happiness.

Throughout the narrative thus far, Giles has been a mere child who
lacks any real capacity to understand either himself or the institution.
Recalling his first term at Wellington, he observes that 'not till I had
been at the place for several terms did it occur to me that Wellington
might have characteristics which were the cause of my depression, and
to question its principles, and to actively combat them'.[39] This slowly
emerging capacity for self-assertion is catalysed into full expression
when Giles is beaten by his housemaster for stealing, a crime which is
common in the boarding house but seldom discovered. The injustice
of the sentence and the public ritual of the punishment are the final
sparks that convert his long-simmering depression into energizing
hatred. He dismisses the beating itself as 'quite an ordinary punishment for a quite obvious crime', but describes the lasting effect it
had upon his character: 'I really hated Wellington for the first time;
before it had merely depressed, frightened, bored me.'[40] Esmond has a
similar experience when he is beaten by a prefect for eating a piece of
chewing gum on the sidelines of a cricket match. Again, the physical
pain of the beating pales beside the absurdity of the elaborate ritual,
which leaves Esmond 'simply incensed with fury'.[41]

When they switched from writing an underground magazine
to a personal memoir, Giles and Esmond altered their prose style to
match the conventions of the genre. In place of strident rhetoric and
broad satire, they adopted a more reflective and personal tone. There

are even some sections in which the authors look ruefully back on their schooldays from the perspective of posterity and laugh at their youthful pomposity. In these passages, any reader who is familiar with the public school memoir can sense the boys' efforts to live up to the expectations of the genre. They are putting on the airs of the wry, ironical old boy, who looks back on his schooldays and wonders at the absurdity of it all – precisely the tone that many of the contributors to Greene's collection adopted. Critics and reviewers played up these aspects of the book. The *Times Literary Supplement* praised the Romillys for their sceptical appraisal of their younger selves and joked that the authors resembled a 'disillusioned sexagenarian' looking back on his schooldays. The reviewer almost seemed to be willing the young authors towards the values of nostalgia and literary good taste, rather than the communism and class warfare that take up so much of the memoir.

Ultimately, however, the boys' still-simmering adolescent rage proves too strong for the dampening effects of the genre. The overriding mood of the narrative is one of emotional desperation, building towards a crescendo of anger and hatred. This is the testament of youth: the proximity of ugly, painful feelings, which have not yet been dimmed by the passage of time and ironized by adult self-awareness. In his essay 'On the Pleasure of Hating' (1821), William Hazlitt observed that, 'without something to hate, we should lose the very spring and thought of action.'[42] According to Hazlitt, hatred has an energizing effect upon the mind and body; it furnishes the necessary jolt of passion that enables us to convert otherwise abstract ideas into concrete actions. Within mainstream political discourse, to hate is to engage in an illegitimate feeling, to open oneself to the charge of illogicality and immaturity. But what the hater loses in terms of nuance and maturity, he gains back in the form of clarity of focus and motivation.

Both Giles and Esmond Romilly embraced the power of political hatred. Their ire, however, was directed not at their parents and teachers – Esmond even declares his affection for the far-right master, Cecil de Sausmarez, who was his perennial adversary in the school debating club – but at the institution itself. In an echo of Graves's *Goodbye to All That*, Giles reflects that the only way effectively to reform a school like Wellington would be to sack all the members of staff and start afresh. In its sensationalist reporting on Esmond's escape from Wellington, the *Daily Mail* cast the Romilly boys as 'abnormal war children', whose delinquent behaviour was the product of parental shell shock during the First World War and their own pathological failure to mature in the appropriate way.[43] In reality, however, theirs was a disciplined hatred directed against carefully chosen targets and channelled into productive forms.

Looking back from the perspective of the early twenty-first century, it is impossible not to be struck by how profoundly wrong Greene, MacNeice, Worsley and the Romilly brothers were when they predicted the inevitable demise of the public school system. Rather than succumbing to the progressive dialectic of history, the public schools managed to scrape through the economic hardships of the 1930s and dodge the wholesale reform of the education system that accompanied the founding of the post-war welfare state. After a period of relative hardship during the 1930s and '40s, the public schools not only survived but flourished in the second half of the twentieth century, fending off competition from the state sector, improving academic standards, relaxing discipline, modernizing facilities, retaining their elite character, and generally going from strength to strength. History has a subtle way of outwitting its most confident analysts and prognosticators. But another thing that is striking about the misplaced confidence of the 1930s left is the way in which that confidence was accompanied by a mixture of idealism, hope and informed critique that is sorely lacking in our more enlightened yet more ambivalent times.

ESMOND ROMILLY'S NOTORIETY as a public school revolutionary did not come to an end in the dingy cafés of Bloomsbury with the final issue of *Out of Bounds*. Nor did it end with a gradual conversion to respectability and a nice career in the liberal establishment, like many of his former comrades (H. W. Stubbs went on to teach classics at the University of Exeter; Philip Toynbee became a successful journalist; Gavin Ewart was a noteworthy poet; and his brother Giles became a foreign correspondent and novelist). The second phase of

Esmond's renegade career was played out in the wider theatre of the Spanish Civil War and the gathering storm of the Second World War. He first departed for Spain at the age of sixteen in October 1936. Esmond was one of a number of current and recently graduated public schoolboys who joined the International Brigades and fought Franco's Nationalists alongside miners from Yorkshire, dockers from Liverpool and shipbuilders from Glasgow. After only a few months in the country, however, Esmond returned home suffering from dysentery and post-traumatic stress after being involved in the bloody fiasco of Boadilla. This battle saw the highest number of casualties of foreign fighters in the entire war. In his account of his experiences in Spain, Esmond describes the sense of 'being in the presence of something horrifying', as he witnessed a member of his platoon die in the midst of a disorderly and leaderless battle.[44]

It was at this point that he renewed his acquaintance with his second cousin, Jessica Mitford – or 'Decca' as she was known to family and friends. Decca was the sixth of the seven Mitford children. Their father, David Freeman-Mitford, 2nd Baron Redesdale, was a formidably conservative peer of the realm, whom Esmond would later refer to as 'the Nazi Baron'. The Mitford daughters were regularly mentioned in the gossip pages of the British press, not only for their debutante appearances at the London season, but for their various accomplishments as novelists, journalists, socialites and Fascists. Nancy Mitford was a glamorous Bright Young Thing and successful novelist; Diana married Oswald Mosley, the leader of the British Union of Fascists, and was interned during the Second World War for her political allegiances; and Unity, or 'Boud' to her friends, was a prominent member of Hitler's social circle.

Decca and Esmond had often met as children at grand weekend retreats at Chartwell, but in adolescence they had little contact. Stewing away in the isolation of her family's estate in rural Gloucestershire, the teenage Jessica avidly followed Esmond's exploits in the press and via borrowed copies of *Out of Bounds*. In her brilliant memoir, *Hons and Rebels* (1960), she recalls the thrill of reading Giles and Esmond's memoir when it was released in 1935:

I almost felt as though I knew Esmond. Rebellious, certainly – the 'holy terror' of Chartwell days grown older; but he was also much more than that. He emerged as a person of unlimited resourcefulness, with that extra degree of good humour which comes from absolute self-confidence in all situations, fearless, indestructible . . .[45]

The attraction clearly lay in Esmond's combination of edgy difference and reassuring familiarity, the 'holy terror' of juvenile delinquency and political radicalism, as well as the public school persona of 'absolute self-confidence' and 'fearless[ness]'. Decca began to save her pocket money in a 'running away fund' and let it be known to the right people that she was planning to bolt.

After a nervous struggle to secure a visa for Decca and lay a false trail for her parents, the couple eloped to Spain, where they worked as freelance reporters. Unsurprisingly, this prompted Esmond's second spell in the tabloid spotlight as a glamorous upper-class runaway. The *Daily Express* was the first newspaper to break the story with a splashy front-page headline, 'Peer's Daughter Elopes to Spain'. The following morning, the *Express* published a more in-depth piece, which included commentary from a former comrade of Esmond's recounting a farewell dinner eaten with the runaway couple that comprised of foie gras sandwiches and champagne.[46] The narrative was already being shaped along what Esmond saw as depressingly familiar lines: the irresponsible children of privilege embarking on a hedonistic spree to the Continent. On the one hand, he understood the value of his own public school background and his wife's aristocratic family as sensationalist bait with which to hook journalists. Esmond's own journalistic work was divided between the factual dispatches he made from the anti-Fascist frontlines and the personality-driven pieces he sold to more gossipy outlets. In this second type of story, he played up the renegade schoolboy persona for all it was worth, larding his speech with both Marxist jargon and boarding school clichés. The danger, however, was that Esmond's self-cultivated image as the *enfant terrible* of Wellington College would become simply another picturesque feature of the public school myth; in short, that the boarding school cliché would drown out the Marxist message. When they were in Spain, Esmond and Decca were continually worried that sensational stories about their elopement were driving genuine news about the conflict off the front pages.

After Spain, the couple returned to London with their newly born daughter and set up home in Rotherhithe, a working-class area in the heart of the London Docklands. Their Rotherhithe flat, a narrow wedge of a building that looked directly out over the Thames, became a gathering point for some of the same cast of surrealist poets, Oxbridge Marxists and raffish loafers that had hung out at Parton Books. But the Romillys also immersed themselves in the more humdrum concerns of the local Labour Party in Poplar and Hackney, where they encountered the 'shorter and paler race of people' who were actually from the East End, rather than casually breezing through.[47] It was also in Rotherhithe that Esmond and Decca experienced their daughter's death from pneumonia at the age of four months. This event was discussed with barely suppressed glee among certain sections of the upper-class society from which the couple had escaped. There was a sharp edge to the way in which distant relatives and family acquaintances deprecated Esmond and Decca's escapades. The silent subtext was that the couple had brought the death of their child upon themselves by choosing to live in the squalor of an East End slum. As Philip Toynbee pointed out, the venomous nature of the response was a register of fear rather than strength, a dawning sense that Esmond and Decca's rebellion signalled a broader shift in the cultural and political landscape.[48]

The news stories continued to flow throughout the short second act of Esmond's life. From their Rotherhithe retreat, Esmond and Decca continued to mount periodic raids on the citadels of the upper classes. On one occasion, Esmond found himself in Windsor for the weekend, where he decided to steal all of the Eton boys' top hats from outside the school chapel. He drafted a letter to *The Times*, which cast the events of the day as a radical left-wing provocation and warned readers to 'Look out for your boaters! We strike Harrow next!'[49] When he and Decca decided to leave for America, Esmond cooked up a scheme to fund their travels with a lecture tour on such sensational themes as 'I Ran Away from a Public School' and 'I was an English

Debutante'. The scheme came to nothing, but when they did arrive in New York, Esmond arranged for a series of articles in the *Washington Post* under the title 'Baby Blue Bloods in Hobohemia', which cast the couple as 'Two Youthful Escapists Who Fled To America With a Song in Their Hearts'.[50] The tension between serious political commitment and hedonistic escapism was still very much in place.

After the death of their daughter, Esmond and Decca toured America for nine months before the u.s. declared war, making ends meet with periodic freebooting campaigns among the rich and respectable, some low-paid sales jobs and a stint serving cocktails in a Florida dive bar. As soon as the conflict began, however, Esmond joined up with the Royal Canadian Air Force, choosing what he called the 'grey' of British Imperialism over the 'black' of German and Italian fascism.[51] In characteristic fashion, he was enraged to be given an automatic commission on account of his public school education, but found that the bureaucratic manoeuvres required to resign his post and enlist as a private were too convoluted to be attempted. He trained as a navigator and was killed in 1941 when his plane went missing over the North Sea en route to a raid on Hamburg.

If Esmond Romilly hadn't existed, someone would surely have invented him. Schoolboy runaway, nephew of the greatest British statesman of the twentieth century, Spanish Civil War veteran, teenage media phenomenon, blue blood provocateur, travelling salesman, scam artist, chancer, chameleon, brat. He is a figure of equal parts historical reality and mythopoetic fantasy. Like Percy Shelley before him, he enjoyed the dubious privilege of dying young – he was 23 at the time of his death – with his youthful charisma and radical ideals still intact. This is a fate that never fails to impart a hint of mythic poignancy to an otherwise fully historical individual. Many of his friends and acquaintances recognized this element of the mythic even before his untimely death. His comrade in arms, Philip Toynbee, cast him as Arthur Rimbaud to his own Paul Verlaine.[52] His former schoolmaster, T. C. Worsley, observed that 'he seemed to spring fully armed with the [Communist] doctrine from Jove's head' and that he stalked the school as 'a lone wolf with a wolf's bite for any hand that fed him, and a wolf's snarl for anyone who reasoned with him'.[53]

In her memoir, written in New York in the late 1950s, many years after her wild youth, Decca put Esmond's delinquency down to his aristocratic background. In another age, she mused, he would have acted out by gambling, whoring and drinking, rather than through political radicalism.[54] But Esmond's delinquency wasn't only the product of the small measure of blue blood that ran in his veins. There was also an air of inspired juvenility to his antics: he turned his own youthfulness into a kind of performance art. Unlike many members of the 1930s intellectual left, Esmond was almost completely uninterested in nuances of meaning, hidden motives, subconscious drives, emotional complexities, subtleties of inflection, liberal balance, reasoned objectivity or nostalgic reverie. His genius for outraging the members of his class was a product of his capacity to commit fully to what would otherwise be a minor and limiting role: that of the schoolboy rebel. He played that role for all it was worth, with a complete lack of concern about seeming juvenile or foolish.

Lindsay Anderson's *if . . .* (1968): Mick and the girl on the school roof
with machine gun.

# SEVEN

# Going Underground

To this day, Peter Gabriel still holds that the most important event in his musical development – maybe even the most important event in his life – was when he saw Otis Redding perform at the RamJam Club in Brixton on 18 September 1966. Gabriel made the journey from Charterhouse School in Godalming, Surrey, one of the nine 'great' schools included in the 1864 Clarendon Commission and alma mater to such luminaries as John Wesley, Ralph Vaughan Williams and Robert Baden-Powell. What he discovered in that sweaty basement in pre-gentrification Brixton – he later recalled that 'there were probably only three white faces in the whole place' – was a vortex of musical energy that provided a blessed release from the stultifying atmosphere of the boarding school.[1] 'You felt your heart being opened in [Redding's] presence,' he later enthused. 'I still feel that emotion when I hear it . . . it was like a factory of energy, love and passion.'[2] This is an archetypal moment echoed in many accounts of boarding school life in the 1950s and '60s, the moment of release and transformation when the sheltered upper middle-class adolescent first encounters the new sounds emanating from Memphis, Detroit, Liverpool or London. For Gabriel, his weekend trip to Brixton was a thrilling encounter with other musics, other races, other selves.

Back at school, the sixteen-year-old Gabriel teamed up with fellow Carthusians Tony Banks, Mike Rutherford, Anthony Phillips and Chris Stewart to form Genesis, who went on to become pioneers of the 'progressive' rock sound of the early 1970s and one of the best-selling bands in the world. On the face of things, it is hard to detect the influence of Gabriel's trip to see Otis Redding or his love for Tamla Motown on Genesis' music. They may have started out at Charterhouse playing rhythm and blues, but Genesis quickly evolved into a decidedly high-concept band, who wrote songs about Victorian manor houses, murderous games of croquet and Ovidian myths about gender-swapping gods. For all of its volume and intensity, their music was highly cerebral, often experimenting with complex narrative structures and unconventional time signatures. Many of these elements seem to have been drawn not from African American soul music, but from the classrooms of Charterhouse, where the band members were exposed to classical poetry, the English literary canon and ecclesiastical music. Mike Rutherford later recalled how compulsory chapel attendance was a 'double-edged sword'. If you could put up with the religion, then the 'drama' of the 'hymns' big chords and chord sequences was fantastic'.[3]

Genesis were often scoffed at by music fans for their polite manners and public school background. Their own drummer, Phil Collins, once dismissed them as a 'bunch of Noel Cowards'.[4] But even if they unapologetically drew on their elite educations as material for their songs, their work was also characterized by a sense of emotional earnestness that they learned from soul music. In an interview with the NME in 1980, Gabriel recalled that, 'I felt I could repress the middle-class English person with soul music . . . I wanted to sit at the piano for hours and hours and scream or whatever it was. Just to release emotions.'[5] This is a strikingly romantic vision of the transformative powers of art, which casts soul music as emotional therapy for the damaged self, an ideal language of rhythm and melody that enables the middle-class white boy from Surrey to commune with the son of a Georgia sharecropper.

In his 1970 book *Revolt into Style*, George Melly located the origins of British pop music with 'cosmopolitan working-class adolescents'.[6] This has become one of the central narratives of pop history: that it helped to dissolve the old assumptions of hierarchy and deference that had defined life in Britain for so long. But while the story usually focuses on the spectacular upward mobility of working and lower middle-class rock stars – often represented in the form of the symbolic ascent from the cramped urban terrace house to the lavishly appointed country manor – pop's promise of class escapism worked both ways. For the sons and daughters of privilege, the new cultures of adolescence that emerged in the 1950s and '60s offered an escape from the values and atmosphere of the public school. In place of discipline, emotional restraint and class loyalty, pop offered hedonism, heightened emotions and a more socially and ethnically diverse community. While the school venerated tradition and wrapped its pupils in an atmosphere of elegant antiquity, pop revelled in the glories of the present and the promise of the future. Music-driven youth cultures may have been working class in origin, but the content of their message and the glitter of their style held out the utopian promise of a new world in which the old distinctions of class, race and gender had evaporated into a heady intensity of youth and freedom.

But it's no easy thing to escape from one's social class. Melly also observed that 'the living in and for the present is what separates pop culture from traditional culture, and at the same time provides both its strength and limitation.'[7] The optimistic focus on the here and now could easily obscure structural inequalities that had built up over centuries. In the 1960s many upper middle-class kids rejected the culture of their parents and teachers, skipped the educational treadmill that led from boarding school to Oxbridge and into the elite professions and embraced a whole range of subcultural lifestyles and radical political creeds. But even as they dropped out of respectable society, they could still draw on the privileges of their class when required: wealthy families, powerful contacts, polished manners, cultural capital and the intangible sense of confidence and self-worth that is the by-product of elite education. As the cultural critic Dan Fox observes, 'code-switching is a white, middle-class privilege that ignores broader problems of gender, race, and sexuality, factors that make chameleon-like mobility difficult for some.'[8] The very ability to refashion one's identity through carefully selected cultural symbols is heightened by the pre-existing privileges of class.

It was precisely this tension that animated Nick Drake's 1971 song 'Poor Boy'. Drake was the son of a colonial family (his father began his career as an engineer with the Bombay Burma Trading Company and his grandfather worked in the Burmese civil service), who was educated at Marlborough and Fitzwilliam College, Cambridge. Unlike the globally successful Genesis, Drake's three albums of exquisite folk-jazz were commercial failures and it was only after his suicide in 1974 that he was recognized as the forgotten voice of the hippy generation. 'Poor Boy' captures the privileged dropout's sense of anxiety about the inauthenticity of his bohemian postures: 'Never sing for my supper / I never help my neighbour / Never do what is proper / Or my fair share of labour.'[9] With its delicate mixture of anguish and irony, Drake's song is the counterpoint to the young Peter Gabriel's experience of seeing Otis Redding at the RamJam Club in Brixton. In 'Poor Boy' the romantic promise of healing and transformation has been replaced with a world-weary resignation to social immobility. Bohemian self-fashioning is revealed as merely a temporary refuge from a class identity that is the product of deep-rooted structures that are beyond the control of the individual.

IN THE DECADES following the Second World War the public school system came under sustained pressure to reform. The war was an important watershed for many of Britain's social institutions. Causing severe hardship for civilians and military alike, the war engendered a widespread sense that Britain's hierarchical and class-bound society would have to change when the fighting ceased. For the collective sacrifice to be worthwhile, a new social order would have to emerge, one that would enable everyone to share in the fruits of victory. The war also encouraged trust in the power and effectiveness of large-scale government planning. Conscription, rationing, the requisition of large houses and estates, the evacuation of children from urban centres, government intervention in key national industries, restrictions on travel and communication: almost all aspects of daily life had come under some form of centralized control or regulation. In this new climate, the old narratives about private education and inherited privilege began to seem more than a little thin. The sanctity of tradition, the privileging of organic growth over rational reform, the tribal ethic of upper-class solidarity and the ideal of gentlemanly leadership all seemed like relics from a pre-war past that had lost their lustre long before the bombs started to fall.

The governmental expression of this new political mood was the Beveridge Report, which was published on 1 December 1942 and immediately became a national best-seller (a rare fate for a government report). Sir William Beveridge, a cerebral Whitehall mandarin enlisted by Winston Churchill to begin planning for peacetime, identified what he called 'five giants on the road to reconstruction': Want, Disease, Ignorance, Squalor and Idleness.[10] These were the deep-rooted social problems that would have to be solved in order to ensure Britain's emergence from the war as a fair-minded and progressive modern democracy. The eventual product of the Beveridge Report, pieced together over the subsequent decades, was the welfare state, with its universal provisions for pensions, health care, education, housing and unemployment.

The first giant to be slain was Ignorance, which was the subject of the 1944 Butler Report on education. This was to be the most far-reaching reform of state education since the Education Act of 1870, which provided universally accessible elementary schooling up to the age of ten, and the Education Act of 1902, which had raised the school leaving age to twelve and authorized newly created Local Education Authorities to fund and build secondary schools. What emerged from the Butler Report was the 'tripartite' system of state education that existed until the introduction of comprehensive schools in the 1960s. This tripartite system divided schools – and, of course, their pupils – into three supposedly equal but different types: the selective grammar school, which taught academic subjects such as Latin, Greek, English, History, Mathematics and the Sciences; the secondary technical school, which taught manual skills and practical subjects in preparation for entry to the trades; and the secondary modern, which provided a general education for the majority of pupils who did not pass the Eleven-plus to attend a grammar school or elect for a technical school (of which there were relatively few).

In the deep background of these reforms was the unlikely figure of Plato and the system of education he envisaged for his ideal republic in the fifth century BCE.[11] Plato's was also a hierarchical, tripartite system, which divided young men and women (the ideal republic was co-educational) into 'gold', 'silver' and 'iron' levels of educational ability.

Only gold status pupils, those capable of the most complex forms of abstract thought, would go on to serve short terms as the republic's enlightened guardians. Of course, Butler and his colleagues abjured Plato's hierarchical structure and spoke positively about the 'parity of esteem' that would exist between the three different types of school. But the tripartite system was based upon a fundamental assumption, inherited from Plato via the Victorian reformers who had begun to build the state education system in the 1860s, that 'the different classes of society, the different occupations of life, require different teaching'.[12] In short, class was built into the system from the beginning.

But what did the Butler Report have to say about the public schools? The answer: nothing at all. Rather than treating education as a universal service to be regulated within a single administrative framework, Butler chose to strike a separate committee to investigate the private education system. When the Fleming Report appeared in July 1944, however, the response was a resounding lack of enthusiasm from all sides. The report suggested, first, that the public schools did not teach enough science and mathematics, a criticism that had been levelled against these classics-obsessed institutions since the dawn of the Industrial Revolution. It suggested that public school-style education should be extended to girls as well as boys – all good and well, but hardly the foundation stone of a New Jerusalem. And finally, it suggested that Local Education Authorities (LEAs) should be allowed to fund up to 25 per cent of all places at public schools for gifted students who couldn't afford the fees. This last item was the centrepiece of the report and Fleming's suggestion for how to unpick the inequities of elite private education. The scheme would, however, be entirely voluntary both on the side of the LEAs and the public schools themselves, and the costs would be borne entirely by local government, rather than the state. This was not so much a bold intervention into the social fabric of a war-weary nation as an airy suggestion about what might be desirable for all concerned, if it wasn't too much trouble. When Fleming's recommendations became law, the uptake for the scheme was negligible at best. By 1948, a mere 155 places at public schools had been taken up by LEAs. Even Butler himself was disappointed with Fleming's work, calling the report 'sensationally ingenuous' and remarking that 'the first-class carriage had been shunted onto an immense siding'.[13]

The Butler and Fleming Reports represented the best opportunity for fundamental reform of the public schools at any point in the twentieth century. There may have been significant opposition and plenty of argument, but there would have been little surprise among politicians, the press, education professionals and the wider public if the private education system had been nationalized, either in whole or in part, in 1944. James Chuter Ede, a Labour education minister in the wartime coalition government, recorded in his diary in 1942 that Winston Churchill himself had privately suggested that 60–70 per cent of all places at public schools should be funded through state scholarships on a purely meritocratic basis.[14]

Butler's failure to reform private education ensured that wealthy parents would always have the option of airlifting their children out of the state system. This not only deprived local comprehensive schools of the influence of articulate parents and their well-behaved kids, but helped to preserve the public schools' mystical aura of separateness from the mainstream of British life. Towards the end of the 1950s and throughout the 1960s, Britain experienced what one historian has termed an 'educational break-out', with large amounts of new money being spent on primary, secondary and higher education, all of which was free to the user and paid for out of general taxation.[15] But in spite of the rising numbers of pupils who graduated with O levels, A levels and university degrees, the very top end of the system remained separate, in terms of culture and ethos, as well as power and prestige. The post-war dream of equality of opportunity remained a fantasy. In 1968 the Newsom Report, the final product of Labour's Public Schools Committee, found that more than 90 per cent of public school pupils had parents in social classes 1 and 2 – that is, the managerial and professional classes.[16] The social profile of the schools was largely unchanged from the mid-nineteenth century. Their demographics were as retro as their uniforms.

In spite of the absence of effective government reform, however, headmasters and boards of governors understood that private education would have to adapt to the changing climate of the times. Their response to the threat of government reform – the Labour Party's election manifestos of 1964 and 1966 both stated its commitment to the abolition of private education – was an informal programme of reform, in which pedagogy, curriculum, discipline and facilities were all updated in order to compete with the rejuvenated state system, attract parents and pupils and present a more modern, user-friendly face to the world at large. Classics migrated still further to the margins of the curriculum. Science came in in a big way, not simply as part of a second-rate 'Modern Side' for dropouts and bums, but as a serious academic subject in its own right. Bounds were extended, restrictions on dress were lifted, students were granted more free time. The militarism that had become such a distinctive feature of many schools in the early twentieth century started to wane. Boys were allowed to opt out of the Cadet Corps in favour of social work and Duke of Edinburgh-style outward-bound schemes. Prefect-fagging, the centuries-old foundation of public school discipline, began to die out for good, especially in the later 1960s and the '70s. Pupils were now encouraged to spend more weekends at home. Some schools installed sixth-form bars. Some even arranged weekend dances with girls bussed in from nearby private schools. Beginning in the 1970s, some of the oldest and most prestigious schools began to admit girls to the sixth form. According to one headmaster, the presence of girls ensured that 'homosexual talk' died out almost overnight.[7]

BUT THESE WERE gradual, piecemeal changes. Old habits die hard in institutions that pride themselves on their long histories and venerable traditions. At the oldest schools, pupils continued to wear old-fashioned uniforms, speak in recondite slang, stage Latin plays and wrestle for scraps of pancake on the appointed Saint's day. Indeed, while the discipline and constraint of the Victorian total institution slowly melted away, the *genius loci* of the school remained intact. The essential character of the place, its mythic topography and mind-haunting architecture provided the unchanging backdrop to these modern developments. The list of bounds at Harrow in the 1960s reads like a page torn from a Victorian school manual. Boys were expressly forbidden from:

Going to the King's Head Hotel
Going to any railway station or its approaches
Standing still on any railway bridge or going on the line
Loitering in the churchyard on Sundays, or standing in groups
    at the outer doors of houses or outside the Chapel doors
Buying any articles (except newspapers) in the streets
Keeping dogs or taking dogs out
Walking more than three abreast up and down the streets
    or London Road
Going in any public conveyance without permission.[18]

This was the old system of discipline and enclosure that had been in place for the previous hundred years or more. The list also furnishes an inverted image of how boys liked to spend their time: loafing in railway stations and churchyards, drinking at the King's Head and dog fancying. Indeed, in the increasingly permissive social climate of the 1960s, discipline itself could become a selling point. John Dancy, the former headmaster of Harrow, observed in a letter to John Betjeman that 'Parents no longer pay for good teaching. They pay for short hair.'[19]

It should come as little surprise, then, that the impact of post-war youth culture on the rarefied environs of the public schools was a slow-burn affair. Insulated by ancient tradition and *genius loci*, public schoolboys and girls were held at one remove from a phenomenon that was both working class in origin and ferociously modern in outlook. In his autobiography *Margrave of the Marshes* (2005), the radio DJ John Peel tells of his schoolfellows' complete lack of interest in his beloved rock 'n' roll records when he was at Shrewsbury School in the late 1950s. He recalls that there was 'a good deal of low-level hostility to popular music' in his boarding house, where the only records were Handel's *Zadok the Priest* and a recording of a wartime speech by George VI.[20] Seeking fellow enthusiasts, Peel played his copy of Earl Bostic's 'Sleep' for the High Society, a group of sixth-form jazz enthusiasts, but was disappointed by their 'spectacularly stuffy' response. The schoolboy codes of connoisseurship and 'cool' didn't yet have room for African American bluesmen and working-class rockers. A pupil at Cheltenham College in the late 1960s would later describe the new youth culture as being 'like a party going on in the next room, and we couldn't go to it'.[21] Even in 1968, much later in the life cycle of pop, there was a sense that modern youth culture circulated in a different orbit than the boarding school.

While the barriers to entry may have been higher for upper-class pupils, the rewards of membership were just as enticing. Tuned in on a pocket radio in a study somewhere in the depths of a Victorian boarding house, pop's break with what Melly called 'traditional culture' took on a particular frisson. Its strangeness and power were amplified by its implicit challenge to the culture of the school. When he first heard Elvis on the radio, John Peel felt as though a 'naked extra-terrestrial' had walked through the door and asked to cohabit.[22] But pop was more than just a new style of music. It was a whole new zeitgeist that ran through records, films, books, art, photography and fashion, all of which privileged the values of youth, pleasure and modernity over those of age, discipline and tradition.

One of the traditional cultures that pop broke away from was the system of managed adolescence that had first emerged in the Victorian public schools. For many generations of young people, it had been the public school, the Scout troop, the Boys' Brigade, the sports club, the borstal, the political youth organization and the cadet force that had furnished the organizational structures of adolescence. This old institutional mode was rapidly outflanked by the new youth culture that emerged post-war, offering an alternative means of identity formation – a new self that was conferred through membership of a new tribe. It was in post-Second World War America that the now ubiquitous figure of the 'teenager' first appeared in magazines, radio shows and advertisements, and what we now recognize as modern youth culture was born.[23] The new sounds and styles that originated on the streets and in the clubs were quickly co-opted by marketing executives who were keen to muscle in on a new trend. But the product of that struggle between the streets and the suits was a powerful new conception of youth, one that was impatient with all attempts to curtail its liberty or control its identity. This was an entirely different prospect than G. Stanley Hall's 1904 concept of the 'adolescent', whose tempestuous psychosocial development harked back to mankind's primitive origins and who thus required careful supervision by adult experts.[24]

The new sounds of pop and rock music became an important part of the under-life of the school, furnishing disaffected boys and girls with a new palette of colours in which to paint the self in opposition to the institution. In his 1971 study of the girls' boarding school system, the sociologist Mallory Wober recorded a conversation with a senior pupil on the pleasures of music as an escape from the rigours of school: 'Music to me means home, freedom, beauty, especially jazz. I love it, it's also romantic and seductive. I like to listen and relax and forget about work here and school life.'[25]

One of the less obvious modi operandi of the boarding school is to curate pupils' sensory experiences. Through the combination of architecture, landscape, art collections, pageantry and ritual, the boarding school creates a complete aesthetic environment that seeks to influence its pupils' taste and behaviour in ways that academic study and organized sports cannot. This is one of the reasons why censorship has long been a feature of boarding school discipline. The authorities place restrictions on access to music, books, newspapers, radio and television in order to avoid disturbing their carefully cultivated air of antiquity and tradition. The jazz musician and broadcaster Humphrey Lyttelton recalled how at Eton in the 1930s jazz music was considered 'as undesirable for the sons of gentlemen as Left Wing politics or Sex'.[26] But while gramophones and wireless sets were banned in the dormitories, certain 'adventurous spirits' built homemade crystal sets, which they hid in their boot lockers and brought out after lights out to listen to the latest jazz and blues sounds.[27] The secret practice of late-night listening seems to have continued through the decades. Wober records numerous instances in the late 1960s and early '70s of girls hiding transistor radios in teddy bears so that they could tune in after lights out; he also describes one case where an enterprising pupil converted the creaking water pipes in her dormitory to act as an antenna to broadcast a radio signal to surrounding rooms.

In many schools, however, pop life existed in an intermediate space between the official structures of the institution and its clandestine under-life. At Charterhouse Mike Rutherford was caned for defying his housemaster's ban on playing his guitar in his study. In his memoir Rutherford explains how he got as much of a kick out of carrying his guitar around the school grounds as actually playing it: 'Leading it through the old stone cloisters felt so clandestine: a real two-fingers up to the masters.'[28] And yet Rutherford met his fellow members of Genesis in Charterhouse's 'Rock Soc', a small student society that was allowed to use school facilities at allotted times in the schedule. At other schools boys and girls petitioned their teachers to allow a weekly viewing of the BBC's *Five Six Special* or ITV's *Cool For Cats*, the first mainstream television pop shows that began to air in the late 1950s. Wober records a junior girl at a Sussex boarding school: 'The most exciting things ... when we watch 'top of the pops' for ten minutes after drawing room ... I looth drawing room it is so booring we are read a book by the housemistress. But I really like this school [*sic*].'[29] At Shrewsbury, John Peel's rock 'n' roll records might not have found many admirers in the High Society, but his interests were tolerated by his enlightened housemaster, who eventually resigned himself to Peel's academic delinquency and let him devote his time entirely to his hobby.

IN THE SHORT time between the late 1950s and the end of the 1960s popular music, fashion and art mutated at an astonishing rate, undergoing a supercharged evolutionary life cycle within the rich new ecosystems of modern youth culture. Music got heavy; hair grew long; the summer of love came and went; the underground split away from the corporatized mainstream; the counterculture blossomed. The arrival of pop in the public schools in the 1950s and early '60s may have been a slow-burn affair, but the hippy styles of the later 1960s spread like wildfire. Indeed, the correlation of taste with social class held true in the brave new worlds of pop, just as it had done in earlier divisions between high- and low-brow culture. Middle-class kids tended to favour the more literary and esoteric ends of the youth cultural spectrum. They tended to be beatniks instead of teddy boys, hippies instead of rockers.

John Rae, former headmaster of Westminster School, describes the late 1960s as a time of constant, low-level 'guerrilla warfare' over the customs and constraints of school life.[30] Countercultural dissent often took the form of a refusal to join in with the collective forms of institutional life: not singing in chapel; not joining clubs; minimal engagement with schoolwork; slouching through cadet corps man-oeuvres. These were all ways of refuting not only the school's petty rules and regulations but the interpersonal relationship between teacher and pupil that was at the heart of the boarding school experience. The hippy culture of the 1960s hit the public schools in a similar way to the aestheticism of the 1920s: it provided an esoteric alternative world in which boys and girls could insulate themselves from their environment. The hippy doctrine of free love furnished a new way to bypass the emotional repression and sexual neurosis of single-sex education; its embrace of Eastern religion was a rejection of compulsory Christianity and an alternative means of engaging with Britain's colonial legacy, albeit one that retained many of the assumptions about the exoticism and 'otherness' of the East that had characterized nineteenth-century orientalism. One of the repeated refrains in Rae's diaries is the struggle to contain the spread of illegal drugs within the boarding school under-life (and keep the resultant scandal out of the national press). Alongside music, fashion and underground magazines, cannabis and LSD provided portals to a psychedelic inner space that was inaccessible to teachers and parents.

We see this refusal to play the game of school life in Lindsay Anderson's 1968 film *if. . .*, which depicts an armed revolution in a traditional boys' boarding school (shot at Anderson's own alma mater, Cheltenham College). Anderson's film is one of the masterpieces of British cinema. It has performed the unlikely feat of installing the fantasy of violent revolution at the heart of the nation's often rather staid mainstream cinematic tradition. But while *if. . .* is most famous today for its scenes of privileged schoolboys wielding machine guns against their masters from the school roof, most of the film is devoted to a minutely observed study of the everyday tensions between the institution's official system of discipline and its illicit under-life. One such scene occurs during the school's annual military manoeuvres, a complex 'war game' that involves the whole school and displays the might of the military-educational complex that held sway in Britain between the late nineteenth and mid-twentieth centuries. When Mick Travis and his gang of dissidents are cornered and 'shot' by a master, they meet him with sullen stares, pause for just long enough to reveal the absurdity of the situation and then drop parodically to the ground. Their lackadaisical response exposes the master's overzealous commitment to the fantasy not only of the war game but of the school itself. The scene adds a new layer of meaning to Sir Henry Newbolt's famous 1897 public school poem 'Vitaï Lampada', which imagines the school cricket field as the ideal training ground for the colonial soldier. With its repeated refrain of 'play up, play up, and play the game', Newbolt's poem encourages its readers not only to play hard at cricket, but to buy in, both ideologically and imaginatively, to the fantasy of school life.[31] With their sullen parody of the military exercise, Travis and co. refuse to play the game.

As with so much of Anderson's visionary work, the boundary between reality and fantasy was blurred: scenes of this sort were replayed in actual schools around the country. The headmaster's speech to Travis and his comrades after they use live rounds during the war game – 'I find that it is often the hair rebels who are first to respond in a crisis' – was a direct quotation from a 1967 book entitled *Eton: How it Works*.[32] John Morris, a junior master at Sedbergh School in Cumbria in 1969, recalled how he and his colleagues struggled to keep the most basic routines of school life up and running amid an atmosphere of widespread disaffection. Morris described the near impossibility of refereeing a rugby match: 'It was a major problem to keep the players actually participating seriously. The ball would be kicked into touch and a suitably long period of time would elapse before anyone would trouble to fetch it.'[33] Simon Farr, who was a pupil at Cheltenham when Anderson was shooting *if. . .*, later recalled that the film's effect on the school was 'incendiary'. The headmaster called *if. . .* a 'brilliant and destructive film', and described how 'our boys, seeing themselves in what seemed to them romantic circumstances, enthusiastically transformed themselves into images of the heroes of the film.'[34] In the wake of the film's release, minor acts of resistance spread throughout the school. A number of sixth-formers refused to act as prefects. There was a mass walkout from a debating society event. Some boys attempted to break into the armoury and rifle range. Little bands of friends re-enacted scenes from the film, especially the imaginary jousting scenes, with their cries of 'Death to tyrants!' and 'England awake!'

When it was released in 1968 *if . . .* was a wildfire success. Anderson's mythic vision was capacious enough to capture both the hermetic world of the public school and the wider current of late 1960s revolutionary sentiment. Anderson later recalled: 'When we wrote it our conclusion seemed like extremest fantasy. When we shot it, in April and May 1968, it seemed like a prophecy.'[35] The year 1968 was the high watermark of student radicalism. This was the year in which Martin Luther King Jr and Bobby Kennedy were assassinated, Russian tanks rolled into Wenceslas Square to suppress the Prague Spring and students occupied university campuses from Berkeley to the LSE to the Sorbonne. The 1968 Cannes film festival was cancelled due to the student uprising in Paris, but in 1969, when the festival reopened, *if . . .* won the Palme d'Or. The British ambassador to France called this 'an insult to the nation'.[36] When Anderson and his screenwriter, David Sherwin, had pitched the film to production companies in 1967, one British producer had threatened to have them horsewhipped for their insolence. The movie was eventually funded by an American company, a fact that Anderson put down to the Americans' imperviousness to the deep-rooted antagonisms of the British class system.

The film was so closely associated with student radicalism that Pauline Kael, the great *New Yorker* film critic, lambasted both Anderson and his production company for 'turning youth onto violent revolt'. 'The market-research people and the press are so eager to sell to "youth",' complained Kael, 'that they'd probably include a machine gun with the admission ticket if it were economically feasible.'[37] Yet Anderson deliberately chose to erase from his film almost all references to contemporary culture and politics. 'We were consciously determined', he explained, '*not* to appear to be reflecting, in journalistic style, revolutionary student action in France or in America.'[38] Anderson depicts the school and its members as though they existed in an ethereal Victorian dreamtime that hovers somewhere beyond the actual time of 1968. The pupils in the film are dressed in outdated uniforms. With their patterned waistcoats and upright carriages, the prefects in particular look like they have just stepped out of the frame of a sepia-tinted photograph. The soundtrack is composed exclusively of Anglican hymns, the *Missa Luba* (sung by Les Troubadours du Roi Baudouin, a choir of Congolese adults and children) and eerie incidental music by Marc Wilkinson for timpani and plucked strings. There are almost no visual or sonic markers of the modern youth culture that was such a powerful force in the lives of most adolescents in 1968.

By distancing the action from contemporary political events, Anderson was making a wider point about the struggle between Travis and the school authorities. His aim was to look beyond the trappings of reform that public schools wore so prominently on their sleeves and reveal the atavistic conservatism of the institution. In *if* . . . the school ceases to be a particular place and becomes instead a mythic crucible in which we can view what Anderson called 'the basic tensions, between hierarchy and anarchy, independence and tradition, liberty and law'.[39] In his preface to the published script of *if* . . ., Anderson highlighted the historical echoes between his protagonists and the generations of schoolboys that preceded them: 'essentially the heroes of *if* . . . are, without knowing it, old-fashioned boys. They are not anti-heroes, or drop-outs, or Marxist-Leninists or Maoists or readers of Marcuse. Their revolt is inevitable, not because of what they *think*, but because of what they *are*.'[40] Anderson casts Travis, Knightly and Walker as 'old-fashioned boys' in the tradition of Hughes's Tom Brown and Kipling's Stalky. With their 'vital energy' and 'sense of fair play', these heroic English lads embody the noble ideal of youth. This is an almost Rousseauian vision of what it means to be young – to remain pure of heart in spite of the corruption of adult institutions. According to Anderson, Travis and co. rebel not because of what they 'think', but because of what they 'are'. Kael was surely wrong in her judgement that Anderson was cynically seeking to exploit student radicalism for his own ends. The opposite is in fact true: Anderson wanted to reconnect the contemporary counterculture with a deeper tradition and a longer history of youthful radicalism, one that transcended politics and is inherent in the existential ideal of youth itself.

Anderson himself embodied many of the contradictions and ironies that have plagued public school-educated radicals throughout the ages. Like so many of his peers, he was a rebel-nostalgist, caught in the double bind of brooding resentment and suppressed love for his old school. In later life he repeatedly stated how happy he had been at Cheltenham in the 1930s. He was a successful student – head of house, member of the sixth form, an Oxford classics scholar. He and Gavin Lambert, his schoolfriend and later collaborator at *Sight and Sound* magazine, were intellectuals, the 'lowest order of human being' in the school's athletic and militaristic culture.[41] But, as with the aesthetes of the 1910s and '20s, senior boys with intellectual or artistic tendencies could find a pretty comfortable niche in the Cheltenham microcosm. Anderson and Lambert ran the drama club and escaped often to the movies, where they entered 'the world according to MGM, where the pursuit of happiness and the blessings of liberty were so confidently taken for granted'.[42] While Lambert found his métier at school as a 'tart', a junior boy who would perform sexual favours for the senior 'toughs', Anderson found it less easy to express his homosexual desires. Both developed a deep hatred for the emotional repression of the school and the social class it served. The scene in *if. . .* of the sadistic maths teacher who whacks pupils on the back of the head and reaches into their shirts to pinch their nipples was taken directly from Anderson's own memories of Cheltenham.[43]

Anderson's radicalism always had a strongly romantic tinge to it: revolution was not simply a matter of casting aside repressive institutions, but also of rejuvenating the self that was warped by their ill effects, of opening up what E. M. Forster called the 'underdeveloped heart' of the public schoolboy.[44] He may have erased all references to contemporary youth culture from his film, but at the heart of his revolutionary vision was a belief that he held in common with the hippy subculture: that a more complete, authentic self lay buried beneath the artificial personae of socially constructed identities. We see this strain of romantic idealism in the famous café scene in *if. . .*, in which Travis and Knightly form an alliance with the working-class girl who serves them coffee. The scene is a glorious mixture of kitchen sink realism and extravagant surrealist fantasy, and concludes with Mick and 'the girl' (who remains unnamed throughout the film) slashing at each other like wild animals and tangling naked on the floor. It begins, however, in stilted fashion. When they first enter the café, Travis and Knightly's interactions with the girl are gauche, even boorish. Knightly is polite and bashful; Travis makes an unconvincing attempt to appear worldly. When the girl turns to make their coffee, the boys ogle her rear. When Travis tries to kiss the girl, she slaps him. Anderson's staging deftly captures the mixture of born-to-rule arrogance and callow inexperience that is the product of the all-male boarding school. But when Mick plays a song on the jukebox, a switch is flipped. The artificial walls of class and gender are dissolved by the primal energies of youth, sex and freedom. As the music of the *Missa Luba* rises about them, Mick and the girl cavort with a primal intensity that threatens to burn right through the celluloid strip itself. The orgiastic café scene prefigures the film's conclusion, in which the girl joins the revolutionary boys on the school roof, from where they strafe parents, pupils, teachers and various assembled worthies with machine gun fire.

The original script for *if...* was titled 'Crusaders', but when it came to present the document to the headmaster of Cheltenham College in the hopes of being allowed to shoot at the school, Anderson and Sherwin got cold feet and cast about for a less radical-sounding alternative. When Anderson pinned a notice on their production company's wall asking for suggestions for something 'very old-fashioned, corny, and patriotic', their secretary, Daphne Hunter, immediately suggested Rudyard Kipling's poem 'If'.[45] But 'If' only became 'If...' later in the day when Anderson returned from an errand, saw the title on the noticeboard and instinctively added the ellipsis. He liked this so much that he immediately decided that it should become the title of the actual film, and not just the defanged version submitted to his alma mater.

What exactly do those three dots add to Kipling's poem? Kipling's original has come to represent the very acme of high-Imperialist machismo, the summation of the masculine values of physical strength, self-control, impartial judgement, community spirit and enlightened rule that were at the heart of the late Victorian and Edwardian public school ethos. The poem itself is composed of a series of conditional statements that set out the ingredients for the ideal masculine type:

If you can talk with crowds and keep your virtue,
Or walk with Kings – nor lose the common touch,
If neither foes nor loving friends can hurt you,
If all men count with you, but none too much;
If you can fill the unforgiving minute
With sixty seconds' worth of distance run,
Yours is the Earth and everything that's in it,
And – which is more – You'll be a Man, my son![46]

The poem enacts a logical progression. If you fulfil these conditions, then you will become fully mature and masculine: 'you'll be a Man, my son.' But when Anderson added the ellipsis at the end of Kipling's title – when 'If' became 'If . . .' – he converted the conditional into the hypothetical mood. What was the title of a poem about the narrow conditions of masculine identity became instead an invitation to open-ended dreaming. What if we were truly free to act in accordance with our authentic and unmediated desires? What if disaffected youth joined forces to change the world at the point of a gun? What if we followed the spirit of fair play to the very letter of its law? What if we abolished private education and the class hierarchy it perpetuates? Everything hinges on the power of that magical hypothetical: what *if* these imagined realities came true. After the first screening of the film at the British Film Institute in 1969, Anderson rushed onto the stage as the curtain fell and implored the audience: 'the rest is up to you.'[47]

BUT THE REVOLUTION did not happen – or at least, not in the way that Anderson might have hoped. Today it is clear that the principal legacy of the 1960s underground was in the domain of popular culture and commerce, rather than reformed social institutions. We enjoy the cultural legacy of the radical sixties in so many facets of our everyday lives – from rock 'n' roll to organic food and from graphic design to 'flexible' business management – while we live in a society in which inequality has risen and the privately educated elite continues to dominate. The musician Robert Wyatt observed that, 'with the best will in the world the people involved might have thought that they were providing an alternative, but they were simply making the

Establishment more flexible'.[48] Wyatt's musings were amply confirmed in 2008 when David Cameron, the Conservative prime minister and alumnus of Eton College, stated in an interview that *if . . .* was his favourite film, claiming to be inspired by its anti-establishment politics and youthful idealism.[49] Cameron said that the film captured his own mood of frustration with the cadet corps when he was at the school in the 1980s. This is a paradigmatic example of the cultural flexibility of the establishment. The radical popular culture of yesterday, with its violent opposition to the old institutions of power and privilege, is co-opted as just another form of heritage culture to be placed along-side all of the other misty-eyed visions of the English past. What was once a radical attack on class privilege and atavistic conservatism is converted into a polite museum piece that is accessible to all and incapable of causing offence.

In spite of its egalitarian ethos and cosmopolitan outlook, the 1960s counterculture replicated many of the hierarchical assumptions that were built into the post-war education system. Since the early nineteenth century the public school had been the training ground for an elite leadership class that disproportionately filled prestigious positions both within the institutions of state – parliament, the civil service, the judiciary, the church, the military and so on – and also within glamorous cultural industries such as publishing, broadcasting and academia. Woven deep into the fabric of public school educa-tion was the assumption that it prepared pupils for future positions of authority and power. They may have instilled their charges with a tempering sense of aristocratic *noblesse oblige* or bourgeois moral conscience, but the leading schools retained a foundational sense of themselves and their charges as being destined to play an active role in the life of the nation.

Butler and Fleming's post-war education reforms left this struc-ture and the assumptions it fostered in place, with the concession that the public schools would now have to compete with the products of the upper tier of the state education system – the grammar school boys and girls. The effects of this hierarchical structure overflowed into the new youth culture, where dissident members of the public school elite used the self-confidence and easy authority that were the products of their privileged educations to found the alternative institutions of the music and fashion industries, art and design. Jonathon Green's oral history of the British counterculture, *Days in the Life* (1988), demonstrates the extent to which it was white, upper middle-class, privately educated dropouts who were the driving force. The aristocratic 'Chelsea set', who combined fashion and art to convert London into a hip global capital; the Oxbridge intellectuals who staged Allen Ginsberg's era-defining 1965 reading at the Royal Albert Hall; Marsha Rowe, Rosie Boycott and Carmen Callil, the founding editors of *Spare Rib*, the iconic feminist magazine: the list of privileged radicals who reshaped British culture in the 1960s is long indeed. Horace Ové, the black British experimental film-maker, observed that: 'All the '60s counterculture leaders would have been leaders, whenever it was. They had that ability. They were bright kids. They were an elite, a hierarchy, and then there were the followers. Although they gave the impression that everybody had a say, there was still an elite.'[50]

While Melly cast the emergence of pop in the 1950s as a response to the experience of educational deprivation and post-war austerity, the hippy culture that emerged in the later 1960s grew out of the middle-class experience of educational privilege and economic affluence. Rosie Boycott, who was expelled from Cheltenham Ladies' College (the sister school to the institution depicted in *if. . .*) before she went on to become one of the nation's leading newspaper editors, captured the mixture of hedonistic abandon and career-oriented calculation that defined the leaders of the counterculture:

> What we were offering was a freedom to do what you wanted: to take drugs if you want, to stay up all night, to work your own hours, to not be regimented, not to have to prove one's success by dressing in a particular way or catching the 8.15 to Waterloo. To prove that there was a different way of running the world. And I assumed that we'd all grow up in some way running the world.[51]

Boycott describes how upper middle-class dropouts saw themselves as cultural exemplars, lifestyle pioneers who demonstrated to the wider world how to live a more satisfying, rounded existence by escaping from the strictures of high-tech capitalist society. The hippy signifiers of psychedelic drugs, free love, Eastern religion and 'far out' musical and graphic styles were extensions of what Richard Neville, the editor of *Oz* magazine, called 'play power', a belief in the radically transformative properties of leisure.[52] Inevitably, it was the sons and daughters of the affluent middle classes who found themselves best positioned to take advantage of play power. In an era before the ubiquity of the unpaid internship, the financial stability ensured by wealthy and supportive parents often enabled an extended period of quasi-adolescence after school or university, a time for prolonged self-discovery and cultural experimentation free from the demands of gainful employment. Thus, for many privileged dropouts in the 1960s and after, what began as a way to escape from the strictures of one's class and education became over time a way to make money, achieve success on one's own terms and enjoy the freewheeling lifestyle associated with the creative arts.

Private education has always been about more than simply the contents of the curriculum. The public school not only equips its pupils with measurable skills and testable knowledge, but subtly moulds their expectations about what constitutes personal success and how it should be achieved. In his 1986 study of public school life, Geoffrey Walford observed how pupils balanced their identification with youth subcultures that challenged the authority of the school with their continued adherence to the principles of hard work and strategic thinking that were necessary for future career success. As Walford put it, 'the boys skilfully construct a cultural form which enables them to retain this solid core of understanding of themselves as people with a future.'[53] They may listen to rock music and smoke behind the bicycle sheds, but in the majority of cases, Walford suggests, they retain a deep-seated commitment to the values of hard work and individual success that are so central to the ethos of the institution. One of the unstated assumptions of elite education is that even extracurricular and leisure activities are ultimately geared towards future success; they are useful ways to build a cv and demonstrate one's 'roundedness' to future employers. Whereas the state school pupil experiences a clear spatial division between work and play, in the boarding school both are included within the same continuous space. Against the backdrop of the elite boarding school, the hippy subculture starts to look a bit like another extracurricular activity.

More than financial assistance and moral support, it was the rarefied forms of cultural capital that accompanied an elite education that contributed to the success of public school graduates in the creative industries. Nowhere was this more apparent than in the careers of the privately educated impresarios who disrupted a music industry that was dominated by staid corporate heavyweights such as Decca and EMI. Brian Epstein, manager of The Beatles, Tony Secunda, manager of Procol Harum, Simon Napier-Bell, manager of the Yardbirds and Marc Bolan, Tony Stratton-Smith, manager of Genesis, Andrew Loog Oldham, manager of The Rolling Stones and Marianne Faithfull, Chris Blackwell, founder of Island Records, and Richard Branson, founder of Virgin Records, were all educated at private boarding schools. The rock 'n' roll rebel may have been a new kind of working-class icon, but his backstage manager was often an ex-public schoolboy on the make.

In the preface that he added for the 2004 reprint of his breathless first draft of pop history, *Awopbopaloobop Alopbamboom* (1969), the journalist Nik Cohn recalled that, 'Rock in the late Sixties was still a spontaneous combustion. Nobody bothered with long-term strategies; hanging on once the thrill was gone was unthinkable.'[54] This is one of the enduring myths of the radical sixties: that the new developments in music, fashion, art and commerce were fuelled by spontaneous enterprise and egalitarian spirit. But in spite of its buccaneering, sometimes semi-criminal ethos, music-driven youth culture was an industry like any other. The public school graduates who took the business by storm in the 1960s and '70s played a game that was just as strategic and calculating as if they had been seeking to climb the career ladder in a traditional corporation. In his memoir *Black Vinyl, White Powder* (2001), Simon Napier-Bell recalls how in an industry that was divided between upper-class executives and working-class talent, 'young men in their twenties with a public school education plus a modicum of unconventionality could cross the divide between the two cultures'.[55] These men practised a new kind of 'code-switching' that enabled them to shift back and forth between the old system of establishment prestige and the new currency of subcultural cool. They were hip denizens of the underground, who also happened to have the right accents, manners and *savoir faire* to make a favourable impression in the company boardroom.

Andrew Loog Oldham was an alumnus of Wellingborough School, an elite boys' grammar school founded in 1595. According to his school friend John Douglas, Wellingborough was 'a damned good apprenticeship for learning the price that the world demands of its rebels'.[56] The school provided a stage for Oldham's oppositional self-fashioning, an enabling background against which his self-crafted image could emerge. In his autobiography, Oldham describes how he learned the rudiments of his sartorial style from his housemaster at Wellingborough, who sported an array of cavalry twill trousers, two-button suits with bone buttons and hacking pockets, lapelled vests, tight trousers and chukka boots. Oldham would later customize this gentlemanly wardrobe on the King's Road in Chelsea, where he worked as an assistant to Mary Quant and Alexander Plunket Greene, two of the pioneers of the emerging London fashion scene. Oldham's intricately crafted persona was an amalgam of his public school background with the new urban types he identified during his holiday adventures on the streets of early 1960s London. In his dealings as the manager of the Stones, he switched back and forth between these two systems of value and style. At one moment he was a hip insider, at another he'd become a corporate shark. In Melly's words, he 'knew how to make head waiters crawl and commissionaires climb down'. He took the lower middle-class Stones and taught them how to 'come on like princes'.[57]

Oldham combined this sharp-suited style with an air of androgyny that he also learned at school. In his memoir, he recalls how at Wellingborough the 'traditional unofficial curriculum was romancing the boys'.[58] While most boys quickly discarded their romantic personae when they left boarding school, adopting more conventional heterosexual postures as soon as the opportunity arose, Oldham retained his effeminacy for strategic effect. He often wore eye shadow and called men 'darling' in order to keep his opponents off balance and engineer an opportunity to steal their girlfriends. By combining traditional gentlemanly style with spiky androgyny, Oldham was at the cutting edge of the new styles of masculinity that emerged in the 1960s. With his sharp suits and kohl-lined eyes, he played a similar game to the one depicted in classic 1960s films and television shows such as Joseph Losey's *The Servant*, Nicolas Roeg and Donald Cammell's *Performance*, and Brian Clemens's *The Avengers*. He vamped the traditional symbols of masculine identity, retaining the crisp tailoring and sharp lines of the gentlemanly uniform, while at the same time infusing it with a hip knowingness and an effete decadence.

Perhaps the biggest challenge to the public school ethos in the 1960s was neither state control nor armed rebellion, but instead a new cultural ideal of masculinity. Youth culture was based on the foundational assumption that identity was a malleable construct, rather than an inherited essence. Marianne Faithfull dubbed Oldham 'a great fabricator of selves', a role that encompassed not only his own restless self-invention but his work with the musicians he managed.[59] In addition to teaching the Stones how to sell sex to teenage girls, he also taught Faithfull how to sell sex to teenage boys. At the age of twenty, still fresh from boarding school, Oldham crafted the press release for Faithfull's first single, 'As Tears Go By', co-written by Mick Jagger and Keith Richards of the Stones:

> Marianne Faithfull is the little seventeen-year-old blonde . . . who still attends a convent in Reading . . . daughter of the Baroness Erisso.
>
> She is lissom and lovely with long blonde hair and a shy smile, and she confesses quietly to a liking for people who are 'long-haired and socially conscious'.
>
> She likes Marlon Brando, Woodbine cigarettes, poetry and going to the ballet, and she loves to wear long evening dresses.
>
> She is a shy, wistful girl with a waif-like beauty all of her own.[60]

Oldham's vision of the 'shy, waif-like beauty' who also has a taste for Woodbines and Marlon Brando is pure schoolboy fantasy, a combination of unthreatening demureness with a strong whiff of debauchery.

This was a not-so-subtle play on gender archetypes that were rooted in the middle-class experience of sexual segregation in the private education system. Faithfull, the daughter of an Austrian aristocrat and an eccentric Welsh academic, was educated at a private Catholic day school in Berkshire, but none of this stopped Oldham from portraying her as an upper-class English waif who had turned to the bad. Faithfull later attributed the intensity of her vilification by the press to Oldham's confected image of her as 'quintessentially English and from a wealthy and protected background'.[61]

Oldham's reputation as a smart exploiter of sexual desire was celebrated in The Rolling Stones' spectacularly obscene 1964 song 'Andrew's Blues', which contrasts the desiccated Sir Edward Lewis, the elderly head of Decca Records, with Oldham, the decadent rock 'n' roll manager. The song contrasts the business smarts and sexual wiles of two former public schoolboys (Lewis was an Old Rugbeian) who were struggling for control of the new musical scene. While Sir Edward's company had famously failed to sign The Beatles in 1962, a clear sign of his being out of touch with the new youth culture, Oldham was a more flexible, dangerous, wised-up kind of operator who had more than just a 'modicum of unconventionality'.

Kit Lambert played a similar double game in his management of The Who, simultaneously escaping from and drawing upon his privileged background. Lambert was an alumnus of Lancing College, a prestigious Sussex boarding school founded during the Victorian boom years, and the son of Constant Lambert, the classical composer and music director of the Sadler's Wells ballet company. When he first met The Who in a sweaty Edgware Road basement club he had almost no familiarity with popular music, whether it be RnB, skiffle or rock. But what he lacked in subcultural knowledge he amply made up for in gentlemanly *sprezzatura*. The Who was a collaborative project that drew on a diverse array of talents from across the segregated strands of the post-war education system. Lambert was the glamorous, effete intellectual from the rarefied world of the public schools. With his well-cut suits and seemingly magical ability to acquire credit with Kensington wine merchants, he came across as a hippyfied survivor from the Brideshead generation. Chris Stamp, his managerial partner, was educated at an East End secondary modern school, the lowest tier of the state system. With his Cockney patter and sharp-edged Mod look, Stamp provided the East End yin to Lambert's West End yang. As for the band themselves, Pete Townshend, Roger Daltrey and John Entwistle were all grammar school boys with intellectual aspirations, although Keith Moon went to a secondary modern and technical college.[62]

It was mainly under Lambert's influence that The Who, led by their ambitious songwriter Townshend, extended their cultural repertoire and incorporated elements from opera and mystical religion into their music. As a child Lambert had been exposed to his father's coterie of musicians and artists, which had included Margot Fonteyn and Sergei Diaghilev. He was steeped in European high culture and spoke fluent French and German. Lambert served as both business manager and cultural guide to The Who, seeking to harness the rasping energy of their music – including Townshend's famously destructive treatment of his guitars – to the high cultural values of his own background. It was Lambert, for instance, who collaborated on the script for the epic 'rock opera' *Tommy*, and it was Lambert again who suggested the band perform the work live at the Metropolitan Opera in New York in June 1970. This was not only a means of making money and generating publicity, but a way of paying homage to his father's work as a classical composer. Just as the dandy-aesthetes of the 1920s had utilized their cultural sophistication – Lucretius *and* jazz, Shelley *and* Soviet cinema – to forge careers in the new mass media landscape of radio and film, Lambert deployed a similarly flexible connoisseurship to thrive in the new ecosystems of youth culture.

In spite of his innovative approach to music management, Lambert's career ultimately fell into the clichéd rock 'n' roll narrative of drug addiction and financial scandal. Lambert and Stamp were fired as The Who's managers in 1974 after a bitter legal dispute over missing royalties. What followed was a prolonged period of addiction and poverty, which culminated with his death from a brain haemorrhage after an altercation in a nightclub in 1981. But in his pomp, Lambert embodied the spirit of generosity and idealism that characterized the best aspects of upper-class bohemianism in the 1960s.

In his autobiography, Keith Richards reflected on Mick Jagger's and his friendship with the 'Chelsea set' and concluded that, 'I've never known if they were slumming or we were snobbing.'[63] There is a tendency within cultural criticism to fit all such exchanges into the transactional model of slumming and snobbing, in which individuals from different class backgrounds extract different kinds of cultural and social capital from each other through their association. But we might see it instead as an exchange of knowledge, rather than prestige, a kind of informal pedagogy in which the different parties learn about facets of experience that would otherwise have been denied them. This isn't simply an attempt to wish away class differences, but rather to acknowledge that at the centre of many of these relationships was a shared enthusiasm for art and culture. Ideas and allusions were exchanged, as well as status and prestige. In his collaboration with The Who, Lambert treated the inherited privileges of his class and education not simply as personal attributes, capacities of taste and intellect that were inherent properties of a unique self, but instead as resources to be shared, gifts to be bestowed. Known to many as 'the Baron' on account of his urbane manners and dandyish style, he acted as a kind of catalytic agent in the swirling seas of the new youth culture, a sparker of connections and maker of deals, who carelessly squandered his ample stock of charm, confidence and culture in order to make things happen for other people, as well as for himself.

We encounter yet another way of combining educational privilege with youth cultural enterprise in the career of Richard Branson, one of modern Britain's most prominent businessmen. Branson is a ubiquitous figure in today's popular media as the founder of the Virgin business empire, which encompasses everything from inter-city rail services to mobile phones, and from fizzy cola to commercial space flight. More than just a successful entrepreneur (although his biographer, Tom Bower, questions exactly how successful the Virgin business model really is), Branson is the figurehead for the liberal vision of capitalist free enterprise as a form of creative self-expression.[64] Branson's memoir, *Losing My Virginity* (1998), is an epic tale of self-actualization through commercial enterprise, a relentless sequence of challenges met, industries disrupted and rules charismatically broken. Branson styles himself as an 'adventure capitalist' who combines the counter-cultural ethos of anti-authoritarianism with a ruthless drive to make money. In doing so, he flaunts his rebellious teenage years at the elite Stowe College as yet another dazzling entry on his nonconformist's cv: 'I have always thought rules were there to be broken and Stowe had as many rules and regulations as the army – many of them, it seemed to Jonny Gems and me, completely anachronistic and pointless.'[65] The central event in the self-created Branson myth is his departure from Stowe at the age of fifteen, mutually agreed upon by headmaster, parents and pupil. Famously, on Branson's final day at the school the headmaster predicted that he would either become a millionaire or end up in jail. The mythic narrative that Branson weaves suggests that it was by rejecting the formal institution of the boarding school that he was able to achieve his full potential in the buccaneering world of the 1960s counterculture. But the narrative of rupture and freedom obscures the continuing legacy of his affluent background and elite education. After all, when Virgin Records was prosecuted for tax evasion in 1971, it was his mother who remortgaged the family's Surrey mansion in order to pay the out-of-court settlement.

Branson left Stowe in order to work full time on the magazine he and his friend Jonny Gems had founded while still at school. *Student* was a countercultural publication with the aim 'of getting every Public School boy more interested in politics and to know about the improvements and "goings on" at every other public school in the country'.[66] In a similar vein to *Out of Bounds*, the paper sought to connect the dissenting elements that were scattered throughout the nation's public school system. To begin with, the magazine was run on Branson's sheer nerve and effrontery. He sold advertising space from a public telephone box on the edge of Stowe's lavish grounds and he conducted correspondence on headed notepaper provided by Jonny Gems's businessman father. The masthead of the first edition claimed that *Student* had correspondents in Europe, the Caribbean, the Middle East, the USA, Russia and Africa, but it is unclear whether these were dedicated reporters or simply acquaintances of Branson's family.

In spite of its small-scale production, *Student* sold tens of thousands of copies and attracted contributions from numerous cultural and political heavyweights. It ran interviews with R. D. Laing, Vanessa Redgrave and Jean-Paul Sartre, and published original work by James Baldwin and Robert Graves. In the first issue, Gavin Maxwell, the author of the children's classic *Ring of Bright Water*, contributed an essay on the ideological effects of formal education: 'all civilised races of mankind are so thoroughly indoctrinated by their education as to render their intellects functionless. Each individual has to a greater or lesser degree, been brainwashed, although we prefer the word "educated", and so have all nations at all times.'[67] The magazine's radical credentials were impeccable.

Yet Branson himself maintained a certain distance from the scene on which he reported. In contrast to previous radical public school magazines, such as *Out of Bounds*, *Eton Candle* and *The Heretick*, *Student* adopted a neutral, disinterested editorial line. Branson's editorial in the first edition announced that the paper's aim was to 'develop as a platform for all shades of opinion, all beliefs and ideas'.[68] Rather than rejecting school authority in favour of a specific creed or cause, such as aesthetic hedonism or communist revolution, *Student* took the classical liberal line of encouraging an open-ended process of debate. The suspicion was, however, that the posture of political disinterest in fact served a deeper strategic goal: careerist ambition. Even when he was still at Stowe neglecting his studies in favour of producing a little magazine, Branson wrote to his concerned father that 'it is, in my opinion, a career like anything else'.[69] From this perspective, liberal disinterest functions not only as a political philosophy but as a productive business practice. By remaining free of limiting political commitments, the entrepreneur is free to invest and expand wherever he chooses. In his memoir, Branson describes *Student* as a 'flexible concept' and explains how 'I wanted to explore this flexibility to see how far I could push it and where it could lead.'[70] In the context of the 1960s counterculture, the values of flexibility, creativity and ceaseless reinvention were radical alternatives to establishment values. But by 1998, when Branson wrote his autobiography, they had become integral to the very ethos of corporate capitalism.

THIS CHAPTER HAS explored a range of different ways in which affluent, white, privately educated graduates embraced the new possibilities of post-war youth culture as an escape from the strictures of their class background and a free-form career path. Peter Gabriel's starry-eyed enthusiasm; Nick Drake's weary irony; Lindsay Anderson's revolutionary idealism; Rosie Boycott's lifestyle leadership; Andrew Loog Oldham's cutting-edge cool; Kit Lambert's spendthrift generosity; Richard Branson's cut-throat careerism: these are all different strategies for weaving together cultural materials drawn from the disparate worlds of youth subculture and educational privilege. In the postures they struck and the values they espoused, these figures formulated different responses to one of the defining experiences of post-war British life: the persistence of class divisions enshrined within the education system. They registered the different degrees of self-awareness, discomfort, guilt, greed and generosity that accompanied the experience of privilege.

But what of those who were denied this experience? How did performers and artists from different walks of life respond to the predominance of privately educated graduates within the creative industries? It seems fitting that this chapter should conclude with at least one voice from beyond the gilded environs of the public school. And what better voice than the rasping, rambling and frequently inspired tones of Lee 'Scratch' Perry, the eccentric genius of Jamaican dub music, much of whose work was published by Chris Blackwell, the Harrow-educated scion of a colonial plantation family and founder of Island Records (named after Alec Waugh's 1955 novel *Island in the Sun*). Blackwell was raised on his parents' Jamaican estate, located in Oracabessa Bay next to Ian Fleming's GoldenEye villa. He began his career as a rebel-entrepreneur at Harrow, where he sold booze and fags to his fellow pupils and was, he later recalled, 'caned by everyone you could be caned by – the head of school, the housemaster, everybody'.[71] When Blackwell was eventually 'asked to leave' Harrow, he used his family's wealth to start his own record company, first in Jamaica and then in Britain. Over time, what began as a small-scale operation importing ska music for the diasporic community in Britain grew into one of the most commercially successful independent record labels in

the world, which helped to make the careers of such luminaries as Bob
Marley, Grace Jones, David Bowie and U2. A recent profile in *Men's
Journal* encapsulates Blackwell's hybridized high-low style: 'Blackwell's
louche beach bum presentation is quickly undercut by an impeccably
well-bred, highly ironized, very British sort of world-weariness ... He
is the Dude by way of *Downton Abbey*, Sir Laurence Olivier wasting
away in Margaritaville.'[72] This is yet another entry in the long list of
performative syntheses of subcultural cool and establishment prestige.

But Perry's song 'Judgment in a Babylon' provides a different perspective on this form of ironic self-presentation. This is all a sham,
claims Perry, a front that enables Blackwell's exploitation of Jamaican
music for his own personal gain. After claiming to have witnessed
Blackwell engaging in a voodoo ceremony, the song proceeds to accuse
him of stealing Bob Marley's royalties and ultimately being responsible for the singer's death from cancer. In the incantatory chorus,
Perry repeatedly denounces Blackwell as a vampire who drinks the
blood of his victims.[73] With their mixture of legalistic argument,
voodoo ritual and paranoid conspiracy theory, Perry's lyrics disrupt
the ethos of cross-cultural exchange and 'one-world' harmony that
Blackwell himself helped to associate with Jamaican music. When
Bob Marley turned up in Blackwell's London office in 1972, he was a
much harder-edged figure than the prophet of ganja-fied world peace
whose image adorned the walls of a million student bedsits in the subsequent decades. This softer, more conciliatory image was the product
of Blackwell's managerial advice, a strategic ploy to help Bob Marley
and the Wailers 'cross over' and appeal to white audiences around the
world. Perry's lyrics course with bitter resentment, casting Blackwell
not as a patron of Jamaican music who helped to make the careers
of otherwise overlooked performers, but instead as a fanged cultural
appropriator who gorges on the life force of his exploited clients.

Perry was later to recant his statements and apologize to Blackwell,
who continued to publish his music and profit from his album sales.
But the sentiments expressed in 'Judgment in a Babylon' were echoed
both by Linton Kwesi Johnson, the dub poet, and Jimmy Cliff, the
reggae singer. Johnson accused Blackwell of 'continuing the tradition
of the white ancestors' and Cliff took aim at his manager in his 1974

song 'Number One Rip-off Man'.[74] Like Perry, both later recanted, but the fact that these sentiments kept bubbling up highlights the uneasy legacy of Blackwell's colonial roots. Blackwell started Island Records with the inheritance he received on his eighteenth birthday (the historian Dominic Sandbrook estimates its value at roughly a million pounds in today's money).[75] Through the start-up funds drawn from the Blackwell family's plantation wealth, Island Records was directly connected to the historical legacies of colonialism and slavery. Blackwell may have done his best to assuage that legacy, to render it irrelevant through the sheer force of his love for Jamaican music and Rastafarian culture, but structural inequalities built up over centuries are stubbornly resistant to goodwill. This is the deep background to Perry's song, the festering historical wound that underwrites the otherwise seemingly hyperbolic language of voodoo and vampirism.

The question that remains, however, is this: is the utopian impulse of radical 1960s youth culture entirely neutralized by our latter-day awareness of its failure to transcend the old distinctions of class and caste? Which side of Chris Blackwell's character is ultimately in the ascendant: his authentic love for Jamaican music or his vampiric appropriation of someone else's cultural tradition? Can at least some of Peter Gabriel's starry-eyed enthusiasm at the RamJam Club survive Nick Drake's weary irony in 'Poor Boy'? As Eric Lott notes in his study of white appropriations of African American culture in the form of black face and minstrelsy, the dividing line between love and theft is frequently blurred.[76] The white, privately educated, upper middle-class experience of 1960s youth culture played out within a similarly blurry set of parameters: enthusiasm and irony; revolution and escapism; idealism and cynicism; love and theft.

Scholars with their brothers and sisters at the Eton–Harrow cricket match at Lords, 1975.

# EIGHT

# The Ordinary Elite

In April 2010 at the Royal Court Theatre in London's Sloane Square, a bold new play thrust into the public spotlight the savage initiation rites and entitled arrogance of the British ruling elite. Laura Wade's *Posh* depicts the riotous antics of an exclusive, all-male undergraduate drinking club at Oxford University, whose members are drawn from a handful of the nation's oldest and most prestigious public schools. The events of the play unfold over the course of the club's end of term fling, a night of hedonistic abandon in a rural gastro-pub that traditionally culminates in club members tearing up furniture, smashing windows, vomiting profusely and flashing a credit card to cover the damages. In the opening scene, Guy, one of the club's senior members, has a drink with his Uncle Jeremy at his London club. As they discuss the past escapades of the Riot Club, Jeremy explains the deeper function of the institution: 'you're connecting yourself to hundreds of years of history – bonding over meat and fire." This is the attraction of the club for its members. It is a sacred initiation rite that forges bonds of allegiance between a hermetic group of soon-to-be-powerful men. With its air of secrecy and ethos of aristocratic hauteur, it is an antidote to the bland anomie of the modern world.

The club derives its name from its founder, Lord Riot, an eighteenth-century aristocratic libertine. Deep into the evening's festivities, Toby, who has passed out drunk on the table, becomes the conduit for Lord Riot's ghost, which returns from beyond the grave to spur on these querulous young men to further feats of rapine and debauchery. 'It's your England. It's yours. Take it back,' belches the unquiet spirit through Toby's slavering mouth.[2] Lord Riot is an emanation from the dark underside of upper-class culture, the same well of appetite and entitlement that bubbled up in the conservative defence of the eighteenth-century public schools and Harry Flashman's opportunistic adventures among the Victorian ruling class. Over the course of the evening the tension builds between the increasingly lairy boys and Chris, the eager-to-please landlord. Deep in his cups, one club member, Alistair, takes exception to Chris's chummy attitude and launches into an astonishing anti-democratic tirade against 'decent hardworking people'.[3] Wade's script subtly articulates the uncertainties and resentments of a group of hyperprivileged young adults in an age of mass democracy. Toby sneers at state-educated undergraduates from Stockport as 'basically children', because they haven't undergone public school character training, which imparts a confidence and maturity that goes beyond simply passing exams.[4] James, the club president, is mercilessly ribbed when his friends discover an application for a trainee position at Deutsche Bank in his bag. This contradicts the club's aristocratic ethos and disrupts their fantasy of freedom from the deadening routines of conventional employment. 'We don't fill out forms,' exclaims Harry, while Guy agrees that this is 'not Riot Club behaviour'.[5]

The play comes to its violent, drunken climax when Chris confronts the boys about their mistreatment of his daughter, who has been waiting tables. When Chris refuses to take the large wad of cash that Alistair presses upon him and starts to threaten them with charges of sexual harassment, Alistair boils over and punches him. The rest of the gang pile on and the landlord is left in a bloody mess on the floor. The final scene takes place a few months later, back at Uncle Jeremy's club. Jeremy has summoned Alistair, who is facing criminal charges for his assault on Chris. Over Scotch and water, Jeremy promises to smooth things over for Alistair by offering the landlord a substantial amount of money and planning permission for an extension to his pub. But this is only a prelude to a further offer to Alistair of a job working for the Conservative Party. Jeremy sounds out Alistair's views about the Riot Club and its wider social role, a test that Alistair passes with flying colours with his clear-eyed analysis of the function of sacred violence in binding together the members of the tribe.

On its first run in the spring of 2010 *Posh* proved a massive popular success, playing to full houses and garnering admiring reviews in the national press. The timing of the production could not have been better, coinciding as it did with the election of the Tory–Liberal coalition, which was headed by a prominent coterie of former public schoolboys: David Cameron (Eton), George Osborne (St Paul's) and Nick Clegg (Westminster) were merely the most immediately recognizable figures in a cabinet of which the majority was privately educated. Wade's play deliberately invoked the infamous Bullingdon Club portrait of Cameron and Boris Johnson, the Old Etonian Mayor of London and prominent Tory politician, taken during their undergraduate days at Oxford in 1987, in which they stand alongside their fellow club members on the steps of Brasenose College, ready for a night of riotous abandon.

Like the Riot Club, the Bullingdon is an undergraduate dining club whose members are drawn from a select group of ancient schools – pukka chaps from Eton, Harrow and Winchester, rather than 'tugs' from minor public schools or 'stains' from grammar and comprehensive schools.[6] In his 1928 novel *Decline and Fall*, Evelyn Waugh depicted the annual meeting of the 'Bollinger' as a glittering whirlwind of shattered windows, smashed-up grand pianos, cigar burns in expensive carpets and desecrated artworks, all of which is accompanied by 'the sound of English country families baying for broken glass'.[7] In Waugh's telling, this is as integral a part of the rituals of upper-class life as hunt meetings, debutante balls and society weddings. In recent years, the exploits of the Bullingdon Club have been updated to include the burning of £50 notes in front of homeless people on street corners, the decoration of new initiates' college rooms with smashed furniture and bodily fluids, and the consumption of illicit drugs, but the same taste for the destruction of property and hedonism persists.[8]

Before Cameron became Prime Minister in 2010 there was a great deal of public debate as to whether it was possible for an Old Etonian to hold high office in today's supposedly more egalitarian culture. In the early days of his leadership of the Conservative Party, measures were taken by the party's retinue of publicists to de-Etonize Cameron. This included everything from cycling to work, husky sledding in the

Arctic, expressions of love for what the Tories used to call 'feral youth' and the suppression of all photographic evidence of membership of the Bullingdon Club. The company that took the photograph and owns the copyright withdrew the image from public circulation in 2007, allegedly on their own initiative, but this only occurred after Cameron entered the public eye.[9] The Bullingdon Club portrait disrupted the approachable, demotic image of the future PM that was presented by the Conservative PR machine. This was a piece of toxic heritage aesthetics, in which the future leaders of the nation appeared in the guise of the late-Imperial ruling class. The black-and-white print, the tailcoats and bow ties, the worn college steps, the air of entitled nonchalance: this is an image of the zombie elite, the old money and old power that refuses to die.

It was this suppressed image that lent *Posh* much of its polemical bite. And yet, in spite of its topicality and critical acclaim, there was a serious flaw in Laura Wade's play: it painted a fundamentally in-accurate picture of how privilege works in contemporary British society. Wade's play colluded in an outdated fantasy – one that was shared by both progressive critics and the characters depicted onstage – about the shadowy influence of the old boys' network and the deep establishment. Since the social and cultural upheavals of the 1960s, a new kind of elitism has emerged in Britain. Inequality may be at its highest level in decades, but the self-presentation of those at the top of the pile has changed. Rather than clinging to the traditional markers of status and prestige – aristocratic hauteur, clannish exclu-sivity and clearly defined accents – modern elites tend to be more self-effacing. In place of the narrowly defined tastes of a prior epoch, most members of today's elite are cultural omnivores, who knowingly mix high and low culture: classical music *and* TV talent shows; literary novels *and* hip hop. Rather than expressing a sense of entitlement, they downplay their privilege and profess their belief in the values of openness, inclusivity and equality of opportunity. Rather than treating wealth and status as their natural rights, they stress the hard work and skill required to achieve their position in society. The sociologists who conducted the BBC's 2013 Great British Class Survey, a massive online study of class identities in contemporary Britain, call this the 'ordinary elite', a social class composed of the top 6 per cent of earners, or roughly 1 million people.[10] With the post-war growth in state education, the expansion of the university system in the 1960s and more transparent hiring practices in prestigious industries such as finance and law, the influence of the old gentlemanly elite, which used to dominate culture and politics, has been reduced to rump status, confined to a few last, albeit well-cellared and extremely comfortable, redoubts.

On the whole, modern Britain is a meritocracy, both in terms of cultural values and institutional practices. As Mike Savage and Karel Williams point out, however, meritocracy can serve as a way of 'justifying the privileges of those at the apex of the hierarchy'.[11] By proclaiming the values of hard work and native intelligence, members of the ordinary elite deflect attention from the social context that enabled their talents to flourish. They may be faintly embarrassed about their class status, but they can still purchase a significant competitive advantage for their children by sending them to a private school. Today, private education gives pupils a head start in life not by granting access to the 'old boy network', nor by instilling in its pupils a sense of born-to-rule arrogance, but instead by preparing them to pass exams, coaching them for university admissions interviews and polishing their CVs with a wide range of extracurricular activities. The days of classics and character, flogging and fagging, are a distant memory. The last vestiges of the total institution have been cast aside in favour of more liberal discipline and improved pastoral care. Boarding has declined and co-education is the norm. Since the 1960s Britain's private schools have been transformed into lavishly equipped academic powerhouses, which prepare the children of the already affluent for success in a highly competitive global marketplace. Research shows that private education provides a significant social and economic advantage to those who can afford it: on average, public school pupils receive higher grades at both GCSE and A level, have much better chances of attending elite universities and earn more per year than their state-educated peers.[12]

In spite of these wide-ranging changes in the fabric of British society, the allure of the old signifiers of class privilege remains strong. *Posh* and the Bullingdon Club portrait sit alongside *Downton Abbey* and 'Keep Calm and Carry On' posters as part of today's postmodern retro culture. Rather than shocking revelations of the shadowy ways of the ruling establishment, they are self-satisfied costume dramas, historical fantasies that revel in the antique kitsch of yesterday's class system. Interestingly, both progressive critics and the members of the Bullingdon Club itself seem to enjoy the anachronism. For critics, the fantasy of the old boys' network provides a clearly defined and instantly recognizable enemy, one that simplifies the complexities of a society that has been profoundly transformed by neoliberal economics and globalization. For the members of the club themselves, the enjoyment is of a different order. By donning the garb of eighteenth-century aristocrats, young men who are being prepared for high-flying careers within the highly technocratic global capitalist system enjoy a brief holiday from the rigours of their training. For one night each term, they enjoy a sojourn in the old world of entitlement, before returning the following morning to the reality of competition and hard work. The voluminous public debate that centred on both *Posh* and the Bullingdon Club portrait served, ultimately, not as enlightening social analysis, but rather as a distraction from the actual ways in which elite education helps to perpetuate privilege in a time of rapidly expanding social inequality. The challenge that writers, artists and critics face today is how to wean popular taste from the comfort food of heritage nostalgia and, more importantly, how to develop new stories, new characters and new symbols that capture the mores of the self-effacing yet hyperprivileged 'ordinary' elite.

TODAY, IF YOU'RE considering sending your child to a public school, there is a wealth of information available to help you make your choice, including prospectuses, guided tours, handbooks, newspaper reviews and websites. Public schools are businesses and, like most other businesses, they rely on branding and publicity to maintain their competitive advantage. In spite of the local differences between schools – single sex, co-ed, boarding, day, city, country, A level, International Baccalaureate, cost, uniform, facilities and so on – their promotional materials paint a remarkably consistent picture of the contemporary public school experience. As the prospective customer settles in with brochures and laptop to survey the options, a complete universe unfolds on glossy magazine paper and screen-wide banner images. Elegant white forms cluster on the distant horizon of a green cricket field. Pupils walk purposefully between classrooms with books tucked under their arms. Crowds gather with hampers and blankets on the river bank for a regatta. Bright-eyed youths perform on stage in period dress, heat test tubes over Bunsen burners, read ancient manuscripts in wood-panelled libraries, huddle at desks sitting exams, stride across dun-coloured moors with heavy backpacks, tune their instruments in orchestra pits, lean into tackles on muddy rugby fields.

These images cast the public school as a perfect marriage between modernity and tradition. In the foreground, boys and girls cultivate their innermost potentials with the very best facilities that money can buy; in the background, framing this symphony of self-actualization, are the landscape and architecture of the traditional public school, with their deep associations of antiquity and belonging. The architecture always has a starring role in the publicity images. It may not be in the foreground of every shot, but even as a background presence it casts a roseate glow upon the activities depicted. The daily round of school life gains a special lustre when set against the backdrop of cold stone cloisters, creamy red chapels, late Victorian boathouses, wood-panelled cricket pavilions and endless acres of deep green playing fields. This is what your money buys: not just a good education, but also a stake in the national past. The modern public school markets itself as a combination of elite educational institution and high-spec heritage experience, a gateway both to the upper reaches of the global economy and the immemorial English past.

The story of today's resurgent private school system begins in 1971 with the founding of ISIS, or the Independent Schools' Information Service, an umbrella group intended to coordinate the efforts of individual associations, such as the Headmasters' Conference and the Girls' Schools Association, which grew out of the reform of the public school system in the Victorian era.[13] ISIS worked with politicians, the press and the schools themselves to present a consistent and appealing image to the world at large. In 1974 the service was reorganized as the Independent Schools' Joint Council, which over time became the central body for promoting the interests of the private education sector, lobbying government, advising on regulatory frameworks, communicating with the press and coordinating with the Independent Schools' Inspectorate. Today, the renamed Independent Schools Council (ISC) represents Britain's private school system as an internationally renowned industry, part of the wider economic mix that helps Britain compete in the global marketplace.

The service was originally founded, however, as a response to the vocal opposition to private education that emanated both from the Labour Party and wide swathes of the general public in the 1960s. The new organization was the product of a growing awareness among school administrators that private education had a serious image problem within the culture at large. PR had not previously been part of a headmaster's traditional skill set. Ambitious headmasters might build the reputation of their school by winning more Oxbridge scholarships and attracting a more fashionable or wealthy clientele, but they had not as a rule been concerned with the reputation of their schools among the public at large. Public relations were considered rather cheap and grubby, far beneath the concern of the scholar-headmaster, whose task it was to cultivate the hearts and minds of a future generation of leaders. But in the political climate of the 1960s, embattled headmasters were prepared to take a new approach. The ISC helped to smooth down some of the rough edges and present a new image of the public school as a dynamic, modern institution.

This effort at rebranding also coincided with what one historian has called an 'academic revolution', which saw private schools refocus their attention on exam results and university entrance instead of the traditional virtues of gentlemanly character and tribal community.[14] In the wake of Butler's post-Second World War education reforms, public schools faced increased competition from the state sector. During the 1950s and '60s education was a dynamic and fashionable arena in which progressive theory was backed up by substantial government spending. In 1969 the education budget exceeded that of the Ministry of Defence for the first time in British history.[15] The 1963 Robbins Report also paved the way for the expansion of higher education on the principle that universities should be open to 'all who were qualified for them by ability and attainment'. It was around this time that the closed scholarships at Oxbridge colleges for boys from particular public schools – Westminster at Christ Church, Oxford; Eton at King's College, Cambridge; Winchester at New College, Oxford – began to be shut down. In this newly competitive and meritocratic climate, the whole ethos of private education shifted. Headmasters still talked in high-flown terms about service and leadership, but this was no longer the pre-eminent goal of a public school education. Character became secondary to qualifications in the order of pedagogical values. One of the less heralded functions of private education in the post-war era has been to prevent the downward social mobility of the less able children of affluent families. The decline of Britain's overseas empire also fuelled the re-evaluation of the purpose of elite education, as the moral idealism of the Victorian institution was replaced by a more materialistic and individualistic ethos.

It was in the 1980s, however, that the independent sector really came into its own. This was a pivotal moment in the recent history of the public school system, a moment of renewed confidence and, for the first time in generations, a sense of being in harmony with the spirit of the age. The year 1979 saw the first of three consecutive election victories for Margaret Thatcher and eighteen years of Conservative government. Headmasters and boards of governors of public schools have always felt more comfortable with a Tory in Downing Street, but for much of the post-war period the educational agenda of both parties had been influenced by Labour's opposition to private schools, as well as the mildly communitarian ethos of the times. One of Margaret Thatcher's most profound impacts upon British public life was to draw the sting from her opponents and undermine the egalitarian assumptions that had been seeded deep within public discourse after the war. The 1980s was the beginning of a decisive shift away from the post-war settlement towards a more competitive society with the values of private ownership and individual enterprise to the fore. The new public school focus on academic excellence and individual achievement chimed perfectly with this sharp-elbowed, get-ahead-at-all-costs vision of society.

Private schools benefited both culturally and materially from the new Conservative government. In 1979 the Conservatives introduced the 'assisted places scheme', a Department of Education initiative that paid for bright state-educated children to attend private schools. Means-tested and based on a competitive scholarship exam, the scheme was designed to mimic the role of the direct-grant grammar schools that had been discontinued by Labour in 1974. This was a pet project of Thatcher herself, the daughter of a petit-bourgeois green-grocer who had risen to Oxford and Westminster via Kesteven and Grantham Girls' School, a state-funded grammar. After a slow start, the assisted places scheme was funding 34,000 pupils at private schools by 1994.[16] Combined with the government funds allocated to pay the school fees of the children of Foreign Office workers and Army officers, this constituted a large state subsidy to the private sector. Educational researchers have questioned the efficacy of the scheme as a means of promoting social mobility, as a disproportionate number of places went to families who passed the means test but already had high levels of education.[17] This was the same criticism that had been levelled against the grammar schools: that they favoured the children of middle-class parents who were rich in cultural capital but relatively poor in economic terms.

More important than financial assistance from the state, though, was the new sense of synergy between the rebranded public school and the popular culture of the day. The early 1980s saw a spate of high-gloss, big budget film and television productions that gloried in a nostalgic vision of upper-class Englishness. ITV's 1981 adaptation of Evelyn Waugh's *Brideshead Revisited* was a huge popular success, drawing upwards of 10 million viewers per episode into the rarefied world of the Oxford aesthetes of the 1920s. In the same year *Chariots of Fire* turned to 1920s Cambridge, this time focusing on the athletes rather than the aesthetes, and the efforts of Eric Liddell and Harold Abrahams to compete in the 1924 Olympics. These two massively successful productions helped to spark a whole new cottage industry of English 'heritage' film-making, which included *A Passage to India* (1982), *The Far Pavilions* (1984), *The Jewel in the Crown* (1984) and *A Room with a View* (1985), all of which looked back to an upper-class milieu before the levelling influences of decolonization and the welfare state. Many of these films were made with American finance and were successful in the overseas cinema and video markets. This was high-gloss heritage for the global village: upper-class English history as soft-core entertainment for the aspirational age. Many also included mildly hand-wringing references to social inequality and class tensions, but the suspicion was that this was merely an excuse to glory in the architecture and elegance of the traditional surroundings of the English upper classes.

The 1980s also saw a renewed confidence in the self-presentation of upper-class fashions. Under the editorship of Tina Brown, *Tatler* magazine, the go-to publication for the old money set, was raised from the ashes and converted into a cutting-edge style bible for the upper classes and their aspiring hangers-on. In 1982 Peter York and Ann Barr published *The Official Sloane Ranger Handbook*, which gently satirized the lifestyles of young, public school-educated men and women.[18] While York and Barr poked mild fun at this upper-crust milieu, with its bad fashion, cosseted lifestyle and bubble-like isolation from the mainstream of British society, they also helped to turn it into an immediately recognizable social group. Alongside the brash, 'loadsamoney' entrepreneur, the Sloane Ranger and the Hooray Henry were part of the wider cast of characters that barged their way into the zeitgeist. The Sloane and the Hooray were joined in 1984 by the 'young fogey', a type first identified by Alan Watkins in the pages of *The Spectator*.[19] Young fogeys were the intellectual elite of the Sloane and Hooray masses, youthful conservatives who looked to the style and culture of the inter-war upper classes for their cues: the novels of Evelyn Waugh, the English Book of Common Prayer, Gothic revival architecture, field sports, tweed jackets, bow ties and the gentlemanly manners of an earlier age. Crucially, however, the renewed prominence of 'gentry' culture was bound up with the individualistic ethos of the consumer economy. Rather than an expression of a deep-rooted class identity, one that had traditionally been based on the nineteenth-century allegiance between the professional middle classes, on the one hand, and the gentry and aristocracy, on the other, the popularity of brands such as Barbour and Burberry were retro signifiers available to anyone who could afford the ticket price.

Ever since the early nineteenth century Britain's public schools have relied on two main arguments to justify their existence: the argument from national service and the argument from individual liberty. The first argument was made most successfully during the high noon of the Victorian era when the ethos of service and leadership fed the needs of an expanding Empire. The second argument gained greater purchase in the post-war period as a defence against state control. When the then Shadow Secretary of State for Education, Roy Hattersley, made a speech to the Headmasters' Conference in 1973 advocating the abolition of private education, he was cast in the press the following morning as an enemy of traditional English liberty and an 'angry young man'.[20] This was perhaps the last time that a senior Labour politician would advocate outright abolition as a viable policy option; from now on the focus would be on reform of the schools' charitable status, ending the assisted places scheme and, more recently, charging VAT on school fees. The argument from liberty resonated strongly with the 1980s ethos of competitive individualism. Greed was good and wealth was nothing to be ashamed of. Your children, too, could enjoy the benefits of a traditional English education if you worked hard, made sacrifices and saved your money. It was simply a matter of individual choice and meritocratic endeavour.

In the 1980s two countervailing forces stimulated the resurgence of the private education sector. Just as the Conservative government reduced funding for state schools, cutting the education budget from 5.5 per cent to 4.8 per cent of GDP between 1980 and 1986, private schools enjoyed a sharp up-tick in fees and enrolments.[21] Over the course of the 1980s school fees rose by 76 per cent.[22] Today, a year's boarding at a top-tier school costs around £30,000, well above the national average annual income, and in the last two decades fees have risen three times faster than the cost of living.[23] This new money has been ploughed into a massive building programme, which sees schools competing against one another to provide ever more opulent facilities and smaller class sizes. Flush with cash from untaxed profits due to their status as charitable trusts, they build swimming pools, squash courts, computer clusters, science laboratories, concert halls, recording studios, theatres and rehearsal spaces. These modern facilities are complemented by a broad and up-to-date curriculum, in which Greek and Latin survive alongside Russian, Mandarin, business studies, art history, design and engineering. In many ways the contemporary public school is a perverse fulfilment of Karl Marx's communist utopia, in which he dreamed he would be able to 'hunt in the morning, fish in the afternoon, rear cattle in the evening, criticize after dinner'.[24] The public school is an adolescent jungle gym in which no intellectual or aesthetic faculty goes uncultivated. For the right price, today's public school student can be a Latin scholar in the morning, receive personalized cricket coaching in the afternoon and cut his or her first album in the recording studio after dinner.

Rather than sticking bullishly to the ways of the past, elite private schools have bent with the prevailing cultural winds. The days when Mike Rutherford could be beaten for playing his electric guitar in the boarding house are long gone. Pop music and youth culture have shifted from the institution's under-life to part of its mainstream culture. Rather than a dissident practice of oppositional self-fashioning – albeit one that could lead to rich returns in the music business – pop music has become just another item on the variegated intellectual menu of an institution that espouses the progressive values of openness, diversity, creativity and cultural omnivorousness. Anthony Seldon, former headmaster of Wellington College and biographer of Tony Blair, describes the values of public schooling not solely in terms of exam results and university admissions but also as a way of cultivating 'roundedness' in pupils. In 2006 Seldon created a splash in the media when he announced that Wellington would augment its curriculum with 'happiness lessons' and focus more on the 'well-being' of its students.[25] The true aim of education, he claimed, was to help students to 'become themselves' through engagement with a tantalizing list of extracurricular activities that ranged from pottery and tennis to drama and ballet. What Seldon failed to mention, however, was that this particular form of self-development is extremely popular with university admissions officers and elite employers, who are always on the lookout for the extra polish that sets a candidate apart from all the others with good exam results. Seldon's version of 'roundedness' is different from the Victorian ideal of the 'well-rounded man', that great paragon of classical learning and gentlemanly polish. Today's ideal type is the multitasking, flexi-skilled, plugged-in go-getter, equipped with both the credentials and *savoir faire* to flourish in a highly competitive job market.

These changes have all taken place against the backdrop of dwindling music and arts provision in the state sector. It was the Conservative Education Act of 1988 that first deemed music lessons 'non-essential' to the state schools' core business of grinding out exam results. In 1993 the government allowed schools to pass the cost of music lessons on to parents, further curtailing access for the less well off. With the additional handicaps of the sale of school playing fields and the National Curriculum's narrow focus on core subjects, the state sector has little chance of matching the opportunities available to those who can afford to pay for better facilities, a longer school day and a broader curriculum. The effects of these disparities were made clear in the 2014 Social Mobility Report, which demonstrated how the privately educated elite is no longer confined to the traditional redoubts of Whitehall, the diplomatic corps, the armed forces and the church, but extends throughout glamorous cultural fields such as publishing, broadcasting, music, film and TV. The Commission found that 54 per cent of all media executives, 44 per cent of all newspaper columnists, 43 per cent of all prominent public figures in film and TV and 22 per cent of all popular music performers were privately educated.

Many historians have noted the incredible capacity of the public school system to adapt to changing social conditions in order to maintain its privilege and independence. If these same historians could see the system today, they would be struck anew by the seamless ease with which it has secured its place in the new globalized economy. Especially at the upper end of the system, British boarding schools are the favoured training grounds for the sons and daughters of the new global elite. The number of foreign students has risen sharply in recent years, up from just over 10 per cent of the total boarding population in the late 1980s to 36 per cent in 2014.[26] Beginning in the late 1990s, public schools also began to expand aggressively into new overseas markets. In 1998 Harrow opened a satellite campus in Bangkok, which provided a traditional English educational experience for the children of Anglophone expats and the new Asian business elite. Other schools have followed suit. Sherborne has a campus in

Qatar, Repton in Dubai, Haileybury in Almaty and Wellington in Tianjin. Dulwich College has a network of seven schools across Asia.[27] These enterprises also help to improve the social profile of the schools back in the UK, with money from overseas business often funnelled back into scholarships for the less well-off at home. Yet the historian David Kynaston has shown that only a tiny fraction of the scholarship support offered by private schools goes towards places for children from disadvantaged backgrounds, while the majority provides fee relief for middle-class families.[28] In addition to excellent tuition and gold-standard qualifications such as the A level and the International Baccalaureate, many of these overseas campuses export the symbolic trappings of the English boarding school. Boys and girls in Shanghai, Abu Dhabi and Seoul walk purposefully between mock-Gothic cloisters with straw boaters on their heads as they discuss their 'beaks' and 'divs'. This is one of the ways in which the new global elite anoints itself by purchasing the trappings of the old forms of cultural capital that fuelled British geopolitical might in the nineteenth and twentieth centuries.

In many ways the story of the post-1980s public schools echoes that of another invented tradition of the Victorian age: association football. In recent years English soccer has been transformed from a decaying working-class culture into a globally branded luxury product, awash with foreign money and international superstars. A residual feature of Britain's deeply entrenched class system – one that was invented in the Victorian public schools, no less – has been transformed through the alchemy of neoliberal capitalism into a high-gloss consumer spectacle for the global marketplace. With their luxury facilities and overseas franchises, the public schools have done something similar for an iconic signifier of upper-class culture. Today, Harrow and Wellington sit alongside Arsenal and Manchester United as part of 'Brand Britain', a portfolio of luxury products that help to export British cultural and economic influence overseas.

And yet the very ease with which the public schools have adapted themselves to the globalized economy is both an example of their famed resilience and a source of potential hazard. Many parents have funded the exorbitant cost of fees on the back of rising property prices, cheap credit, investment portfolios and bonuses. In the wake of the 2008 financial crisis, there is talk of an unsustainable 'bubble' in the private education sector.[29] While the system grows in the South East, it shrinks in the North, which is cut off from the globalized turbo-economy of Greater London. The historian David Turner has observed a new fault line within the already restricted class of people who might contemplate sending their children to public school. Increasingly the professional middle classes, such as doctors, lawyers and civil servants, struggle to afford the exorbitant fees that are easily met by the City of London financial elite and the global super-rich. This is another reason why the language of the 'old boys' club' and the 'establishment' is so inadequate. Rather than a unified and homogeneous class, the ordinary elite is made up of numerous different groups, who jostle for position and compete for opportunities within an ever-shifting economic and cultural terrain. If, as many economists predict, rising levels of inequality will further polarize British society between the professional elite and the precariat in the coming decades, then the competition for positional goods such as elite schools will become even more intense, as anxious middle-class parents seek to protect their children from the greater risks of downward social mobility in this more polarized economic landscape. For all of its antique elegance, and for all of its espousal of the values of happiness and self-fulfilment, the modern public school is a zone of fierce competition.

SINCE THE 1960S Britain's elite schools have undergone a process of radical transformation, during which they have retained the symbolic trappings of tradition while modernizing almost all aspects of their curriculum, ethos and discipline. And yet, in spite of these changes, it is the archetypal Victorian boarding school – a boarding school of the imagination that was forged in countless novels, diaries, memoirs, cartoons, films and plays throughout the nineteenth and twentieth centuries – that continues to dominate within popular culture. The old glamour remains strong, not just for culturally conservative fans of the Brideshead aesthetic and gentry-style clothing brands, but for progressive writers, artists and activists who wish to critique the social injustice of private education.

Before the success of *Posh* in 2010, one of the angriest pop cultural critiques of the public school was The Jam's 'The Eton Rifles', which reached number three in the charts in 1979. The song describes a scrap between punks on a Right to Work march in Slough in 1978 and a group of Eton schoolboys. Paul Weller's lyrics bristle with resentment at the unearned privileges of the ruling class, while also expressing his wry acknowledgement of the asymmetrical nature of the struggle: the punks might win a scrap in the streets, but the game of life is stacked against them.[30] And yet, with his references to the cadet force, athleticism and the old boys' network, Weller snarls at the old system of public school character-building. The lyrics to 'The Eton Rifles' would have made just as much sense in 1879 as they did in 1979. When The Jam performed the song on *Top of the Pops*, Rick Buckler, the drummer, wore a striped blazer and straw boater, while the backing singers sported the bright red coats and golden buttons of Harry Flashman and the Victorian military. With its thunderous chords and whip-smart delivery, 'The Eton Rifles' was a stirring anthem that rallied popular opposition to unearned privilege, but it did so by focusing on a series of cultural references that have become increasingly out of step with the realities of modern Britain.

Arguably no one has done more to rehabilitate the image of the traditional British public school than best-selling author, Labour Party donor and vocal supporter of progressive causes, J. K. Rowling. So successful were Rowling's novels, and such was the intensity of their young fans' absorption in the institutional life of Hogwarts, that they have been credited with stimulating a brief up-tick in enrolments at private boarding schools, both in Britain and overseas.[31] Rowling rehabilitated the long out-of-date genre of the public school story for a contemporary audience by symbolically punishing those of Hogwarts' pupils who still clung to the old assumptions of entitlement and exclusivity. Rowling's moral universe relies on a sharp distinction between the ways in which different groups of pupils respond to privilege. Harry, Ron and Hermione are representatives of a benign meritocratic elite, one which embraces diversity in the form of ethnic minority characters such as Parvati Patil and Lee Jordan, and combines the traditions of Hogwarts with an openness to the modern world. The powerful sense of solidarity that many readers felt with this group of characters inspired them to write their own stories set in the Harry Potter universe and form online communities of editors and readers. Some fan fiction sites even held creative writing contests and awarded funds towards university scholarships to the winners.[32] In this way Rowling's stories seemed to offer everyone the chance to become a member of the Hogwarts elite.

This sense of openness and inclusivity is contrasted in the novels themselves with the entitlement of Draco Malfoy and his comrades in Slytherin House, who denounce Hogwarts' progressive admissions policies and proclaim the inherent superiority of a select group of ancient wizarding families. With his straw-blond hair and fantasies of biological superiority, Malfoy is a representative of the darkest aspects of upper-class privilege – the faith in blood and soil that was espoused by the most atavistic members of the aristocracy before its final collapse as a social force after the Second World War. In Rowling's Manichaean world, the forces of evil are designed to evoke associations with mid-twentieth-century fascism and the horrors of totalitarianism. Rowling even named her own daughter after Jessica Mitford, the aristocratic anti-fascist who ran away with Esmond Romilly to report on the Spanish Civil War. And yet, the self-effacing Harry is no less the product of privilege than Draco Malfoy. After all, he is able to afford Hogwarts' fees due to a large inheritance from his famous wizarding parents that drops into his lap as if from nowhere. In spite of his suffering at the hands of the petit bourgeois Dursleys, Harry is a member of the lucky few who are blessed with magical talents and can afford to attend an elite school of witchcraft and wizardry. When he arrives at Hogwarts, he thrives in the cut and thrust of an institution that is based on the principle of constant competition – between houses, pupils, schools and the universal forces of good and evil. He is, without a doubt, a member of the ordinary elite. It would be foolish to look to Harry Potter for a latter-day version of Percy Shelley or Esmond Romilly's radical critique of public school culture, but it is nevertheless striking that Rowling shares with both Laura Wade and Paul Weller the tendency to focus her ire on the old forms of class privilege, rather than its suppler and more insinuating modern forms.

In 2007 cinema audiences were treated to another reboot of the boarding school archetype, this time in the form of *St Trinian's*, directed and produced by Oliver Parker and Barnaby Thompson. This starred Rupert Everett as both Camilla Fritton, the school's redoubtable headmistress, and Carnaby Fritton, her pusillanimous art dealer brother. The film's plot, such as it is, revolves around an elaborate attempt made by the girls of St Trinian's to steal Vermeer's *Girl with a Pearl Earring* from the National Gallery – it's actually in The Hague, but this allows for yet another Colin Firth gag – in order to raise enough money to prevent the school from falling into bankruptcy and being forced to close. Like *Harry Potter*, the film divides its schoolgirl characters into good and bad models of privilege. The hedonistic, anti-establishment ethos of St Trinian's is shared by the school's various subcultural cliques, including the Emos, the Geeks, the Posh Totty and the Chavs. As Owen Jones has pointed out, the use of the term 'chav' to refer to members of the white working class is one of the few acceptable forms of bigotry in contemporary Britain, one that is voiced both at polite middle-class dinner parties and in the scurrilous headlines of the tabloid press.[33] In *St Trinian's*, however, the Chavs and the Posh Totty play for the same team, united in their opposition to intrusive government inspectors and other, more traditional boarding schools.

The foil for St Trinian's 'good' boarding school girls is Annabelle Fritton, daughter of Carnaby and niece of Camilla, who is transferred to the school after being bullied at her previous institution, Cheltenham Ladies' College. When she first arrives at St Trinian's, Annabelle exclaims in horror, 'it's like Hogwarts for pikeys', invoking another classist epithet, but this time without the sense of recuperative inclusiveness.[34] Over the course of the film, however, her snobbery is eroded and she joins in the traditional St Trinian's pursuits of brewing bootleg vodka and stealing priceless works of art. In a similar fashion to Rowling's depiction of Hogwarts, *St Trinian's* encourages a diverse modern audience to take imaginative possession of the exclusive space of the boarding school by focusing its critique on the old modes of privilege and entitlement.

Yet in spite of its outlandish plotting and too-easy populism, *St Trinian's* is one of the canniest representations of the modern public school in recent memory, which refers by name to some of the country's most prestigious institutions, including Eton, Ampleforth, Cheltenham Ladies' College and Bedales. As cover for their daring art heist, the girls of St Trinian's enter a TV quiz show – 'School Challenge' – the final of which is held in the great hall of the National Gallery. In an extended montage sequence, we see how the girls cheat their way to the final, using their detailed knowledge of the social profile of particular private schools in order to prosper. For example, to get the better of Eton, one of the few remaining single-sex boarding schools, they use their sexual wiles to snog these privileged but unworldly young men into a state of befuddlement. Against the crunchy, co-educational Bedales, the girls resort to spiking their opponents' tea with magic mushrooms. When it comes to answering the host's questions, Chas, Caspar and Rupert are left dreamily staring into space. When one of the boys absent-mindedly presses his buzzer, the quiz host, played by Stephen Fry, delivers the immortal line, 'Caspar, are you buzzing?'[35]

In these scenes the film exhibits a more nuanced understanding of the contemporary public school world than its earlier depictions of Annabelle's snobbish entitlement. This sense of knowing familiarity extends to the film's adult characters, especially Rupert Everett's dual performance as Carnaby and Camilla Fritton, and Colin Firth's turn as a stern school inspector. Everett and Firth make knowing reference to their youthful appearances in *Another Country*, the 1984 film adaptation of Julian Mitchell's play about Guy Burgess's schooldays. A scene shot on the school roof also invokes Lindsay Anderson's *if. . . .* Within the film's self-aware visual style, yesterday's anti-establishment critique becomes fodder for today's knowing pastiche. The subversive energy of Searle's original cartoons is converted into self-conscious winks and insider jokes about the dissident public school culture of the past.

*St Trinian's* is based on the assumption that popular youth culture is no longer a threat to the public school ethos but part of its very lifeblood. In many ways *St Trinian's* is the perfect encapsulation of the new style of elitism that defines the contemporary private school experience. With its diverse cast, girl power ethos, knowing self-referentiality and sugar-rush pop soundtrack, it has all of the glitz and glitter one would expect from a big budget film aimed at a global youth audience. But that well-calibrated appeal is the product of a wider cultural ecosystem that is dominated by the 'ordinary elite'. A quick glance at the film's closing credits reveals just how deep the synergy between pop culture and private education runs. Among the young actors who play the girls of St Trinian's are graduates from some of the nation's most expensive private schools, including Godolphin, Wimbledon High School, Bedales, Latymer Upper School and Cheltenham Ladies' College. Oliver Parker is descended from the British aristocracy and Barnaby Thompson is an old boy of St Paul's public school. The predominance of privately educated cast members reflects the wider trend that was captured in the Social Mobility and Child Poverty Commission's 2014 report, 'the closed shop at the top' of British society that extends throughout the cultural industries.

Just to be clear, I'm not somehow 'against' privately educated musicians, actors, directors, writers, curators or cultural administrators. If I was, I probably should never have written this book, as I was also the lucky recipient of an expensive liberal education at an ancient seat of learning. What I am against, however, is a national education policy that tacitly surrenders large portions of the most glamorous and desirable professions to those whose parents can afford to pay for private education. This is not only unfair to the great majority of schoolchildren who have to compete on an uneven playing field, it is also bad for the health of popular culture, as it limits the range of experiences and voices that are available within the mainstream.

Among the many conclusions drawn by sociologists from the BBC's Great British Class Survey was that cultural capital – the subtle markers of taste, style and knowledge that correlate with class status – takes new forms in today's society. Rather than being predominantly associated with high cultural forms and narrowly defined tastes, cultural capital is now more frequently associated with 'cosmopolitan and ironic forms which appear to be pluralist and anti-elitist'.[36] But this new ethos of openness and inclusivity goes hand in hand with rising inequality and the continued dominance of the privately educated elite. In his study of educational privilege in the United States, Shamus Rahman Khan observes that 'ironically, exclusivity marks the losers in the hierarchical, open society'.[37] To be too categorical in one's judgements, too exclusive in one's tastes or too fiercely committed to a single, unpopular cause is to be at odds with the values of the contemporary cultural elite. This is a cultural system, in short, that has little room for the bitter passions and ugly resentments that fuelled so much of the radical public school culture of the past.

# Afterword

George Orwell and Cyril Connolly were close friends at both
prep school and Eton, united by their shared love of books and
opposition to the dull conformism of boarding school life. In *Enemies
of Promise* Connolly holds up Orwell as a heroic anti-establishment
rebel: 'I was a stage rebel, Orwell a true one.'[1] While Connolly put on
the louche airs of the dandy-aesthete and remained in thrall to the
aristocratic glamour of 'Pop', Eton's famous sixth-form club, Orwell
was implacable in his rejection of the school and all it stood for. When
it came to assessing the lasting impact of their schooldays on their
later lives, however, Connolly and Orwell parted company.

In his famous essay 'Inside the Whale' (1940) Orwell discussed
Connolly's theory of permanent adolescence, which argued that the
public school was such an emotionally scarring experience that it
stunted the characters of its former pupils for the rest of their lives.
In spite of his rebellious schooldays and left-wing politics, Orwell was
having none of it. 'Your natural impulse,' he remarks, 'is to look for
the misprint. Presumably there is a "not" left out, or something. But
no, not a bit of it! He means it!'[2] While Orwell granted that there
was some truth in Connolly's claim that public school was the most
significant experience in a 'cultured middle-class life', he added that
this state of affairs was simply a reflection of the decadence of the
left-wing intelligentsia. It was only against the backdrop of the 'depth
of softness' at which this group had arrived that the rigours of public
schooling could seem degrading or traumatic. The standard pattern of
middle-class education – 'public school, university, a few trips abroad,

then London' – fatally impaired the young man's capacity to under-stand the real struggles of life: 'hunger, hardship, solitude, exile, war, prison, persecution, manual labour'.[3]

Orwell's objection could just as easily be applied to this book. The resentments and discomforts of the privately educated elite pale in significance when set against the wider backdrop of poverty, war and environmental degradation that define the contours of so many human lives. The poems, plays, novels, magazines, songs, cartoons and films that I have discussed in this book record the experiences of a tiny fraction of an already small subsection of the population: those who rebelled against or expressed their displeasure with their private educations. By focusing on the sentiments of a small number of privileged malcontents, have I not painted a distorted picture of the public school and its position within British culture and society? Have I not given undue weight to the special pleading of a vocal minor-ity, amplified the grievances of overly sensitive artistic types with a skewed sense of moral righteousness? Surely public school education wasn't always so brutally alienating and irredeemably philistine. Surely there were many boys who happily rubbed along, instead of rebelling against their masters and harbouring lifelong grudges. And what of the positive contributions that public schools have made to society? What of the charitable missions, the scholarships for the deserving poor, the lives devoted to service and leadership?

A different kind of historical study would have addressed these questions in more detail. It would have been more scrupulous about maintaining a sense of balance, would have striven to give equal weight to supportive and critical voices, would have cultivated an air of rigorous scholarly disinterest. Many of the works that I have drawn on for my research take precisely this approach. I have chosen to be more one-sided, however, not only due to my conviction that private education wilfully perpetuates social injustice, and is hence an appropriate target for partisan attack, but as a way to capture the sheer intensity of feeling that the public school experience has gener-ated over the years. Throughout its long history, the public school has always been a zone of myth and fantasy, a source of fallible childhood memories and bitter adult resentments. Where its supporters have imagined it as a repository of national values and organic tradition, its critics have cast it as a ghostly presence that haunts the mind and stunts the growth. But we should not be too hasty in dismissing these feelings as *mere* fantasies. And we should not disregard the powerful feelings of nostalgia and resentment that echo throughout public school culture on the grounds that they are *only* subjective, or emerge against a backdrop of social and economic privilege, or are somehow too cloyingly emotional for serious discussion. To do so would be to acquiesce in the quiet code of suppression that has played such a central role in British culture throughout the years, the upper lip that was first stiffened at boarding school and kept buttoned in later life. Difficult, ugly, even embarrassing feelings can be the source of new knowledge about ourselves and the world in which we live. They can also provide the impetus to action and change.

Orwell ended his boarding school memoir 'Such, Such Were the Joys' (1952) with a gesture of minimization and forgetting. In spite of the pungent reek of the memories he dredged up for his readers, he concluded by noting 'how small everything has grown, and how terrible is the deterioration in myself.'[4] For me, however, the institution still looms large, both in my own childhood memories and in my political beliefs about how British society might be made fairer and more cohesive. Today, when I return to my alma mater, which is close to my family home, my peevish resentment prevents me from entering the grounds, so I stalk the boundaries of the school, casting ambivalent glances over the iron fence that divides it from the world at large. There is a particular spot that I like to frequent, right next to the school chapel and fives courts but still on the public pathway that skirts the edge of the official school grounds. On one side of the path, a steep bank runs down to the River Severn through a tangled undergrowth of brambles and nettles; on the other, the passer-by is afforded a fleeting glimpse of the lush grass of the school cricket fields, the soft red stone of the chapel and the Gothic geometries of the fives courts. Whenever I stand on this spot, I feel as though I am on the boundary between two worlds. On the one side is the river, the town, everyday life; on the other is the enchanted world of the school, with its carefully cultivated air of antiquity and privilege. In spite of the efforts of marketers and modernizers, the public school remains a place apart from the mainstream of British society, a rarefied world open only to a select group of young people who have access to opportunities and experiences the likes of which most of the population can only dream about. As long as it does, this iconic British institution will continue to be a powerful source of myth and fantasy, controversy and resentment.

# REFERENCES

INTRODUCTION: PERMANENT ADOLESCENCE

1 Leslie Stephen, 'Thoughts of an Outsider: Public Schools', *Cornhill Magazine*, 27 (1873), p. 283.
2 Jonathan Gathorne-Hardy, *The Old School Tie: The Phenomenon of the Public School* (New York, 1977), p. 49.
3 George Orwell, 'Inside the Whale', in *A Collection of Essays* (Orlando, FL, 1981), p. 239.
4 'Elitist Britain?', www.gov.uk, 28 August 2014.
5 The case against public school education has been made with great clarity and force in recent years by both David Kynaston and Alan Bennett. David Kynaston, 'What Should We Do with Private Schools?', *The Guardian*, 5 December 2014; Alan Bennett in 'Fair Play', *London Review of Books*, 19 June 2014, pp. 29–30.
6 Cyril Connolly, *Enemies of Promise* (Chicago, IL, 2008), p. 253.
7 Isabel Quigly, *The Heirs of Tom Brown: The English School Story* (London, 1982); Jeffrey Richards, *Happiest Days: The Public Schools in English Fiction* (Manchester, 1988).
8 Dominic Sandbrook, *The Great British Dream Factory: The Strange History of our National Imagination* (London, 2015).
9 Stanley Cohen, *Folk Devils and Moral Panics* (London, 2011).
10 Thomas Hughes, *Tom Brown's Schooldays* (New York, 2008), p. 99.
11 Pierre Bourdieu, *Distinction: A Social Critique of the Judgement of Taste* (Cambridge, MA, 1984). The most up-to-date application of the concept of 'habitus' to elite education has been in the American context of St Paul's School in Connecticut: Shamus RahmanKhan, *Privilege: The Making of an Adolescent Elite at St Paul's School* (Princeton, NJ, 2013).
12 Evelyn Waugh, *A Little Learning: An Autobiography* (Boston, MA, 1964), p. 84.
13 Alex Renton, 'Abuse in Britain's Boarding Schools', www.guardian.com, 4 May 2014.
14 Joy Shaverien, *Boarding School Syndrome: The Psychological Trauma of the 'Privileged' Child* (London, 2015).
15 Alex Renton, 'The Damage Boarding Schools Do', www.guardian.com, 20 July 2014.

16 Nick Duffell, *Wounded Leaders: British Elitism and the Entitlement Illusion* (London, 2014).
17 Robert Graves, *Goodbye to All That* (London, 2000), p. 36.


1 *Floreat Seditio*

1 My principal source for the details of Winchester's great rebellion of 1793 is Arthur F. Leach, *A History of Winchester College* (London, 1899), pp. 396–407. Leach gives a detailed and spirited account of the 1793 rebellion, as well as shorter accounts of similar uprisings that took place at the school around that time. The report of the Usher who found the boys 'metamorphosed into serpents' is on p. 399. The 1793 rebellion is also discussed in more recent histories of the public schools. These include Edward Mack, *Public Schools and British Opinion, 1780–1860* (London, 1938), pp. 79–89; Jonathan Gathorne-Hardy, *The Old School Tie: The Phenomenon of the Public School* (New York, 1977), p. 57; John Chandos, *Boys Together: English Public Schools, 1800–1864* (New Haven, CT, 1984), pp. 176–91. The background on the revolutionary symbolism of the red cap of liberty comes from Jennifer Harris, 'The Red Cap of Liberty: A Study of Dress Worn by French Revolutionary Partisans, 1789–94', *Eighteenth-century Studies*, xiv/3 (1981), pp. 283–312.
2 Quoted in Leach, *A History of Winchester College*, p. 403.
3 Hugh Cunningham, *Children and Childhood in Western Society since 1500* (London, 2005); Colin Heywood, *A History of Childhood: Children and Childhood in the West from Medieval to Modern Times* (Oxford, 2003); Jenny Holt, *Public School Literature, Civic Education, and the Politics of Male Adolescence* (Farnham, 2008); Jon Savage, *Teenage: The Creation of Youth, 1875–1945* (London, 2007).
4 G. Stanley Hall, *Adolescence: Its Psychology and Its Relations to Physiology, Anthropology, Sociology, Sex, Crime and Religion* (New York, 1904).
5 Philippe Ariès, *Centuries of Childhood: A Social History of Family Life* (New York, 1962), p. 25.
6 John R. Gillis outlines the social and demographic conditions, including surplus wealth, elite educational institutions and reduced birth rate, which enabled the emergence of early forms of youth culture among the late eighteenth-century European upper classes. John R. Gillis, *Youth in History: Tradition and Change in European Age Relations, 1770–Present* (New York, 1974).
7 Jean-Jacques Rousseau, *Emile; or, On Education*, trans. Alan Bloom (New York, 1979), pp. 211–12.
8 Stephen Gill, ed., *Wordsworth: The Major Works* (New York, 2000), p. 550.
9 Robert Shoemaker, *The London Mob: Violence and Disorder in Eighteenth-century England* (New York, 2007), p. 21.
10 *A Sketch of the Rights of Boys and Girls, by Launcelot Light of Westminster School, and Laetitia Lookabout of Queen's Square, Bloomsbury* (London, 1792), pp. 8, 9, 23 and 29.
11 Ibid., p. 23.

12 Ibid., p. 24.
13 Maxwell Lyte, *A History of Eton College* (New York, 1889), especially Chapter Sixteen, 'Eton Life in the Eighteenth Century', pp. 294–304.
14 Ian Gilmour, *The Making of the Poets: Byron and Shelley in Their Time* (London, 2002), p. 78.
15 Ibid., p. 79.
16 Lyte, *A History of Eton College*, p. 301.
17 Quoted in Chandos, *Boys Together*, p. 103.
18 Ibid., p. 221.
19 Arnold Whitridge, *Doctor Arnold of Rugby* (New York, 1926), p. 84.
20 M. V. Wallbank, 'Eighteenth-century Schools and the Education of the Governing Elite', *History of Education*, VIII/1 (1979), pp. 1–19.
21 Holt, *Public School Literature*, p. 18.
22 Edward Gibbon, *The Autobiography and Correspondence of Edward Gibbon, the Historian* (London, 1869), p. 20.
23 G. R. Parkin, *Edward Thring, Headmaster of Uppingham School: Life, Diary, Letters* (London, 1898), p. 22.
24 Jeffrey Richards, *Happiest Days: The Public Schools in English Fiction* (Manchester, 1988), p. 9.
25 William Tucker, *Eton of Old, 1811–1822* (London, 1901), p. 40.
26 John Moultrie, *Dream of Life, Lays of the English Church, and Other Poems* (London, 1843), p. 57.
27 James Fitzjames Stephen, 'Tom Brown's Schooldays', *Edinburgh Review*, 107 (January 1858), p. 178.
28 Ibid.
29 Thomas Hobbes, *Leviathan* (London, 1982), p. 89.
30 Moultrie, *Dream of Life*, p. 57.
31 William Golding, *Lord of the Flies* (New York, 1997), p. 102.
32 Sidney Smith, 'Public Schools', *The Works of the Revd. Sidney Smith*, vol. 1 (London, 1859), p. 187.
33 Quoted in Chandos, *Boys Together*, p. 39.
34 The details of Shelley's pyromaniac assault on Doctor Bethel's tree are taken from Richard Holmes, *Shelley: The Pursuit* (London, 1974), p. 24. Other details of Shelley's schooldays are taken from: Gilmour, *The Making of the Poets*, and Anne Wroe, *Being Shelley: The Poet's Search for Himself* (New York, 2008).
35 Percy Shelley, *Zastrozzi and St Irvyne* (Oxford, 1986).
36 Thomas Jefferson Hogg, *The Life of Percy Bysshe Shelley* (London, 1858), p. 28.
37 Donald H. Reiman, Neil Freistat and Nora Crook, eds, *The Complete Poetry of Percy Bysshe Shelley*, vol. III (Baltimore, MD, 2012), p. 25.
38 [J. T. Coleridge], 'Shelley's Revolt of Islam', *Quarterly Review*, 21 (April 1819), p. 470.
39 *New Statesman*, 16 January 1937.
40 Donald Thomas, *Swinburne: The Poet and His World* (Chicago, IL, 1999), p. 26.
41 Robert Graves, *Goodbye to All That* (London, 2000), p. 239.

42 Louis MacNeice, *The Strings are False: An Unfinished Autobiography* (London, 1996), p. 98.


## 2 THOMAS ARNOLD'S SCHOOLDAYS

1 Details of the Marlborough rebellion are taken from: A. G. Bradley, A. C. Champneys and J. W. Baines, *A History of Marlborough College: During Fifty Years: From its Foundation to the Present Time* (London, 1893); and J. A. Mangan, 'Bullies, Beatings, Battles, and Bruises: "great days and jolly days" at one Mid-Victorian Public School', in *Disreputable Pleasures: Less Virtuous Victorians at Play*, ed. Mike Huggins and J. A. Mangan (New York, 2004), pp. 3–32.
2 J. R. de S. Honey, *Tom Brown's Universe: The Development of the English Public School in the Nineteenth Century* (New York, 1977), p. 104.
3 Ibid.
4 Mangan, 'Bullies, Beatings, Battles, and Bruises', p. 23.
5 De Honey, *Tom Brown's Universe*, p. 13.
6 Arthur Penrhyn Stanley, *The Life and Correspondence of Thomas Arnold* (London, 1844), p. 93.
7 Ibid., p. 123.
8 Edward C. Mack and W.H.G. Armytage, *Thomas Hughes* (London, 1952), p. 23.
9 Thomas Arnold, 'Public School Discipline', in *Thomas Arnold on Education*, ed. T. W. Bamford (London, 1970), p. 129.
10 David Newsome, *Godliness and Good Learning: Four Studies on a Victorian Ideal* (London, 1961).
11 Terence Copley, *Black Tom: Arnold of Rugby: The Myth and the Man* (London, 2002), pp. 123–5.
12 Bamford, *Thomas Arnold on Education*, p. 79.
13 Ibid., p. 80.
14 Stanley, *The Life and Correspondence of Thomas Arnold*, p. 81.
15 Quoted in Copley, *Black Tom*, p. 28.
16 Ibid., p. 32.
17 Thomas Arnold, 'Sermon XII', *Sermons*, vol. II, 3rd edn (London, 1844), p. 114; quoted in Bamford, *Thomas Arnold on Education*, p. 51.
18 Stanley, *The Life and Correspondence of Thomas Arnold*, p. 103.
19 Bamford, *Thomas Arnold on Education*, p. 121.
20 Jonathan Gathorne-Hardy, *The Old School Tie: The Phenomenon of the Public School* (New York, 1977), p. 77.
21 Isabel Quigly, *The Heirs of Tom Brown: The English School Story* (London, 1982), p. 78.
22 Jonathan Rose, *The Intellectual Life of the British Working Classes* (New Haven, CT, 2010), p. 328.
23 George Orwell, 'Boys' Weeklies', in *A Collection of Essays* (Orlando, FL, 1981), pp. 279–308.
24 [Charles Hamilton], 'Frank Richards Replies to George Orwell,' *Horizon*, 1/5 (May 1940).
25 Quoted in John J. MacAloon, *This Great Symbol: Pierre de Coubertin*

*and the Origins of the Modern Olympic Games* (London, 2008), p. 53.

26 Thomas Hughes, *Tom Brown's Schooldays* (London, 2008), p. 198.

27 Ibid., p. 189.

28 Ibid., p. 130.

29 Ibid., p. 198.

30 P. G. Wodehouse, *Tales of St Austin's* (Auckland, 2012), pp. 192–9.

31 Hughes, *Tom Brown's Schooldays*, p. xxxix.

32 P. G. Wodehouse, *Mike* (New York, 1909), p. 15.

33 For more on Rugby, Tennessee, see Mack and Armytage, *Thomas Hughes*, pp. 237–50.

34 John J. MacAloon, ed., *Muscular Christianity in the Colonial and Post-colonial Worlds* (London, 2008).

35 Thomas Hughes, *The Manliness of Christ* (Boston, MA, 1880), p. 47.

36 Ibid., p. 8.

37 Lytton Strachey, *Eminent Victorians* (Radford, VA, 2008), p. 130.

38 Cyril Connolly, *Enemies of Promise* (Chicago, IL, 2008), p. 47.

39 C.L.R. James, *Beyond a Boundary* (London, 2005), p. 24.

40 Ibid., p. 35.

41 Ibid., p. 215.

42 Ibid., p. 39.

43 Ibid., p. 55.

44 George MacDonald Fraser, *Flashman* (New York, 1984), p. 11.

45 Ibid., p. 67.

46 Ibid., p. 14.

47 George MacDonald Fraser, *Flashman at the Charge* (New York, 1986), p. 45.

48 Ibid., p. 79.

49 W.H.D. Rouse, *A History of Rugby School* (London, 1898), pp. 177–86.

50 George MacDonald Fraser, 'The Last Testament of Flashman's Creator: How Britain Has Destroyed Itself', *Daily Mail*, 5 January 2008.

### 3 THE SECRET LIFE OF THE VICTORIAN SCHOOLBOY

1 Erving Goffman, *Asylums: Essays on the Social Situation of Mental Patients and Other Inmates* (New York, 1990), p. xiii.

2 Ibid., p. 12.

3 Ibid., p. 188.

4 This criticism is made by Michael Ignatieff in 'Total Institutions and Working Classes: A Review Essay', *History Workshop Journal*, XV (1983), pp. 167–73. Goffman's use of the 'method of ideal types' is in *Asylums*, p. 5.

5 Goffman, *Asylums*, p. 199.

6 Deana Heath, *Purifying Empire: Obscenity and the Politics of Moral Regulation in Britain, India, and Australia* (Cambridge, 2010), p. 70.

7 Colin Shrosbree, *Public Schools and Private Education: the Clarendon Commission, 1861–64, and the Public Schools Act* (Manchester, 1988).

8 Quoted in Edward Mack, *Public Schools and British Opinion since 1860* (Westport, CT, 1941), p. 38.

9 Quoted in Josephine Kamm, *How Different from Us: A Biography of Miss Buss and Miss Beale* (London, 1958), p. 76.

10 For the history of girls' schools, see Gillian Avery, *The Best Type of Girl: A History of Girls' Independent Schools* (London, 1991).

11 Ibid., p. 115.

12 W. H. Auden, 'Honour (Gresham's School, Holt)', in *The Old School: Essays by Divers Hands*, ed. Graham Greene (London, 1934), p. 11.

13 Malcolm Seaborne, 'The Architecture of the Victorian Public School', in *The Victorian Public School: Studies in the Development of an Educational Institution*, ed. Brian Simon and Ian Bradley (Dublin, 1975), p. 177.

14 Quoted ibid., p. 181.

15 Arnold Lunn, *The Harrovians: A Tale of Public School Life* (Los Angeles, CA, 2010), p. 41.

16 Patrick Joyce, *The State of Freedom: A Social History of the State since 1800* (Cambridge, 2013), p. 274.

17 Quoted in Alisdaire Hickson, *The Poisoned Bowl: Sex and the Public School* (London, 1996), p. 24.

18 E. M. Forster, 'Notes on the English Character', in *Abinger Harvest* (Orlando, FL, 1964), p. 5.

19 Quoted in J. R. de S. Honey, *Tom Brown's Universe: The Development of the English Public School in the Nineteenth Century* (New York, 1977), p. 55.

20 Vyvyen Brendon, *Prep School Children: A Class Apart over Two Centuries* (London, 2009).

21 Honey, *Tom Brown's Universe*, p. 167.

22 William Acton, *The Functions and Disorders of Reproductive Organs, in Childhood, Youth, Adult-age, and Advanced Life, Considered in the Physiological, Social, and Moral Relations* (Philadelphia, PA, 1857), p. 48.

23 Henry Maudsley, 'Illustrations of a Variety of Insanity', *Journal of Mental Science*, XIV/66 (1868), p. 153.

24 Edward Thring, 'The Felon's Creed, and the Redeemer', in *Sermons Preached at Uppingham School*, vol. II (Cambridge, 1886), p. 15.

25 Thomas Laqueur, *Solitary Sex: A Cultural History of Masturbation* (New York, 2003), p. 21.

26 Robert Graves, *Goodbye to All That* (London, 2000), p. 39.

27 Hickson, *The Poisoned Bowl*, p. 57.

28 Clive Dewey, '"Socratic Teachers": The Opposition to the Cult of Athletics at Eton, 1870–1914, Part I', *International Journal of the History of Sport*, XII/1 (1995), pp. 51–80.

29 Hickson, *The Poisoned Bowl*, p. 61.

30 Stephen Marcus, *The Other Victorians: A Study of Sexuality and Pornography in Mid-nineteenth-century England* (New York, 1974), p. 2.

31 Edward Lyttelton, *The Causes and Prevention of Immorality in Schools* (London, 1887), p. 20.

32 Frederick W. Farrar, *Eric; or, Little by Little: A Tale of Rosslyn School* (Edinburgh, 1858), p. 102.

33 Quoted in Hickson, *The Poisoned Bowl*, p. 29.

34 Phyllis Grosskurth, ed., *The Memoirs of John Addington Symonds* (London, 1984), p. 84.

35 Ibid., p. 94.
36 Christopher Tyerman, *A History of Harrow School, 1324–1991* (Oxford, 2000), p. 247.
37 Grosskurth, ed., *The Memoirs of John Addington Symonds*, p. 114.
38 James Brinsley-Richards, *Seven Years at Eton, 1857–1864* (London, 1883), p. 72.
39 See Tyerman, *A History of Harrow School*, p. 196; and Ian Gibson, *The English Vice: Beating, Sex, and Shame in Victorian England and After* (London, 1978)
40 Heather Ellis, 'Corporal Punishment in the English Public School in the Nineteenth Century', in *Childhood and Violence in the Western Tradition*, ed. Laurence Brockliss and Heather Montgomery (Oxford, 2010), pp. 141–50.
41 Charles Alix Wilkinson, *Reminiscences of Eton (Keate's Time)* (London, 1888), p. 24.
42 Ibid., p. 23.
43 Deborah Lutz, *Pleasure Bound: Victorian Sex Rebels and the New Eroticism* (New York, 2011), p. 124.
44 Ian McCalman, *Radical Underworld: Prophets, Revolutionaries, and Pornographers in London, 1795–1840* (Cambridge, 1988), p. 215; Walter Kendrick, *The Secret Museum: Pornography in Modern Culture* (New York, 1987), p. 77.
45 Gibson, *The English Vice*, p. 125.
46 Ibid., p. 236.
47 Ibid.
48 *The Mysteries of Verbena House; Or, Miss Bellasis Birched for Thieving* (London, 2011), p. 28.
49 Ibid., p. 143.
50 Ibid., p. 28.
51 Lisa Sigel, *Governing Pleasures: Pornography and Social Change in England, 1815–1914* (New Brunswick, NJ, 2002), p. 77.
52 *The Romance of Chastisement; Or, Revelations of the School and Bedroom. By an Expert* (London, 1870), p. 9.
53 Marcus, *The Other Victorians*, p. 260.
54 George Bernard Shaw, *Misalliance and The Fascinating Foundling* (London, 1995), p. 60.
55 Goffman, *Asylums*, p. 211.

#### 4 CLASSICS AND NONSENSE

1 James Brinsley-Richards, *Seven Years at Eton, 1857–1864* (London, 1883), p. 1.
2 Ibid., p. 4.
3 Ibid., p. 1.
4 Ibid., p. 3.
5 Clive Dewey, '"Socratic Teachers": The Opposition to the Cult of Athletics at Eton, 1870–1914, Part 1', *International Journal of the History of Sport*, XII/1 (1995), p. 60.

6  M. L. Clarke, *Classical Education in Britain, 1500–1900* (Cambridge, 1959), p. 4.

7  Edward Bulwer-Lytton, *England and the English* (London, 1833), p. 255.

8  Ibid., p. 256.

9  Christopher Stray, *Classics Transformed: Schools, Universities, and Society in England, 1830–1960* (Oxford, 1998), p. 71.

10  Patrick Joyce, *The State of Freedom: A Social History of the State since 1800* (Cambridge, 2013), p. 258.

11  Quoted in J. R. de S. Honey, 'Tom Brown's Universe: The Nature and Limits of the Victorian Public Schools Community', in *The Victorian Public School: Studies in the Development of an Educational Institution*, ed. Brian Simon and Ian Bradley (Dublin, 1975), p. 23.

12  Stray, *Classics Transformed*, p. 2.

13  Charles Darwin, *Autobiographies*, ed. Michael Never (London, 2002), p. 10.

14  J. d'E. Firth, *Winchester College* (London, 1949), p. 109.

15  Charles Alix Wilkinson, *Reminiscences of Eton (Keate's Time)* (London, 1888), p. 62.

16  E. F. Benson, *David Blaize* (London, 1989), p. 154.

17  Ibid., p. 167.

18  George Melly, *School Experiences of a Fag at a Private and a Public School* (London, 1854), p. 127.

19  Thomas Hughes, *Tom Brown's Schooldays* (New York, 2008), p. 262.

20  Ibid., p. 261.

21  Ibid., p. 262.

22  Ibid., p. 263.

23  Henry Salt, *Memories of Bygone Eton* (London, 1928), p. 87.

24  W.H.D. Rouse, *The Teaching of Latin at the Perse School, Cambridge* (London, 1910), p. 22; quoted in Stray, *Classics Transformed*, p. 187.

25  Wilkinson, *Reminiscences of Eton*, p. 63.

26  Ibid.

27  Clarke, *Classical Education in Britain*, p. 53.

28  Stray, *Classics Transformed*, p. 97.

29  Ibid., p. 26; Peter Raby, *Samuel Butler: A Biography* (Iowa City, IA, 1991), pp. 25–6.

30  Jean-Jacques Lecercle, *Philosophy of Nonsense: The Intuitions of Victorian Nonsense* (New York, 2002).

31  Quoted in Jenny Woolf, *The Mystery of Lewis Carroll: Discovering the Whimsical, Thoughtful, and Sometimes Lonely Man who Created Alice in Wonderland* (New York, 2010), p. 23.

32  Ibid., p. 24.

33  Lecercle, *Philosophy of Nonsense*, p. 3.

34  This argument is made by Catherine Robson in *Men in Wonderland: The Lost Girlhood of the Victorian Gentleman* (Princeton, NJ, 2001).

35  Iona Opie and Peter Opie, *The Lore and Language of Schoolchildren* (Oxford, 1959), p. 18.

36  Charles Stevens, *Winchester Notions: The Dialect of Winchester College*, ed. Christopher Stray (London, 1998).

37 Jonathan Gathorne-Hardy, *The Old School Tie: The Phenomenon of the Public School* (New York, 1977), p. 309.

38 Arnold Lunn, *The Harrovians: A Tale of Public School Life* (Los Angeles, CA, 2010), p. 47.

39 Ibid.

40 Bulwer-Lytton, *England and the English*, p. 161.

41 Rudyard Kipling, *The Complete Stalky and Co.*, ed. Isabel Quigly (New York, 2009).

42 Walter Ong, 'Latin Language Study as a Renaissance Puberty Rite', *Studies in Philology*, LVI/2 (1959), pp. 103–24.

43 George Orwell, 'Such, Such Were the Joys', in *A Collection of Essays* (Orlando, FL, 1981), p. 5.

44 Winston Churchill, *My Early Life: 1874–1904* (New York, 1996), p. 10.

45 Ibid., p. 11.

46 Evelyn Waugh, *Decline and Fall* (London, 2012), p. 32.

47 Harry Thompson, *Peter Cook: A Biography* (London, 1997), p. 24.

48 Roger Wilmut, ed., *The Complete Beyond the Fringe* (London, 1993).

49 Thompson, *Peter Cook*, p. 6.

## 5 ATHLETES AND AESTHETES

1 The best and most complete account of public school athleticism is J. A. Mangan, *Athleticism in the Victorian and Edwardian Public School: The Emergence and Consolidation of an Educational Ideology* (Cambridge, 1981).

2 Edward Thring, *Education and School* (London, 1867), p. 33.

3 Quoted in Jonathan Gathorne-Hardy, *The Old School Tie: The Phenomenon of the Public School* (New York, 1977), p. 155.

4 William Acton, *The Functions and Disorders of Reproductive Organs, in Childhood, Youth, Adult-age, and Advanced Life, Considered in the Physiological, Social, and Moral Relations* (Philadelphia, PA, 1857), p. 29.

5 James George Cotton Minchin, *Our Public Schools: Their Influence on English History* (London, 1901), p. 113.

6 Thomas Hughes, *The Manliness of Christ* (Boston, MA, 1880), p. 20.

7 Erving Goffman, *Asylums: Essays on the Social Situation of Mental Patients and Other Inmates* (New York, 1990), p. 12.

8 Oscar Wilde, *The Picture of Dorian Gray*, ed. Isobel Murray (Oxford, 1998), p. xxiii.

9 John Betjeman, 'The Silver Age of Aesthetes: A Picture of Oxford during the Twenties' (1938), quoted in Bevis Hillier, *Young Betjeman* (London, 2003), p. 131.

10 Harold Acton, *Memoirs of an Aesthete* (London, 2008), p. 79.

11 Marie-Jacqueline Lancaster, *Brian Howard: Portrait of a Failure* (London, 2007), p. 32.

12 Henry Green, *Pack My Bag* (New York, 1993), p. 152.

13 Ibid., p. 108.

14 Robert Graves, *Goodbye to All That* (London, 2000), p. 43.

15 Green, *Pack My Bag*, p. 152.

16  Louis MacNeice, *The Strings are False: An Unfinished Autobiography* (London, 1996), p. 96–7.
17  Selina Hastings, *Evelyn Waugh: A Biography* (London, 1994), p. 70.
18  Quoted in D. J. Taylor's 'Introduction' to Lancaster, *Brian Howard*, p. xiv.
19  Lancaster, *Brian Howard*, pp. 35–6.
20  See, in particular, Jon Savage, *Teenage: The Creation of Youth, 1875–1945* (London, 2007), pp. 234–48; and Ronald Blythe, *The Age of Illusion: Some Glimpses of Britain between the Wars, 1919–1940* (Oxford, 1983), pp. 15–42.
21  The figures for Eton come from Peter Parker, *The Old Lie: The Great War and the Public School Ethos* (London, 2007), p. 16; the figures for Harrow are from Savage, *Teenage*, p. 152.
22  *Eton Candle* (1922), p. 79.
23  Ian Kelly, *Beau Brummell: The Ultimate Man of Style* (New York, 2006).
24  Martin Green, *Children of the Sun: A Narrative of 'Decadence' in England after 1918* (Mount Jackson, VA, 2008), p. 13.
25  A.J.P. Taylor, *English History, 1914–1945* (Oxford, 2001), p. 260.
26  Green, *Pack My Bag*, p. 152.
27  Dick Hebdige, *Subculture: The Meaning of Style* (London, 2003), p. 2.
28  Ibid., p. 3.
29  Alec Waugh, *The Loom of Youth* (London, 2012).
30  Quoted in Gathorne-Hardy, *The Old School Tie*, p. 308.
31  MacNeice, *The Strings are False*, p. 241.
32  Harold Nicolson, *Some People* (London, 2010), p. 29.
33  Quoted in Cyril Connolly, *Enemies of Promise* (Chicago, IL, 2008), p. 208.
34  Anthony Blunt, 'From Bloomsbury to Marxism', *Studio International*, 186 (November 1973), p. 164.
35  Acton, *Memoirs of an Aesthete*, p. 109.
36  Connolly, *Enemies of Promise*, p. 116.
37  Noel Annan, *Our Age: English Intellectuals between the World Wars: A Group Portrait* (New York, 1990), p. 11.
38  Ibid., p. 8.
39  See Introduction, n.4 above.
40  Henry Fairlie, 'The Establishment', *The Spectator*, 23 September 1955.
41  Q. D. Leavis, 'The Background of Twentieth Century Letters', *Scrutiny* (June 1939), p. 76 [review of Connolly, *Enemies of Promise*].
42  Richard Usborne, *Clubland Heroes: A Nostalgic Study of Some Recurrent Characters in the Romantic Fiction of Dornford Yates, John Buchan, and Sapper* (London, 1974).
43  Ibid., p. 91.
44  Sapper, *Bulldog Drummond* (Callington, Cornwall, 2001), p. 14.
45  John Buchan, *The Thirty-nine Steps* (London, 2007), p. 149.
46  Sapper, *Bulldog Drummond*, p. 9.
47  Ibid., p. 12.
48  Ian Fleming, *Casino Royale* (Las Vegas, NV, 2012), p. 130.
49  Quoted in Miranda Carter, *Anthony Blunt: His Lives* (London, 2001), p. 15.
50  Ian Fleming, *You Only Live Twice* (Las Vegas, NV, 2012), p. 204.

51 Bernard Bergonzi, 'The Case of Mr. Fleming', *Twentieth Century* (March 1958), pp. 220–28; quoted in Andrew Lycett, *Ian Fleming* (London, 1995), p. 320.

52 Paul Johnson, 'Sex, Snobbery and Sadism', 5 April 1958, p. 431; quoted in James Chapman, 'Bond and Britishness', in *Ian Fleming and James Bond: The Cultural Politics of 007*, ed. Edward P. Comentale, Stephen Watt and Skip Willman (Bloomington, IN, 2005), p. 131.

53 Cyril Connolly, 'Bond Strikes Camp', *London Magazine*, III/1 (April 1963).

54 Ian Fleming, *Live and Let Die* (Las Vegas, NV, 2012), p. 71.

55 Ian Fleming, *Goldfinger* (Las Vegas, NV, 2012), p. 184.

56 Fleming, *You Only Live Twice*, p. 173.

57 Ian Fleming, *Moonraker* (Las Vegas, NV, 2012), p. 208.

58 John le Carré, *Tinker, Tailor, Soldier, Spy* (New York, 2011), p. 12.

59 Ibid., p. 273.

60 Ibid., p. 29.

61 Ibid., p. 115.

62 Ibid., p. 117.

63 Ibid., p. 368.

64 Ibid., p. 157.

## 6 RED MENACE

1 Philip Toynbee, *Friends Apart: A Memoir of the Thirties* (London, 1954), p. 18.

2 *Out of Bounds*, I/1 (1934), p. 1.

3 *Daily Mail*, 2 February 1934.

4 Toynbee, *Friends Apart*, p. 15.

5 *Sunday Graphic*, 15 April 1934.

6 Giles Romilly and Esmond Romilly, *Out of Bounds: The Education of Giles and Esmond Romilly* (London, 1935), p. 196.

7 *Out of Bounds*, I/1 (1934), p. 37; *Out of Bounds*, I/2 (1934), p. 34.

8 Romilly and Romilly, *Out of Bounds*, p. 214.

9 *Out of Bounds*, I/1 (1934), p. 2.

10 The demographics of the BUF are described in Jon Savage, *Teenage: The Creation of Youth, 1875–1945* (London, 2007), p. 305. For details on the Socialist youth organizations of the 1920s and '30s, see Arthur Marwick, 'Youth in Britain, 1920–1960: Detachment and Commitment', *Journal of Contemporary History*, V/1 (1970), pp. 37–51.

11 Toynbee, *Friends Apart*, p. 17.

12 Romilly and Romilly, *Out of Bounds*, p. 204.

13 Ibid., p. 53.

14 T. C. Worsley, *Flannelled Fool: A Slice of Life in the Thirties* (London, 1985), pp. 91–2.

15 Brian Simon, *Education and the Social Order, 1940–1990* (New York, 1991), p. 32.

16 Christopher Tyerman, *A History of Harrow School, 1324–1991* (Oxford, 2000), p. 412.

17 Harold Laski, *The Danger of Being a Gentleman, and other Essays* (New York, 1967), p. 23.
18 Kevin Ingram, *Rebel: The Short Life of Esmond Romilly* (New York, 1986), p. 82.
19 Noel Annan, *Our Age: English Intellectuals Between the World Wars: A Group Portrait* (New York, 1990), p. 183.
20 Paul Mason, *Why It's Still Kicking Off Everywhere: The New Global Revolutions* (London, 2013), p. 66.
21 Graham Greene, ed., *The Old School: Essays by Divers Hands* (London, 1934), p. 7.
22 Louis MacNeice, *The Strings are False: An Unfinished Autobiography* (London, 1996), p. 85; T. C. Worsley, *Barbarians and Philistines: Democracy and the Public Schools* (London, 1940), p. 169.
23 Patrick Leigh-Fermor, *A Time of Gifts: On Foot to Constantinople* (London, 2004), p. 5.
24 Romilly and Romilly, *Out of Bounds*, p. 309.
25 Ibid., p. 96.
26 Cyril Connolly, *Enemies of Promise* (Chicago, IL, 2008), p. 150.
27 Steven Johnson, *The Ghost Map: The Story of London's Most Terrifying Epidemic – How it Changed Science, Cities, and the Modern World* (New York, 2006), p. 128.
28 C. S. Lewis, *Surprised by Joy: The Shape of My Early Life* (New York, 2012), p. 173.
29 Regenia Gagnier, *Subjectivities: A History of Self-representation in Britain, 1832–1920* (London, 1991), p. 190.
30 L. P. Hartley, 'The Conformer', in *The Old School*, ed. Graham Greene, p. 85.
31 Ibid.
32 C. Day-Lewis, *The Buried Day* (London, 1960), p. 111.
33 Ibid.
34 Christopher Isherwood, *Lions and Shadows: An Education in the Twenties* (London, 2013), p. 51.
35 Ibid., p. 227.
36 Romilly and Romilly, *Out of Bounds*, p. 12.
37 Ibid., p. 47.
38 Ibid.
39 Ibid.
40 Ibid., p. 73.
41 Ibid., p. 120.
42 William Hazlitt, *On the Pleasure of Hating* (London, 2004), p. 105.
43 Romilly and Romilly, *Out of Bounds*, p. 248.
44 Quoted in Ingram, *Rebel*, p. 144.
45 Jessica Mitford, *Hons and Rebels* (New York, 2004), p. 100.
46 *Daily Express*, 1 March 1937.
47 Mitford, *Hons and Rebels*, p. 172.
48 Toynbee, *Friends Apart*, p. 116.
49 Quoted in Ingram, *Rebel*, p. 181.
50 *Washington Post*, 28 January 1940.

51  Ingram, *Rebel*, p. 219.
52  Toynbee, *Friends Apart*, p. 33.
53  Worsley, *Flannelled Fool*, p. 98.
54  Mitford, *Hons and Rebels*, p. 281.


7 GOING UNDERGROUND

 1  Daryl Easlea, *Without Frontiers: The Life and Music of Peter Gabriel* (New York, 2014), p. 35.
 2  Ibid.
 3  Mike Rutherford, *The Living Years: The First Genesis Memoir* (New York, 2014), p. 28.
 4  Easlea, *Without Frontiers*, p. 71.
 5  Ibid., p. 35.
 6  George Melly, *Revolt into Style: The Pop Arts in Britain* (London, 2012), p. 2.
 7  Ibid., p. 5.
 8  Dan Fox, *Pretentiousness: Why it Matters* (Minneapolis, MN, 2016), p. 67.
 9  Nick Drake, 'Poor Boy' on *Bryter Later* (Island Records, 1971).
10  For a thorough and fair-minded account of the history of the welfare state in Britain, see Nicholas Timmins, *The Five Giants: A Biography of the Welfare State* (London, 2001).
11  In his book *Philosophers and Kings*, Gary McCulloch explains the centrality of Plato's model of education for leadership to the nineteenth- and twentieth-century public school. He also argues that by rejecting this model in favour of a purely academic ethos the post-Second World War grammar schools placed their pupils at a competitive disadvantage in relation to the graduates of public schools, where the ethos of leadership training persisted. Gary McCulloch, *Philosophers and Kings: Education for Leadership in Modern England* (Cambridge, 1991).
12  Quoted in Timmins, *The Five Giants*, p. 73.
13  Ibid., p. 86.
14  Ibid., p. 76.
15  Brian Simon, *Education and the Social Order, 1940–1990* (New York, 1991).
16  Ibid., p. 323.
17  Quoted in David Turner, *The Old Boys: The Decline and Rise of the Public School* (New Haven, CT, 2015), p. 211.
18  John Rae, *The Public School Revolution* (London, 1981), p. 115.
19  Quoted in Jonathan Gathorne-Hardy, *The Old School Tie: The Phenomenon of the Public School* (New York, 1977), p. 401.
20  John Peel, *Margrave of the Marshes* (Chicago, IL, 2007), p. 49.
21  Simon Worrall, 'Not If . . . but When', *The Times*, 27 May 2008.
22  Peel, *Margrave of the Marshes*, p. 48.
23  Jon Savage, *Teenage: The Creation of Youth, 1875–1945* (London, 2007), p. xiii.
24  G. Stanley Hall, *Adolescence: Its Psychology and Its Relations to Physiology, Anthropology, Sociology, Sex, Crime and Religion* (New York, 1904).
25  Mallory Wober, *English Girls' Boarding Schools* (London, 1971), p. 84.

26  Humphrey Lyttelton, *I Play as I Please: The Memoirs of an Etonian Trumpeter* (London, 1954), p. 55.
27  Ibid., p. 53.
28  Rutherford, *The Living Years*, p. 36.
29  Wober, *English Girls' Boarding Schools*, p. 121.
30  Rae, *Public School Revolution*, p. 93.
31  Henry Newbolt, 'Vitaï Lampada', in *Empire Writing: An Anthology of Colonial Literature, 1870–1918*, ed. Elleke Boehmer (New York, 1998), p. 287.
32  J.D.R. McConnell, *Eton: How it Works* (London, 1967).
33  Rae, *Public School Revolution*, p. 106.
34  Worrall, 'Not If... but When'.
35  Lindsay Anderson, *Never Apologise: The Collected Writings*, ed. Paul Ryan (London, 2004), p. 114.
36  Gavin Lambert, *Mainly about Lindsay Anderson: A Memoir* (London, 2000), p. 146.
37  Pauline Kael, 'School Days, School Days', *New Yorker*, 15 March 1969, p. 152.
38  Anderson, *Never Apologise*, p. 109.
39  Ibid., p. 120.
40  Ibid., p. 122.
41  Lambert, *Mainly about Lindsay Anderson*, p. 10.
42  Ibid., p. 12.
43  Anderson, *Never Apologise*, p. 120.
44  E. M. Forster, 'Notes on the English Character', in *Abinger Harvest* (Orlando, FL, 1964), p. 5.
45  Lambert, *Mainly about Lindsay Anderson*, p. 141.
46  Rudyard Kipling, *Poems* (New York, 2007), p. 171.
47  Ibid., p. 22.
48  Quoted in Jonathon Green, *Days in the Life: Voices from the English Underground, 1961–1971* [1988] (London, 1998), p. 425.
49  Andrew Pulver, 'Does David Cameron's taste in films match his values? If ... only', www.guardian.co.uk, 6 January 2012.
50  Quoted in Green, *Days in the Life*, p. 188.
51  Quoted ibid., p. 257.
52  Richard Neville, *Play Power* (London, 1971).
53  Geoffrey Walford, *Life in Public Schools* (London, 1986), p. 84.
54  Nik Cohn, *Awopbopaloobop Alopbamboom: The Golden Age of Rock* (London, 2004), p. 3.
55  Simon Napier-Bell, *Black Vinyl, White Powder* (London, 2001), p. 90.
56  Andrew Loog Oldham, *Stoned* (London, 2001), p. 46.
57  Melly, *Revolt into Style*, p. 94.
58  Oldham, *Stoned*, p. 31.
59  Marianne Faithfull with David Dalton, *Faithfull* (London, 1994), p. 21.
60  Quoted ibid., p. 31.
61  Ibid., p. 12.
62  The details on Lambert's life and career come from Andrew Motion, *The Lamberts: George, Constant and Kit* (London, 1986).

63 Keith Richards, *Life* (New York, 2010), p. 202.

64 Tom Bower, *Branson: Behind the Mask* (London, 2014).

65 Richard Branson, *Losing My Virginity: The Autobiography* [1998] (London, 2009), p. 39.

66 Ibid., p. 43.

67 Gavin Maxwell, 'Education Axed', *Student Magazine*, 1/1 (January 1968), p. 36.

68 'Editorial' in ibid., p. 6.

69 Branson, *Losing My Virginity*, p. 47.

70 Ibid., p. 64.

71 Quoted in Dominic Sandbrook, *The Great British Dream Factory: The Strange History of our National Imagination* (London, 2015), p. 78.

72 Mark Binelli, 'Chris Blackwell: The Barefoot Mogul', www.mensjournal. com, 1 August 2017.

73 Lee 'Scratch' Perry, 'Judgment in a Babylon' (Lion of Judah, 1981).

74 Linton Kwesi Johnson, 'Roots and Rock: The Marley Enigma', in *The Rock History Reader*, ed. Theo Cateforis (New York, 2013); Jimmy Cliff, 'Number One Rip-off Man' on *Music Maker* (Rhino/Warner Bros, 1974).

75 Sandbrook, *The Great British Dream Factory*, p. 78.

76 Eric Lott, *Love and Theft: Blackface Minstrelsy and the American Working Class* (New York, 2013).

## 8 THE ORDINARY ELITE

1 Laura Wade, *Posh* (London, 2010), p. 38.

2 Ibid., p. 141.

3 Ibid., p. 125.

4 Ibid., p. 52.

5 Ibid., p. 110.

6 Sonia Purnell, *Just Boris: A Tale of Blond Ambition* (London, 2011), p. 68.

7 Evelyn Waugh, *Decline and Fall* (New York, 2012), p. 2.

8 The rituals and status of the modern Bullingdon Club are discussed by Barney Ronay in 'Young, Rich, and Drunk', www.theguardian.com, 8 May 2008. The detail of the burning of £50 notes is reported in Tom McTague, 'Bullingdon Club Initiation Ceremony Claim', www.mirror. co.uk, 23 February 2013.

9 'Cameron Student Photo is Banned', *Newsnight*, BBC News, 2 March 2007.

10 Mike Savage et al., *Social Class in the 21st Century* (London, 2015).

11 Mike Savage and Karel Williams, eds, *Remembering Elites* (London, 2008), p. 7.

12 David Turner, *The Old Boys: The Decline and Rise of the Public School* (New Haven, CT, 2015), pp. 240–41.

13 John Rae, *The Public School Revolution* (London, 1981), p. 67.

14 Ibid., p. 155.

15 Nicholas Timmins, *The Five Giants: A Biography of the Welfare State* (London, 2001), p. 301.

16 Turner, *The Old Boys*, p. 223.

17  Melissa Benn, *The School Wars: The Battle for Britain's Education* (London, 2011), p. 67.
18  Ann Barr and Peter York, *The Official Sloane Ranger Handbook: The First Guide to What Really Matters in Life* (London, 1982).
19  Alan Watkins, 'Diary', *The Spectator*, 19 May 1984.
20  Quoted in Rae, *Public School Revolution*, pp. 50–52.
21  Turner, *The Old Boys*, p. 221.
22  Ibid., p. 249.
23  Benn, *The School Wars*, p. 145.
24  Karl Marx and Friedrich Engels, *The German Ideology, including Theses on Feuerbach* (New York, 1998), p. 53.
25  Anthony Seldon, 'Lessons in Life: Why I'm Teaching Happiness', www.independent.co.uk, 18 April 2006.
26  Turner, *The Old Boys*, p. 231.
27  For details on overseas expansion, see Jim Pickard, 'UK Schools Expand their Operations Abroad', *Financial Times*, 6 September 2013; 'Private Schools Turn to Foreign Pupils as Recession Bites', *The Independent*, 25 April 2013; Justin Harper, 'Boom in British Schools Overseas', *The Telegraph*, 20 August 2013.
28  David Kynaston and George Kynaston, 'Education's Berlin Wall: The Private Schools Conundrum', www.newstatesman.com, 3 February 2014.
29  Turner, *The Old Boys*, p. 251.
30  The Jam, 'The Eton Rifles' (Polydor, 1979).
31  See, for example, Richard Garner, 'Boarding Schools Miss their Harry Potter Magic', www.independent.co.uk, 28 April 2004.
32  Henry Jenkins, *Convergence Culture: Where Old and New Media Collide* (New York, 2006), pp. 169–205.
33  Owen Jones, *Chavs: The Demonization of the Working Class* (London, 2016).
34  *St Trinian's*, dir. Oliver Parker and Barnaby Thompson (Ealing Studios, 2007).
35  Ibid.
36  Savage et al., *Social Class in the 21st Century*, p. 51.
37  Shamus Rahman Khan, *Privilege: The Making of an Adolescent Elite at St Paul's School* (Princeton, NJ, 2013), p. 16.

## AFTERWORD

1  Cyril Connolly, *Enemies of Promise* (Chicago, IL, 2008), p. 163.
2  George Orwell, 'Inside the Whale', in *A Collection of Essays* (Orlando, FL, 1991), p. 239.
3  Ibid., p. 240.
4  Orwell, 'Such, Such Were the Joys', in *A Collection of Essays*, p. 47.

# SELECT BIBLIOGRAPHY

Acton, Harold, *Memoirs of an Aesthete* (1948) (London, 2008)

Acton, William, *The Functions and Disorders of Reproductive Organs, in Childhood, Youth, Adult-age, and Advanced Life, Considered in the Physiological, Social, and Moral Relations* (Philadelphia, PA, 1857)

Anderson, Lindsay, *Never Apologise: The Collected Writings*, ed. Paul Ryan (London, 2004)

Annan, Noel, *Our Age: English Intellectuals between the World Wars: A Group Portrait* (New York, 1990)

Anon., *A Sketch of the Rights of Boys and Girls, by Launcelot Light of Westminster School, and Laetitia Lookabout of Queen's Square, Bloomsbury* (London, 1792)

Anon., *The Romance of Chastisement; Or, Revelations of the School and Bedroom. By an Expert* (London, 1870)

Ariès, Philippe, *Centuries of Childhood: A Social History of Family Life* (New York, 1962)

Arnold, Thomas, 'On the Discipline of Public Schools', *Quarterly Journal of Education*, 9 (1835), pp. 280–92; cited in *Thomas Arnold on Education*, ed. T. W. Bamford (Cambridge, 1970)

Auden, W. H., 'Honour (Gresham's School, Holt)', in *The Old School: Essays by Divers Hands*, ed. Graham Greene (London, 1934), pp. 1–12

Avery, Gillian, *The Best Type of Girl: A History of Girls' Independent Schools* (London, 1991)

Barr, Ann, and Peter York, *The Official Sloane Ranger Handbook: The First Guide to What Really Matters in Life* (London, 1982)

Benn, Melissa, *The School Wars: The Battle for Britain's Education* (London, 2011)

Bennett, Alan, 'Fair Play', *London Review of Books*, XXXVI/12 (19 June 2014), pp. 29–30

Benson, E. F., *David Blaize* [1916] (London, 1989)

Binelli, Mark, 'Chris Blackwell: The Barefoot Mogul', www.mensjournal.com, 1 August 2017

Blunt, Anthony, 'From Bloomsbury to Marxism', *Studio International*, 186 (November 1973), pp. 164–8

Blythe, Ronald, *The Age of Illusion: Some Glimpses of Britain between the Wars, 1919–1940* (Oxford, 1983)

Bourdieu, Pierre, *Distinction: A Social Critique of the Judgement of Taste* (Cambridge, MA, 1984)

Bower, Tom, *Branson: Behind the Mask* (London, 2014)

Bradley, A. G., A. C. Champneys and J. W. Baines, *A History of Marlborough College during Fifty Years: From its Foundation to the Present Time* (London, 1893)

Branson, Richard, *Losing My Virginity: The Autobiography* [1998] (London, 2009)

Brendon, Vyvyen, *Prep School Children: A Class Apart over Two Centuries* (London, 2009)

Brinsley-Richards, James, *Seven Years at Eton, 1857–1864* (London, 1883)

Buchan, John, *The Thirty-nine Steps* (London, 1916)

Bulwer-Lytton, Edward, *England and the English* (London, 1833)

Carter, Miranda, *Anthony Blunt: His Lives* (London, 2001)

Chandos, John, *Boys Together: English Public Schools, 1800–1864* (New Haven, CT, 1984)

Chapman, James, 'Bond and Britishness', in *Ian Fleming and James Bond: The Cultural Politics of 007*, ed. Edward P. Comentale, Stephen Watt and Skip Willman (Bloomington, IN, 2005), pp. 129–43

Churchill, Winston, *My Early Life, 1874–1904* [1930] (New York, 1996)

Clarke, M. L., *Classical Education in Britain, 1500–1900* (Cambridge, 1959)

Cohen, Stanley, *Folk Devils and Moral Panics* (London, 2011)

Cohn, Nik, *Awopbopaloobop Alopbamboom: The Golden Age of Rock* (1969) (London, 2004)

[Coleridge, J. T.], 'Shelley's Revolt of Islam', *Quarterly Review*, 21 (April 1819), pp. 460–71

Connolly, Cyril, *Enemies of Promise* [1938, revd 1948] (Chicago, IL, 2008)

——, 'A London Diary', *New Statesman*, 16 January 1937

Copley, Terence, *Black Tom: Arnold of Rugby: The Myth and the Man* (London, 2002)

Cotton Minchin, James George, *Our Public Schools: Their Influence on English History* (London, 1901)

Cunningham, Hugh, *Children and Childhood in Western Society since 1500* (London, 2005)

Darwin, Charles, *Autobiographies*, ed. Michael Never (London, 2002)

Day-Lewis, Cecil, *The Buried Day* (London, 1960)

Dewey, Clive, '"Socratic Teachers": The Opposition to the Cult of Athletics at Eton, 1870–1914, Part 1', *International Journal of the History of Sport*, XII/1 (1995), pp. 51–80

Duffell, Nick, *Wounded Leaders: British Elitism and the Entitlement Illusion* (London, 2014)

Easlea, Daryl, *Without Frontiers: The Life and Music of Peter Gabriel* (New York, 2014)

Ellis, Heather, 'Corporal Punishment in the English Public School in the Nineteenth Century', in *Childhood and Violence in the Western Tradition*,

ed. Laurence Brockliss and Heather Montgomery (Oxford, 2010),
    pp. 141–50

Etonensis [George Augustus Sala and James Campbell Reddie],
    *The Mysteries of Verbena House: or, Miss Bellasis Birched for Thieving* (1882)
    (London, 2011)

Fairlie, Henry, 'The Establishment', *The Spectator*, 23 September 1955

Faithfull, Marianne, with David Dalton, *Faithfull* (London, 1994)

Farrar, Frederick W., *Eric, or Little by Little: A Tale of Rosslyn School*
    (Edinburgh, 1858)

Firth, J. d'E., *Winchester College* (London, 1949)

Fleming, Ian, *Casino Royale* (1953) (Las Vegas, NV, 2012)

——, *Goldfinger* [1959] (Las Vegas, NV, 2012)

——, *Live and Let Die* [1954] (Las Vegas, NV, 2012)

——, *Moonraker* [1955] (Las Vegas, NV, 2012)

——, *You Only Live Twice* [1964] (Las Vegas, NV, 2012)

Forster, E. M., 'Notes on the English Character', in *Abinger Harvest* (1936)
    (Orlando, FL, 1964), pp. 3–14

Fox, Dan, *Pretentiousness: Why it Matters* (Minneapolis, MN, 2016)

Fraser, George MacDonald, *Flashman* [1969] (New York, 1984)

——, *Flashman at the Charge* [1973] (New York, 1986)

——, 'The Last Testament of Flashman's Creator: How Britain Has Destroyed
    Itself', *Daily Mail*, 5 January 2008

Gagnier, Regenia, *Subjectivities: A History of Self-representation in Britain,
    1832–1920* (London, 1991)

Gathorne-Hardy, Jonathan, *The Old School Tie: The Phenomenon of the Public
    School* (New York, 1977)

Gibbon, Edward, *The Autobiography and Correspondence of Edward Gibbon,
    the Historian* (London, 1869)

Gibson, Ian, *The English Vice: Beating, Sex, and Shame in Victorian England
    and After* (London, 1978)

Gill, Stephen, ed., *Wordsworth: the Major Works* (New York, 2000)

Gillis, John R., *Youth in History: Tradition and Change in European Age
    Relations, 1770–Present* (New York, 1974)

Gilmour, Ian, *The Making of the Poets: Byron and Shelley in Their Time*
    (London, 2002)

Goffman, Erving, *Asylums: Essays on the Social Situation of Mental Patients
    and Other Inmates* (New York, 1990)

Golding, William, *Lord of the Flies* [1954] (New York, 1997)

Graves, Robert, *Goodbye to All That* [1929] (London, 2000)

Green, Henry, *Pack My Bag* (New York, 1993)

Green, Jonathon, *Days in the Life: Voices from the English Underground,
    1961–1971* [1988] (London, 1998)

Green, Martin, *Children of the Sun: A Narrative of 'Decadence' in England
    after 1918* (Mount Jackson, VA, 2008)

Greene, Graham, ed., *The Old School: Essays by Divers Hands*
    (London, 1934)

Grosskurth, Phyllis, ed., *The Memoirs of John Addington Symonds*
    (London, 1984)

Hall, G. Stanley, *Adolescence: Its Psychology and Its Relations to Physiology, Anthropology, Sociology, Sex, Crime and Religion* (New York, 1904)

Harris, Jennifer, 'The Red Cap of Liberty: A Study of Dress Worn by French Revolutionary Partisans, 1789–94', *Eighteenth-century Studies*, XIV/3 (1981), pp. 283–312

Hastings, Selina, *Evelyn Waugh: A Biography* (London, 1994)

Hazlitt, William, *On the Pleasure of Hating* [1821] (London, 2004)

Heath, Deana, *Purifying Empire: Obscenity and the Politics of Moral Regulation in Britain, India, and Australia* (Cambridge, 2010)

Hebdige, Dick, *Subculture: The Meaning of Style* (London, 2003)

Heywood, Colin, *A History of Childhood: Children and Childhood in the West from Medieval to Modern Times* (Oxford, 2003)

Hickson, Alisdare, *The Poisoned Bowl: Sex and the Public School* (London, 1996)

Hillier, Bevis, *Young Betjeman* (London, 2003)

Hobbes, Thomas, *Leviathan* [1651] (London, 1982)

Hogg, Thomas Jefferson, *The Life of Percy Bysshe Shelley* (London, 1858)

Holmes, Richard, *Shelley: The Pursuit* (London, 1974)

Holt, Jenny, *Public School Literature, Civic Education, and the Politics of Male Adolescence* (Farnham, 2008)

Honey, J. R. de S., *Tom Brown's Universe: The Development of the English Public School in the Nineteenth Century* (New York, 1977)

—, 'Tom Brown's Universe: The Nature and Limits of the Victorian Public Schools Community', in *The Victorian Public School: Studies in the Development of an Educational Institution*, ed. Brian Simon and Ian Bradley (Dublin, 1975), pp. 19–33

Hughes, Thomas, *The Manliness of Christ* (Boston, 1880)

—, *Tom Brown's Schooldays* [1857] (New York, 2008)

Ignatieff, Michael, 'Total Institutions and Working Classes: A Review Essay', *History Workshop Journal*, XV (1983), pp. 167–73

Ingram, Kevin, *Rebel: The Short Life of Esmond Romilly* (New York, 1986)

Isherwood, Christopher, *Lions and Shadows: An Education in the Twenties* (London, 2013)

James, C.L.R., *Beyond a Boundary* (London, 2005)

Jenkins, Henry, *Convergence Culture: Where Old and New Media Collide* (New York, 2006)

Johnson, Steven, *The Ghost Map: The Story of London's Most Terrifying Epidemic – How it Changed Science, Cities, and the Modern World* (New York, 2006)

Jones, Owen, *Chavs: The Demonization of the Working Class* (London, 2016)

Joyce, Patrick, *The State of Freedom: A Social History of the State since 1800* (Cambridge, 2013)

Kael, Pauline, 'School Days, School Days', *New Yorker*, 15 March 1969, p. 152

Kamm, Josephine, *How Different from Us: A Biography of Miss Buss and Miss Beale* (London, 1958)

Kelly, Ian, *Beau Brummell: The Ultimate Man of Style* (New York, 2006)

Kendrick, Walter, *The Secret Museum: Pornography in Modern Culture* (New York, 1987)

Khan, Shamus Rahman, *Privilege: The Making of an Adolescent Elite at St Paul's School* (Princeton, NJ, 2013)

Kipling, Rudyard, *The Complete Stalky and Co.*, ed. Isabel Quigly (New York, 2009)

——, *Poems* (New York, 2007)

Kwesi Johnson, Linton, 'Roots and Rock: The Marley Enigma', in *The Rock History Reader*, ed. Theo Cateforis (New York, 2013), pp. 153–4

Kynaston, David, 'What Should We Do with Private Schools?', *The Guardian*, 5 December 2014

Kynaston, David, and George Kynaston, 'Education's Berlin Wall: The Private Schools Conundrum', www.newstatesman.com, 3 February 2014

Lambert, Gavin, *Mainly about Lindsay Anderson: A Memoir* (London, 2000)

Lancaster, Marie-Jacqueline, *Brian Howard: Portrait of a Failure* (London, 2007)

Laqueur, Thomas, *Solitary Sex: A Cultural History of Masturbation* (New York, 2003)

Laski, Harold, *The Danger of Being a Gentleman, and other Essays* [1939] (New York, 1967)

Leach, Arthur F., *A History of Winchester College* (London, 1899)

Le Carré, John, *Tinker, Tailor, Soldier, Spy* [1974] (New York, 2011)

Lecercle, Jean-Jacques, *Philosophy of Nonsense: The Intuitions of Victorian Nonsense* (New York, 2002)

Leigh-Fermor, Patrick, *A Time of Gifts: On Foot to Constantinople* [1977] (London, 2004)

Lewis, C. S., *Surprised by Joy: The Shape of My Early Life* [1955] (New York, 2012)

Lott, Eric, *Love and Theft: Blackface Minstrelsy and the American Working Class* (New York, 2013)

Lunn, Arnold, *The Harrovians: A Tale of Public School Life* [1913] (Los Angeles, CA, 2010)

Lutz, Deborah, *Pleasure Bound: Victorian Sex Rebels and the New Eroticism* (New York, 2011)

Lycett, Andrew, *Ian Fleming* (London, 1995)

Lyte, Maxwell, *A History of Eton College* (New York, 1889)

Lyttelton, Edward, *The Causes and Prevention of Immorality in Schools* (London, 1887)

Lyttelton, Humphrey, *I Play as I Please: The Memoirs of an Etonian Trumpeter* (London, 1954)

MacAloon, John J., *This Great Symbol: Pierre de Coubertin and the Origins of the Modern Olympic Games* (London, 2008)

——, ed., *Muscular Christianity in the Colonial and Post-colonial Worlds* (London, 2008)

McCalman, Ian, *Radical Underworld: Prophets, Revolutionaries, and Pornographers in London, 1795–1840* (Cambridge, 1988)

Mack, Edward, *Public Schools and British Opinion, 1780–1860* (London, 1938)

——, *Public Schools and British Opinion since 1860* (Westport, CT, 1941)

Mack, Edward C., and W.H.G. Armytage, *Thomas Hughes* (London, 1952)

MacNeice, Louis, *The Strings are False: An Unfinished Autobiography* (1965) (London, 1996)

McConnell, J.D.R., *Eton: How it Works* (London, 1967)

McCulloch, Gary, *Philosophers and Kings: Education for Leadership in Modern England* (Cambridge, 1991)

Mangan, J. A., *Athleticism in the Victorian and Edwardian Public School: The Emergence and Consolidation of an Educational Ideology* (Cambridge, 1981)

—, 'Bullies, Beatings, Battles, and Bruises: "great days and jolly days" at one Mid-Victorian Public School', in *Disreputable Pleasures: Less Virtuous Victorians at Play*, ed. Mike Huggins and J. A. Mangan (New York, 2004), pp. 3–32

Marcus, Stephen, *The Other Victorians: A Study of Sexuality and Pornography in Mid-nineteenth-century England* (New York, 1974)

Marwick, Arthur, 'Youth in Britain, 1920–1960: Detachment and Commitment', *Journal of Contemporary History*, v/1 (1970), pp. 37–51

Marx, Karl, and Friedrich Engels, *The German Ideology, including Theses on Feuerbach* [1932] (New York, 1998)

Mason, Paul, *Why It's Still Kicking Off Everywhere: The New Global Revolutions* (London, 2013)

Maudsley, Henry, 'Illustrations of a Variety of Insanity', *Journal of Mental Science*, xiv/66 (1868), pp. 149–62

Maxwell, Gavin, 'Education Axed', *Student*, 1/1 (January 1968), pp. 36ff

Melly, George [1926–2007], *Revolt into Style: The Pop Arts in Britain* (1970) (London, 2012)

Melly, George [1830–1894], *School Experiences of a Fag at a Private and a Public School* (London, 1854)

Mitford, Jessica, *Hons and Rebels* [1960] (New York, 2004)

Motion, Andrew, *The Lamberts: George, Constant and Kit* (London, 1986)

Moultrie, John, *Dream of Life, Lays of the English Church, and Other Poems* (London, 1843)

Napier-Bell, Simon, *Black Vinyl, White Powder* (London, 2001)

Neville, Richard, *Play Power* (London, 1971)

Newbolt, Henry, 'Vitai Lampada', in *Empire Writing: An Anthology of Colonial Literature, 1870–1918*, ed. Elleke Boehmer (New York, 1998), pp. 287–8

Newsome, David, *Godliness and Good Learning: Four Studies on a Victorian Ideal* (London, 1961)

Nicolson, Harold, *Some People* [1957] (London, 2010)

Oldham, Andrew Loog, *Stoned* (London, 2001)

Ong, Walter, 'Latin Language Study as a Renaissance Puberty Rite', *Studies in Philology*, lvi/2 (1959), pp. 103–24

Opie, Iona, and Peter Opie, *The Lore and Language of Schoolchildren* (Oxford, 1959)

Orwell, George, 'Boys' Weeklies', in *A Collection of Essays* (Orlando, FL, 1981), pp. 279–308

—, 'Inside the Whale', in ibid., pp. 210–52

—, 'Such, Such Were the Joys', in ibid., pp. 1–47

Parker, Peter, *The Old Lie: The Great War and the Public School Ethos* (London, 2007)

Parkin, G. R., *Edward Thring, Headmaster of Uppingham School: Life, Diary,*
     *Letters* (London, 1898)
Peel, John, *Margrave of the Marshes* (Chicago, IL, 2007)
Purnell, Sonia, *Just Boris: A Tale of Blond Ambition* (London, 2011)
Quigly, Isabel, *The Heirs of Tom Brown: The English School Story*
     (London, 1982)
Rae, John, *The Public School Revolution* (London, 1981)
Reiman, Donald H., Neil Freistat and Nora Crook, eds, *The Complete Poetry*
     *of Percy Bysshe Shelley*, vol. III (Baltimore, MD, 2012)
Renton, Alex, 'Abuse in Britain's Boarding Schools', www.guardian.com,
     4 May 2014
——, 'The Damage Boarding Schools Do', www.guardian.com, 20 July 2014
Richards, Frank [Charles Hamilton], 'Frank Richards Replies to George
     Orwell', *Horizon*, 1/5 (May 1940), pp. 346–55
Richards, Jeffrey, *Happiest Days: The Public Schools in English Fiction*
     (Manchester, 1988)
Richards, Keith, *Life* (New York, 2010)
Robson, Catherine, *Men in Wonderland: The Lost Girlhood of the Victorian*
     *Gentleman* (Princeton, NJ, 2001)
Romilly, Giles, and Esmond Romilly, *Out of Bounds: The Education of Giles*
     *and Esmond Romilly* (London, 1935)
Ronay, Barney, 'Young, Rich, and Drunk', www.theguardian.com, 8 May 2008
Rose, Jonathan, *The Intellectual Life of the British Working Classes*
     (New Haven, CT, 2010)
Rouse, W.H.D., *A History of Rugby School* (London, 1898)
——, *The Teaching of Latin at the Perse School, Cambridge* (London, 1910)
Rousseau, Jean-Jacques, *Emile; or, On Education*, trans. Alan Bloom
     (New York, 1979)
Rutherford, Mike, *The Living Years: the First Genesis Memoir* (New York, 2014)
Salt, Henry, *Memories of Bygone Eton* (London, 1928)
Sandbrook, Dominic, *The Great British Dream Factory: The Strange History*
     *of our National Imagination* (London, 2015)
Sapper, *Bulldog Drummond* (1920) (Callington, Cornwall, 2001)
Savage, Jon, *Teenage: The Creation of Youth, 1875–1945* (London, 2007)
Savage, Mike, and Karel Williams, eds, *Remembering Elites* (London, 2008)
Savage, Mike, et al., *Social Class in the 21st Century* (London, 2015)
Seaborne, Malcolm, 'The Architecture of the Victorian Public School', in
     *The Victorian Public School: Studies in the Development of an Educational*
     *Institution*, ed. Brian Simon and Ian Bradley (Dublin, 1975), pp. 177–87
Seldon, Anthony, 'Lessons in Life: Why I'm Teaching Happiness',
     www.independent.co.uk, 18 April 2006
Shaverien, Joy, *Boarding School Syndrome: The Psychological Trauma of the*
     *'Privileged' Child* (London, 2015)
Shaw, George Bernard, *Misalliance and The Fascinating Foundling*
     (London, 1995)
Shelley, Percy, *Zastrozzi and St Irvyne* [1810] (Oxford, 1986)
Shoemaker, Robert, *The London Mob: Violence and Disorder in Eighteenth-*
     *century England* (New York, 2007)

Shrosbree, Colin, *Public Schools and Private Education: The Clarendon Commission, 1861–64, and the Public Schools Act* (Manchester, 1988)

Sigel, Lisa, *Governing Pleasures: Pornography and Social Change in England, 1815–1914* (New Brunswick, NJ, 2002)

Simon, Brian, *Education and the Social Order, 1940–1990* (New York, 1991)

Smith, Sidney, *The Works of the Revd. Sidney Smith*, vol. I (London, 1859)

Stanley, Arthur Penrhyn, *The Life and Correspondence of Thomas Arnold* (London, 1844)

Stephen, James Fitzjames, 'Tom Brown's Schooldays', *Edinburgh Review*, 107 (January 1858), pp. 172–93

Stephen, Leslie, 'Thoughts of an Outsider: Public Schools', *Cornhill Magazine*, 27 (1873), pp. 281–92

Stevens, Charles, *Winchester Notions: The Dialect of Winchester College*, ed. Christopher Stray (London, 1998)

Strachey, Lytton, *Eminent Victorians* [1918] (Radford, VA, 2008)

Stray, Christopher, *Classics Transformed: Schools, Universities, and Society in England, 1830–1960* (Oxford, 1998)

Taylor, A.J.P., *English History, 1914–1945* [1965] (Oxford, 2001)

Thomas, Donald, *Swinburne: The Poet and His World* (Chicago, IL, 1999)

Thompson, Harry, *Peter Cook: A Biography* (London, 1997)

Thring, Edward, *Education and School* (London, 1867)

—, 'The Felon's Creed, and the Redeemer', in *Sermons Preached at Uppingham School*, vol. II (Cambridge, 1886), pp. 11–16

Timmins, Nicholas, *The Five Giants: A Biography of the Welfare State* (London, 2001)

Toynbee, Philip, *Friends Apart: A Memoir of the Thirties* (London, 1954)

Tucker, William, *Eton of Old, 1811–1822* (London, 1901)

Turner, David, *The Old Boys: The Decline and Rise of the Public School* (New Haven, CT, 2015)

Tyerman, Christopher, *A History of Harrow School, 1324–1991* (Oxford, 2000)

Usborne, Richard, *Clubland Heroes: A Nostalgic Study of Some Recurrent Characters in the Romantic Fiction of Dornford Yates, John Buchan, and Sapper* (London, 1974)

Wade, Laura, *Posh* (London, 2010)

Walford, Geoffrey, *Life in Public Schools* (London, 1986)

Wallbank, M. V., 'Eighteenth-century Schools and the Education of the Governing Elite', *History of Education*, VIII/1 (1979), pp. 1–19

Watkins, Alan, 'Diary', *The Spectator*, 19 May 1984

Waugh, Alec, *The Loom of Youth* [1917] (London, 2012)

Waugh, Evelyn, *A Little Learning: An Autobiography* (Boston, MA, 1964)

—, *Decline and Fall* [1928] (London, 2012)

Whitridge, Arnold, *Doctor Arnold of Rugby* (New York, 1926)

Wilde, Oscar, *The Picture of Dorian Gray*, ed. Isobel Murray (Oxford, 1998)

Wilkinson, Charles Alix, *Reminiscences of Eton (Keate's Time)* (London, 1888)

Wilmut, Roger, ed., *The Complete Beyond the Fringe* (London, 1993)

Wober, Mallory, *English Girls' Boarding Schools* (London, 1971)

Wodehouse, P. G., *Mike and Psmith* (New York, 1909)

—, *Tales of St Austin's* (1903) (Auckland, 2012)

# ACKNOWLEDGEMENTS

I'd like to thank everyone who offered encouragement and advice over the course of this book's writing. In particular, thank you to Sukhdev Sandhu, Phil Chessum and Frans De Bruyn, all of whom read drafts of varying lengths. Thanks, in particular, to Sukhdev for inviting me to talk about posh rock stars at the Colloquium for Unpopular Culture at New York University. Thanks also to Shamus Khan for his fructiferous response to my talk. Thank you to the members of the Montreal-Ottawa Romanticism Working Group, who offered insightful commentary on my ideas even as the project drifted further and further away from the Romantic era: Ina Ferris, Jonathan Sachs, Andrew Piper, Paul Keen, Ian Dennis, Fiona Ritchie, Mark Salber Philips, Lauren Gillingham, Julie Murray, Michael Nicholson, April London, Joel Faflak, Marcie Frank, Naomi Levine, Greg Ellerman and Peter Sabor. Thanks also to my colleagues at the University of Ottawa who listened to 'works-in-progress' talks drawn from chapters Four and Seven of the book: Jennifer Panek, Anne Raine, Keith Wilson, David Jarraway, Robert Stacey, Andrew Taylor, Nick von Maltzahn and Florian Grandena. I am very grateful for the generous support of the University of Ottawa Faculty of Arts. Thank you to the pink-haired librarian in the Rare Books and Manuscripts section of the British Library, who gave me the slightest of winks when locating the lost volume of Victorian flagellation pornography that I had travelled 3,000 miles to peruse. Thank you to my research assistant and fellow Romilly fan, Jason Liboiron. And thank you to my agent, Sally Holloway, for her incisive editing and unflagging commitment to this project. But above all, thank you to Sara Landreth, than whom no better partner in the serious business of living, writing and raising children could ever be imagined. I love you.

*Permissions*

The Nick Drake lyrics for 'Poor Boy', 1970, are reproduced by permission of Bryter Music/BMG Publishing.

# PHOTO ACKNOWLEDGEMENTS

The author and publishers wish to express their thanks to the below sources of illustrative material and/or permission to reproduce it. Some locations of artworks are also given below, in the interests of brevity:

Photo Howard Coster: p. 170; from Maria Edgeworth, *The Parent's Assistant; or, Stories for Children* (London, 1856): p. 22; from Thomas Hughes, *Tom Brown's School Days* (London, 1911): p. 50; photo László Moholy-Nagy: p. 140; photo Jimmy Sime: p. 112; Homer Sykes/Getty Images: p. 234; photo Philip Wolmuth: p. 6; from R. G. van Yelr, *The Whip and the Rod* (London, 1941): p. 78; United Archives GmbH/Alamy Stock Photo: p. 200.

# INDEX

Page numbers in *italics* refer to illustrations